Praise for *Down and Out in the Great Depression*

"The book is unique. Nowhere else can we read of despair as recorded by those who were feeling it hardest, unfiltered by memory."—*Southern Living*

"These are the forgotten men, women and children of the Depression years."—*Newsday*

"There is a poignancy which occasionally pushes past the confines of history and turns into street poetry, art, delirium."—*Los Angeles Herald Examiner*

"A much more vivid account than most historical works can provide."—*Houston Post*

"Compelling human drama as well as important history."—*Hartford Courant*

"By rescuing the struggles of individuals from the anonymity of statistics, this volume preserves the Depression as it was experienced—with sorrow, anguish, hatred, faith, and humor."—*The New Republic*

"Some of the letters are heartbreaking with their revelations of deprivation, illness, and old age; some provoke a smile, and all are enormously affective."—*Progressive*

"The letters bear a sense of urgency that recollections of the Depression lack, and Robert McElvaine's solid introduction and method of organization deepen their meaning."—*Christian Century*

"McElvaine has done a masterful job."—*Sojourners*

"First-rate explanatory essays by the editor."—*The New Yorker*

"*Down and Out in the Great Depression* is a remarkable testament to a time that no longer seems so distant and, at times, strikes awfully close to home."—*Philadelphia Inquirer*

"The dispirited reality of the Waltons' age is vividly outlined."—*Kansas City Star*

"These letters are a moving testimony."—*Times Literary Supplement*

*These unhappy times call for the building
of plans . . . that build from the bottom up
and not from the top down, that put their faith
once more in the forgotten man at the bottom
of the economic pyramid.*
Franklin D. Roosevelt, April 1932

The forgotten man is still forgotten.
J. W. C., worker, to Eleanor Roosevelt, March 1935

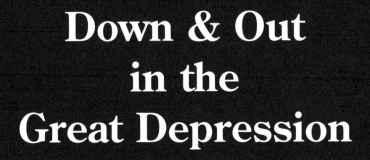

Down & Out in the Great Depression

Letters from the Forgotten Man

Edited by Robert S. McElvaine

Twenty-fifth Anniversary Edition

With a New Foreword by the Editor

The University of North Carolina Press
Chapel Hill

The Library of Congress has cataloged the original edition of this book as follows:
Main entry under title:
Down and out in the Great Depression
Includes index.
1. United States—Social life and customs—1918–1945—Sources.
2. United States—Social conditions—1933–1945—Sources.
3. Depressions—1929—United States—Sources.
I. McElvaine, Robert S., 1947– . II. Title.
E 169.D746 973.91 82-7022

ISBN 978-0-8078-5891-2

12 11 10 09 08 5 4 3 2 1

In Memory of My Mother,
Ruth Ludewig McElvaine,
1902–1978
one who loved history and
taught me that love

Contents

Illustrations

Foreword to the
Twenty-fifth Anniversary Edition

Rereading *Down and Out* in full after a quarter century is, for me, an experience both nostalgic and stimulating. I have read portions of it many times in the intervening years, mainly in conjunction with the use of the letters in courses I have taught, but I had not read it from cover to cover since it was published.

I find nothing that particularly embarrasses me, and I am not reluctant to stand by what I wrote then and how I said it. In my opinion, it still holds up well. In any case, I believe it is best to leave a book like this unchanged, to let it serve as a document of the time in which it was produced, as well as a documentary record of the time it is about.

It is highly unusual for a book to stay in print for twenty-five years, and the fact that this one has done so provides some indication of the impact it has had. The book was pathbreaking in giving voice to "ordinary" people expressing their views and feelings at the time a major historical event was taking place. Their stories remain every bit as relevant to readers today as they were when *Down and Out* was first published.

I was fairly certain that I was on to something important when I started reading the letters in 1970, and I tried to interest publishers in the idea of a collection of them while I was working on my dissertation, but—quite understandably—no one I approached was willing to take a chance on a concept from an unknown, untested would-be author without seeing a manuscript. I, in turn, could not take a chance on devoting time to a project that might never pan out when I had neither my degree nor a job. After I obtained both, the latter kept me too busy through the mid-1970s to return to the letters.

It was a National Endowment for the Humanities summer seminar in 1978 at the University of California at Berkeley that launched the project. The late Lawrence W. Levine, who directed the seminar, took a great interest in the letters and gave me the encouragement and guidance I needed to produce a book manuscript and begin to seek a publisher. Larry was a pioneer in the history of "the folk"—finding ways to give voice to those who had previously been silent in (or entirely absent from) the pages of history. He quickly became my intellectual model and mentor. His interest in the letters was completely genuine, as he showed when he and his wife, Cornelia, did their own book based on similar letters and Franklin Roosevelt's fireside chats, published in 2002. Larry was to become my closest friend in the historical profession. The death of this wonderful, humane man in 2006 was an enormous loss to me, as it was to our profession and, indeed, to the world.

Although the book was to have a large influence and great success, publishers to whom I submitted a draft manuscript did not initially foresee its potential. The letters, editors at several presses told me, were just too depressing. I argued that the book was, after all, about the Depression and it had not been a fun time. But the editors persisted: Who would want to read such depressing stuff? I pointed to the enormous success of Studs Terkel's *Hard Times: An Oral History of the Great Depression*, but to no avail.

When I submitted the manuscript to the University of North Carolina Press, the reaction was very different. The editors loved it, and when one of the two academics to whom they had sent it for review returned an unfavorable report, they took the unusual step of sending it to a third reader. This action produced a second favorable report. At last what these Americans of the Depression era had had to say was moving toward publication.

After all the problems finding support among editors and academic readers, when *Down and Out* was published, reviewers gave it a very different reception. On the question of whether the letters were "just too depressing," Jonathan Yardley provided a clear answer in his review in the *Washington Post Book World*. Reading the letters, he said, is "an experience that pays rich if painful rewards." In the *New York Times Book Review*, Arthur Schlesinger, Jr., called *Down and Out* "a compelling contribution to our history." Glowing reviews appeared in publications from the *New Yorker* to *Christian Century*, from *Sojourners* to *Newsweek*. In all, *Down and Out* garnered more than a hundred reviews, all but one of them highly favorable.

Appearances on three NPR programs, the Studs Terkel Program on WFMT in Chicago, and many other media outlets followed. "McElvaine has captured these voices as no one else ever has," Terkel said. Other comments came rapidly. Perhaps my favorite was from Pete Seeger:

"Here is history written by the people who had to live it, in the U.S.A. of the 1930s. *Down and Out* is a hell of a good book."

Down and Out stimulated wide interest among historians in the treasure trove of letters written during the Depression. It opened a new and continuing approach to the field of Depression Studies. Several book-length collections of letters from the era have been published in the quarter century since *Down and Out* first appeared. Among them are Gerald Markowitz and David Rosner, *Slaves of the Depression: Workers' Letters About Life on the Job* (Ithaca: Cornell University Press, 1987); Lawrence W. Levine and Cornelia R. Levine, *The People and the President: America's Conversation with FDR* (Boston: Beacon Press, 2002); Robert Cohen, ed., *Dear Mrs. Roosevelt: Letters from Children of the Great Depression* (Chapel Hill: University of North Carolina Press, 2002); Cathy D. Knepper, ed., *Dear Mrs. Roosevelt: Letters to Eleanor Roosevelt through Depression and War* (New York: Carroll and Graf, 2004); and Elna C. Green, ed., *Looking for the New Deal: Florida Women's Letters during the Great Depression* (Columbia: University of South Carolina Press, 2007).

Over and over again people—historians, students, and general readers alike—with whom I come in contact (and, in recent years, many who send me e-mails) tell me how moving they find the letters to be, and how they *feel* the Depression in them as they never have before. Particularly because this is the same way I felt when I first read the letters, I find such reactions gratifying. My own students have frequently been obviously moved by reading the letters, and many other professors have told me of similar reactions from their students.

But I can take little credit for the impact the letters have had—and surely will continue to have—on readers. This book was written by Americans of the 1930s. The book is theirs, not mine. All I did was find the letters, select them, and struggle to get them published. Twenty-five years later, I have no doubt that that quest was well worth the effort.

Robert S. McElvaine
May 2007
Wellington, New Zealand

Preface

What follows is not, despite the volume's title, the story of a singular "forgotten man." There was too much diversity among the down and out of the Depression for such a term to be accurate. Rather, it is a collection of portions of the stories of 173 forgotten men, women, and children of the 1930s. It is an attempt to let these people speak for themselves. They have been forgotten for so long not because they were silent but because their stories were not valued as they should have been.

The book is based on the belief that the social history of a people in a given historical period must begin with the testimony of the people themselves. "If you want Negro history," a former slave once told a Fisk University interviewer, "you will have to get [it] from somebody who wore the shoe, and by and by from one to the other you will get a book."[1] This is a wise method. What follows is an effort to employ it in the case of victims of the Great Depression.

The "nameless masses" of the thirties are treated herein as individuals. The initials of those who signed their letters are given to show that the writers were genuine historical actors, not merely props in a play directed entirely from above them. The letters are reproduced exactly as they were written, not for the amusement of readers, but in order to give an accurate impression of the writers and the full flavor of their stories. No ridicule is intended.

The letters contained in the book were selected from the following manuscript collections: the President's Emergency Committee on Employment Central Files, the President's Organization for Unemployment Relief General Correspondence, the Federal Emergency Relief Administration Central Files, and the Civil Works Administration Administrative Correspondence Files, all in the National Archives, Washington, D.C., the Eleanor Roosevelt Papers in the Franklin D. Roosevelt Library, Hyde Park, N.Y., the Robert F. Wagner Papers in the Georgetown University Library, Washington, D.C., and the Norman Thomas Papers in the New York Public Library.

Included with the letters reproduced in the book is a small selection of the photographic art of the 1930s. This rich source has only recently begun to receive its due consideration by historians. The photographs can provide an invaluable part of the feeling of life in the Depression, which is the main purpose of this volume. Sometimes a picture may be worth a thousand words, but sometimes, too, a paragraph may be worth a thousand pictures. It is hoped that a combination of these two types of evidence will help us to gain a better understanding of what life was like for the down and out in the 1930s.

Those who helped make this book possible are too numerous to list. Several, though, deserve special thanks. A significant part of the research for the book was done with the generous support of a grant from the Eleanor Roosevelt Institute. Research and writing were completed with the assistance of a grant from the National Endowment for the Humanities in the summer of 1979 and during an N.E.H. seminar at Brown University in 1980–81. Grants from the Millsaps College Faculty Research Fund were also helpful. I am deeply indebted to the following persons who have read and criticized earlier drafts of my work, parts of which appear in this volume: David Brody of the University of California, Davis; Richard Dalfiume of the State University of New York at Binghamton; Len De Caux of Glendale, California; Melvyn Dubofsky and Charles Forcey, both of the State University of New York at Binghamton; Staughton Lynd of Niles, Ohio; James T. Patterson and Joan W. Scott, both of Brown University; and James Weinstein of San Francisco. David Shannon of the University of Virginia provided an early suggestion that led me to begin my explorations of the letters. The late Robert Starobin shared with me many of his penetrating ideas on methods that can be used to study the history of the "inarticulate." (The reason for the quotation marks should be apparent to anyone who reads the pages that follow.)

I am especially grateful to Professor Lawrence Levine and the members of a National Endowment for the Humanities summer seminar, "The Folk in American History," that he led at the University of California, Berkeley, in 1978. This outstanding seminar and Professor Levine's keen interest in my work inspired me to complete the book and provided me with much of the time needed to do so.

Portions of the material presented in this book were contained in papers delivered at meetings of the American Historical Association at New Orleans in 1972 and at Dallas in 1977. Comments from other participants in those sessions and from members of the audiences were very helpful in advancing my thinking on the subject. Students in my classes in American social history and twentieth-century American history at Millsaps College have been a continuing source of new insights as I have worked out my ideas with their assistance.

The staffs of the following libraries and archives have been most helpful and cooperative: the Franklin D. Roosevelt Library, the National Archives, New York Public Library, New York State School of Industrial and Labor Relations Library, Georgetown University Library, State University of New York at Binghamton Library, Millsaps-Wilson Library, University of California at Berkeley Library, Cornell University Library, Rockefeller Library at Brown University, Georgia State University Library, Atlanta Public Library, Emory University Library, and the Louisiana State University Library.

My greatest debt is owed to my wife, Anne, who was fortunate enough to be born too late to live through the 1930s, but who has cheerfully suffered through many years of reliving the Great Depression. My daughters, Kerri, Lauren, and Allison, neither lived through the Depression nor provided much direct assistance with the book, but they might never forgive me if their names did not appear in it.

It should go without saying, but cannot be allowed to, that I alone am responsible for those errors of fact or idiosyncrasies of interpretation that remain.

Acknowledgments

p. i   Franklin D. Roosevelt, 7 April 1932, radio address, Albany, N.Y., in *The Public Papers and Addresses of Franklin D. Roosevelt,* comp. by Samuel I. Rosenman (New York: Russell and Russell, 1938), 1:625. J. W. C., worker, to Eleanor Roosevelt, March 1935, in Box 2697, Eleanor Roosevelt Papers, Franklin D. Roosevelt Library.

p. ii   No work today, unemployed youth, Washington, D.C., 1938, by John Vachon, Library of Congress.

p. 1   Family bound for Krebs, Oklahoma, from Idabel, Oklahoma, 1939, by Dorothea Lange, Library of Congress.
Unemployed man, 1935, as quoted in Melvin J. Vincent, "Relief and Resultant Attitudes," *Sociology and Social Research* 19 (Sept. –Oct. 1935): 28–29.

p. 33   Breadline, New York City, 25 December 1931; ten thousand people were fed in this Christmas breadline. United Press International.

p. 34   E. J. Sullivan, "The 1932nd Psalm," *Seamen's Journal* 46 (October 1932): 259.

p. 35   "Hooverville," New York City, 8 December 1930, United Press International. Herbert Hoover, 4 March 1933, as quoted in George Wolfskill, *Happy Days Are Here Again* (Hinsdale, Ill.: Dryden Press, 1974), p. 1.

p. 49   Coal miner's child taking home a can of kerosene, Purseglove, Scott's Run, West Virginia, 1938, by Marion Post-Wolcott, Library of Congress.

p. 51   "El" station interior, New York City, 1936, by Bernice Abbott, Museum of The City of New York Picture Collection.
Oscar Wilde, *The Ballad of Reading Gaol* (New York: E. P. Dutton, 1928), p. 72.

p. 67   Ill-housed, ill-clad, ill-nourished: mother and two children of a family of nine living in a one-room hut built on an abandoned Ford Chasis, Highway 70, Tennessee, 1936, by Carl Mydans, Library of Congress.
Bob Miller, in *Hard Hitting Songs for Hard-Hit People,* ed. Alan

Lomax, Woody Guthrie, and Pete Seeger (New York: Oak Publications, 1967), pp. 38–39.

p. 79 Ex-slave, by Dorothea Lange, Oakland Museum.
Afro-American folksong, Paul Oliver, *Conversation with the Blues* (New York: Horizon Press, 1965), p. 146.

p. 95 Ninety-one years old, Orange County, North Carolina, 1939, by Marion Post-Wolcott, Library of Congress.
Jane Addams, as quoted in David Hackett Fischer, *Growing Old in America* (New York: Oxford University Press, 1978), p. 157.

p. 113 A Christmas dinner in tenant farmer's home, southeastern Iowa, 1936, by Russell Lee, Library of Congress.
Margot Hentoff, "Kids, Pull Up Your Socks: A Review of Children's Books," *New York Review of Books* 18 (20 April 1972): 15.

p. 121 Unemployed worker during the Great Depression, by Dorothea Lange, Franklin D. Roosevelt Library.
Archibald MacLeish, "Speech to Those Who Say Comrade," in MacLeish, *Public Speech* (New York: Holt, Rinehart and Winston, 1936).

p. 122 Helen Keller, *Out of the Dark* (Garden City, N.Y.: Doubleday, Page, 1907, 1920), p. 11.

p. 123 Waiting outside rural relief station, Urbana, Ohio, 1938, by Ben Shahn, Library of Congress.
One of the down and out, comment made to Dorothea Lange, as quoted in *The Bitter Years, 1935–1941: Rural America as Seen by the Photographers of the Farm Security Administration*, ed. Edward Steichen (New York: The Museum of Modern Art, 1962), p. viii.

p. 124 Herbert Spencer, *Social Statics* (New York: D. Appleton & Co., 1882), pp. 415–16.

p. 143 One of the judges at the horse races, Warrenton, Virginia, 1941, by Marion Post-Wolcott, Library of Congress.

p. 155 Lumberjack in saloon, Craigville, Minnesota, 1937, by Russell Lee, Library of Congress.
A small-town housewife, 1933, Muncie, Indiana, quoted in Robert S. Lynd and Helen Merrell Lynd, *Middletown in Transition: A Study in Cultural Conflicts* (New York: Harcourt Brace, 1937), p. 112.

p. 173 Oldtimers near courthouse, San Augustine, Texas, 1939, by Russell Lee, Library of Congress.
John Steinbeck, *The Grapes of Wrath* (New York, P. F. Collier & Son, 1939), p. 164.

p. 183 Riot at Fisher Body Plant, Cleveland, Ohio, 31 July 1939, United Press International.

"Mammy's Little Baby Loves a Union Shop," CIO Strike Song, in Kermit Eby, "They Don't Sing Anymore," *Christian Century* 69 (27 February 1952): 246.

p. 201 FDR campaigns at entrance to Midtown Tunnel, New York City, 28 October 1940, by Ben Heller, Franklin D. Roosevelt Library.

p. 202 Florence King, *Southern Ladies and Gentlemen* (New York: Stein and Day, 1975), p. 12.

Mrs. G. W. B. to Eleanor Roosevelt, July 1936, Eleanor Roosevelt Papers, Box 2716, Franklin D. Roosevelt Library.

Franklin D. Roosevelt, 1936, as quoted in George Wolfskill, *Happy Days Are Here Again* (Hinsdale, Ill.: Dryden Press, 1974), p. 143.

p. 203 Waiting for relief checks, Imperial Valley, California, 1937, by Dorothea Lange, Library of Congress

Restaurant waiter, Lowell, Massachusetts, 1939, as quoted in Benjamin Appel, *The People Talk* (New York: E. P. Dutton, 1940), p. 83.

p. 215 Happy days are finally here, 1941, by Jack Delano, Library of Congress.

New York businessman, 1935, as quoted in John T. Flynn, "Other People's Money," *New Republic* 85 (11 December 1935): 129.

p. 231 Happy days are here again, Pittsburgh, Pennsylvania, 1941, by Jack Delano, Library of Congress.

p. 233 Unemployed trapper, Placquemines Parish, Louisiana, 1935, by Ben Shahn, Library of Congress.

INTRODUCTION

We're about down and out and the only
good thing about it that I see is that
there's not much farther down we can go
Unemployed man, 1935

Americans' interest in the Great Depression of the 1930s has been extraordinary. Recently Franklin D. Roosevelt surpassed Abraham Lincoln as the most written-about president in our history.[1] Popular fascination with the thirties is greater than with any other era of American history save the Civil War and, possibly, the American Revolution.

Yet, despite all the writings on the thirties, until recently there have been few indications of the thoughts and feelings of "ordinary" Americans, the people whom Roosevelt collectively called, in those days before women's liberation, the "forgotten man." There are volumes on almost every leading figure in the Roosevelt administration and on most New Deal intellectuals, not to mention memoirs of widely varying merit by almost every government official who survived long enough to write them. Abundant verbiage also exists on political episodes, economic developments, state and local deals (old or new), and interest groups such as labor, big business, small business, and farmers. The organized left of the thirties has meanwhile received at least its share of attention from historians. Many of these studies are of enormous value. Indeed, an essay such as this introduction would be impossible without them.[2]

The forgotten Americans, however, have remained largely forgotten. The task of trying to remember them is a formidable one. The sources of traditional history—governmental records, organization files, collections of personal papers, diaries, memoirs, newspapers—yield only spotty information about the problems and attitudes of the "down and out."

Still, the paucity of data has not deterred historians from generalizing about working-class attitudes during the Depression. In the late 1950s, for example, Arthur M. Schlesinger, Jr., concluded that the dominant mood of the unemployed early in the Depression was despair. "People," he declared, "were sullen rather than bitter, despairing rather than violent." Such Americans, Schlesinger believed, "sat at home, rocked dispiritedly in their chairs, and blamed 'conditions.'"[3] Other historians have generally joined Schlesinger in commenting on the remarkable docility of the forgotten man, after which they have quickly forgotten him again.

One reason many historians have felt competent to discuss the mood of Depression America is that they were there. Until recently, those who wrote about the Depression had lived through it. Personal experience is irreplaceable, but it brings disadvantages as well as benefits. Few of the historians who lived through the Depression and later wrote about it were actually among the poor of the period. And for those who had personally faced harsh conditions, the very fact that they had escaped them was likely to color their recollections of people's attitudes in the thirties.

Today a new generation of historians is studying the Depression, dealing with the thirties solely as history. Our memories can neither aid nor hinder us in examining the decade. Often all we have known of the Depression has been what our parents told us, which usually took the form of moral lessons.[4] The lack of personal experience makes it essential for us to seek new methods of understanding what life was actually like during the Great Depression.

How can we get below the surface of traditional histories and uncover the problems, thoughts, and emotions of those "ordinary" Americans who left no record in the usual places? Certain possibilities are available. Scientific public-opinion polls began in 1935. The results of such surveys are enlightening, but the individual human being rapidly vanishes in the numbers, charts, and graphs. Although statistics are a necessary part of history, history is not only a social science; it is also one of the humanities. Historians must attempt to relate, in human terms, the lives that are summarized in the social scientists' tables. Cabell Phillips cogently made this point: "Mass unemployment is both a statistic and an empty feeling in the stomach. To fully comprehend it, you have to both see the figures and feel the emptiness."[5]

But how to relate those lives, how to feel that emptiness? Some attempts have been made. One of the most noted is Studs Terkel's *Hard Times: An Oral History of the Great Depression*, drawn from interviews with survivors of the thirties. The lost human element of the Depression begins to revive in Terkel's pages. Yet his method also has its drawbacks. Most important, the interviews took place thirty years or more after the events they described. Memories are notoriously fallible. This is especially true when unpleasant experiences are involved. The "bad old days" are more readily forgotten than the good. The intervening years may well have introduced inaccuracies into the recollections of many of Terkel's Depression victims. People living in desperation can better explain at the time what it is like than they can decades afterward.[6]

The same difficulty exists with other oral history interviews conducted decades after the fact, such as Alice and Staughton Lynd's *Rank and File*.[7] The problem can be avoided by turning to sources that were written as people lived through the Depression. Three types of this kind of evidence stand out. Many psychologists and sociologists conducted studies of particular groups of unemployed people during the Depression.[8] These are extremely helpful in any attempt to reconstruct life and attitudes in the thirties, but they rarely give us any *direct* contact with Depression victims. Interviews conducted in the late 1930s by people employed by the WPA Federal Writers' Project provide us with revealing glimpses into the lives of "ordinary" Americans. Three collections of these interviews—the Federal Writers' Project, *These Are Our Lives*; Tom E. Terrill and Jerrold Hirsch, *Such As Us*; and Ann Banks, *First Person America*—have been published.[9] They are invaluable contributions, yet the reader remains one step removed from the Depression sufferers. Their thoughts were filtered through the interviewers, who had no tape recorders and simply wrote down later what they remembered. The memories and degrees of creativity (less useful here than in many types of writing) of the interviewers varied greatly.

A similar difficulty exists with the other major source of contemporary information on the lives and beliefs of the poor in the thirties, the reports of FERA and WPA investigators written for Federal Relief Administrator Harry Hopkins. Some of the most useful of these reports are reproduced by Richard Lowitt and Maurine Beasley in *One Third of a Nation: Lorena Hickok's Reports on the Great Depression*.[10] Although these reports provide insights not available elsewhere, we see the problems and aspirations of the poor through the eyes of middle-class investigators. We still have not gotten directly in touch with the contemporary views of those who suffered through the Depression.

One of the few means available to obtain such immediate testimony is to examine letters written to public figures in the 1930s. The words of men, women, and children as they described their problems to persons they believed to be concerned afford a better feeling of what life was like for Depression victims than does any other available source. Particularly revealing are letters addressed to Eleanor and Franklin Roosevelt, who made repeated efforts to get citizens to write to them. During his fireside chats, the president often spoke of the mail he received from the public and encouraged others to write. Mrs. Roosevelt, too, "made a special effort to build up her mail." Some people felt more comfortable writing to the first lady. "I have often heard it said," wrote a Chicago woman in 1935, "that if a common citizen writes a letter to the President it is read by his secretary and then thrown in the waste basket." Therefore she and many others addressed their correspondence to Mrs. Roosevelt. Or, as another woman put it, "Centuries back Catholics prayed to the Virgin Mary because they thought she might intercede with a diety who could not take time to hear every petitioner. In some such spirit we turn to you."[11]

In the New Deal years, both the volume of mail reaching the White House and the high percentage of it coming from the poor were unprecedented.

This was not attributable simply to the Depression. President Roosevelt gave many people a feeling that he was their personal friend and protector, that they could tell him things in confidence. The results were clear enough in the letters from the public. "At no time," a New Hampshire woman wrote in 1934, "have the people been so free to write and feel that the President or his wife would be interested to know what each community were doing." An Alabama woman agreed: "Never before have we had leaders in the White House to whom we felt we could go with our problems, for never before have our leaders seemed conscious of the masses," she declared. "The knowledge that my President is trying to uplift 'the forgotten man' has made me bold to write to you."[12]

The fact that the letters were generally answered promptly (and, with rare exception, were actually signed by the president) was of great service to Roosevelt in maintaining his popularity and the people's sense of contact with him. Many felt that they knew the president personally, Lorena Hickok reported from New Orleans in 1934. She attributed this in large measure to Roosevelt's radio addresses, in which he spoke to people "in such a friendly, man-to-man fashion." Listeners felt, Hickok said, that FDR was "talking to each one of them, personally." She also mentioned the replies to the letters that people sent to the White House. Many Americans cherished their form letters from the offices of Franklin or Eleanor Roosevelt. "And these people take them all very seriously," noted Hickok, "as establishing a personal relation."[13]

"From his first hours in office," one historian has written, "Roosevelt gave people a feeling that they could confide in him directly." And confide they did. In the week following FDR's inauguration, 450,000 letters poured into the White House. For years the average remained at 5,000 to 8,000 communications each day. Under Roosevelt the White House staff for answering such letters quickly increased from one person, who had been adequate in past administrations, to fifty. After allowing for literacy rates and population changes, FDR received nearly four times as many letters as Lincoln or Wilson, previously the leading recipients of White House mail. Letters from the public were very important to Roosevelt, who saw the mail as a way to gauge fluctuations in public sentiment. According to his aide Louis Howe, FDR "always maintained that a personal letter from a farmer or a miner or little shopkeeper or clerk who honestly expresses his conviction, is the most perfect index to the state of the public mind." The president therefore had the mail analyzed on a regular basis and sometimes read a random sampling of letters himself "to renew his sense of contact with raw opinion."[14]

Under normal conditions, better-educated people from the middle and upper classes are overrepresented among political letter writers. But Normalcy died in October 1929, and the Depression provided the strong motive that the poorly educated need to write. For a variety of reasons, among them the economic situation and the public's identification of the Roosevelts as friends of the poor, more than half of those who wrote to the New Deal White House were members of the working class.[15]

The economic motives for writing the president are easily stated. By early 1933, approximately one-quarter of the nation's workers were without jobs. This amounted to between 13 and 14 million people.[16] When their families are included, the number of Americans without a dependable source of income in early 1933 reaches at least 40 million. But what do such numbers mean? How can anguish and hunger be graphed? Underlying the statistics are countless human stories. A few of them will be told in the pages that follow.

Letters from "ordinary" people can provide us with an understanding of life and thought in the Depression that can be gained in no other way. Like other sources of information about the down and out, though, the letters have their drawbacks and limitations.

Some 15 million letters from the public are preserved in the Franklin D. Roosevelt Library.[17] Many others, originally addressed to the White House but passed along to federal agencies for action or reply, are housed in the National Archives. Working-class Americans also wrote letters to many other public figures during the Depression. Such people as New York Senator Robert Wagner and Socialist leader Norman Thomas, who were especially identified with workers' problems, received many interesting communications from forgotten men and women.

Of these millions of letters, approximately 15,000 were examined at random in the preparation of the present volume. Certainly no claim can be made that this represents a scientific sampling of opinion in the thirties. Although the letters surveyed were selected at random, there was nothing random about the act of writing the letters in the first place. Unlike the answering of questions in a poll, the writing of a letter obviously requires a conscious decision. Mail comes from people who are especially interested in the subjects about which they write, while polling organizations ask "everyone" without regard for level of concern. Letters, moreover, like any form of literature, are written for a purpose, with a strategy behind them. When reading a letter like the ones reproduced in this book, one should try to discern the writer's motives.[18]

One must also be wary of reaching conclusions based solely upon letters because pressure groups tried to influence the president through letter-writing campaigns. Such attempts are usually easy enough to detect. They tended to produce letters arriving in large batches and containing similar phrases. Occasionally, though, special interest groups were more clever. In an attempt to block the Public Utilities Holding Company bill, for example, "representatives of utility interests scrawled letters on scratch paper with pencil and mailed them to Congressmen in Washington." Such artful deception appears to have been rare, however, and the exercise of sufficient caution makes it reasonably safe to assume that our sample of letters consists almost entirely of genuine communications from unorganized individuals.[19]

Despite all the warning flags, the letters can be used to great advantage. "If we are concerned with historical change," Edward Thompson has said, "we must attend to the articulate minorities. But these minorities arise from a less articulate majority whose consciousness may be described as being, at this time, 'sub-political.'" Unscientific samplings that bring us into direct contact with the thoughts of expressive working-class people can thus provide "indispensable insights into the moods and habits of thought" of other people as well.[20] If the letters are used to complement the other sorts of evidence mentioned earlier, we can begin to see the Depression through the eyes of those who lived it.

The letters chosen for this volume were selected because they represent themes that emerged from the larger body of letters examined. It is to these themes that we now must turn.

It is, first of all, clear that victims of the Depression were a heterogeneous lot. There were differences in race, religion, ethnicity, and age; between men and women, rural and urban residents, and the poor and those who considered themselves "middle class."

Some of these distinctions are apparent in Part I, where the views on causes and cures of the Depression among the more well-to-do seem to differ significantly from those of the poor. The main purpose of Part I, however, is to provide a background of attitudes in the Hoover years so that the themes that emerge in the far more numerous letters of the Roosevelt years may be placed in some perspective.

The varied nature of the problems facing Americans of different backgrounds is explored in Part II. Not all of the differences are readily apparent in the letters, but some come through strikingly. There is evidence, at least early in the Depression, of a serious split between proud middle-class homeowners and the poor. Homeowners complained that frugal folk (such as themselves) could get no assistance, while the profligate lower class received charity. (See Chapter 2.) This division appears to have narrowed in the mid-thirties, when a large portion of the middle class joined the poor in supporting the New Deal. A 1936 survey of Chicago residents, for example, found a marked "tendency for the middle income group to agree with the lower group on questions pertaining to the present distribution of wealth and influence."[21]

Men and women differed in their reactions to the Depression. Both wrote letters seeking assistance, but women represented by far the larger percentage of those who sought help. Almost all the letters asking for clothing came from women and were addressed to Eleanor Roosevelt (Chapter 3). Providing money, on the other hand, was thought to be a man's duty, and men seem to have been more numerous among those requesting financial aid than among those asking for clothing. The fact that women appear to have outnumbered men in both areas was probably the result of socially defined sex roles. A man who asked for help was admitting his failure as a provider; a woman who "begged" was simply trying to help her family. What appeared to be weakness for a man was acceptable for a woman.

Perhaps the most important difference between the attitudes of blacks and whites was that the former had no doubt that race played an important part in their plight (Chapter 4). White workers were much slower to perceive that their problems were shared by many others in the working class. After Roosevelt took office, however, a significant number of whites began to see themselves, as blacks had long seen themselves, as members of a downtrodden *group*.

The reactions of older Americans, whose letters appear in Chapter 5, to economic collapse differed from those of their younger countrymen. Their letters show that older Americans were especially tied to the nation's traditions of self-reliance, hard work, and thrift. The distinction was noted by a WPA subforeman in Texas at the end of the Depression: "On this government work lots of men lay down on the job, young men especially. The older workers seem to appreciate what they get but the young ones just try to get by until quitting time."[22] The older Depression victims' letters also indicate that they were often bitter because they were not enjoying the positions they had expected age would bring them. The combination of belief in traditional values and resentment that they no longer seemed operational appears to have resulted in a remarkable willingness on the part of the elderly to turn to the government. In this way they hoped to regain the places to which they believed they were entitled. Individualists could seek help from the government in the form of pensions because they saw this as something that was rightfully theirs, not as charity.

Older people differed in at least one other way from younger Americans in their reactions to the Depression. The former had seen better times and could, perhaps, be more philosophical about the disaster. Young people, on the other hand, had little hope of ever seeing good times.[23] The same distinction could cut the other way as well: if things ever got better, the young would presumably still be around to enjoy better times while the old might not be.

At the opposite end of the age scale from the elderly, children experienced the Depression in a distinct manner. The feelings of shame that overcame many fathers in the Depression can be seen through the eyes of their children in the letters reproduced in Chapter 6. They saw problems in simpler terms than did adults: not "We are poor," but "I don't have skates." In some of their letters, children expressed feelings of sympathy for parents, reversing the usual pattern of a parent comforting a child. Children were open in their descriptions of how the Depression had forced their families to give up, however reluctantly, status symbols and pleasures in order to survive. It is also evident in the letters that it was sometimes socially acceptable for children, as for women, to seek assistance when pride would not allow the traditional provider to turn to charity.

Part III shows the wide variety of reactions to the Depression. The attitudes of Americans toward relief form a separate category among responses to the Depression, in part, at least, because there was no necessary or definite relationship between views of relief and attitudes toward the Depression, the New Deal, or the socioeconomic system. It was possible to be critical of relief policies without attacking the system. More than one contemporary study of relief clients found active, emotional attitudes toward relief combined with passive reactions to the Depression itself. It is not true, however, that acceptance of relief necessarily constituted acceptance of the economic system.[24]

The attitudes of people on relief encompassed a wide spectrum that is evident in several contemporary sociological and psychological studies of relief clients. One social psychologist divided the reactions of a sample of people on relief (all of whom had been self-supporting before the Depression) into five groups. At one extreme were the fatalists, "whose courage has been definitely 'blown to pieces.'" Most such people apparently maintained their adherence to the traditional middle-class values and hence blamed themselves, at least to an extent, for their problems. Another group that clung to the old beliefs accepted relief only "with reluctance." People of the other three types identified in this study, however, had cast off personal responsibility for their condition. One category was bitter, believing "society [had] inflicted so much woe on them that it owes them a living; they will demand more and more." This was the type of relief recipient that worried Lorena Hickok. They were, she reported, "gimmes." "The more you do for the people the more they demand." Some of these clients had come to think that the government owed them a living. "And," Hickok said, "they want more."[25] Such people are well represented in the letters in Chapter 7.

The holders of the last two types of attitudes specified in the 1935 study also had moved beyond self-blame. One group, apparently "among the more intelligent," saw the Depression as something beyond their control. They accepted "their situations with philosophical rationalizations." Finally, some people on relief had "become intensely irritated at the whole social order." Such discontented Americans, however, were not necessarily rebellious. "Not a few," the author reported, had "taken to alcoholic drinking as a refuge."[26]

Other studies of the attitudes of relief clients found more or less parallel types.[27] The differences in views about welfare were determined in part by differences in the backgrounds of the people interviewed. The Lynds found in attitudes toward relief in Muncie a sharp class distinction, a cleavage that presumably was present elsewhere in the nation. The business class wanted "to wipe out public relief at the earliest possible moment"; working-class residents not only favored relief, they also tended to be critical of the inadequacy of funds.[28]

Another element causing variations in attitudes toward relief was the condition of a person before the Depression. Those who had been successful in earlier years were, at least in the early thirties, more likely to blame themselves for their plight and become broken and passive than were those who had suffered frequent unemployment prior to 1929. This distinction between "new poor" and "old poor" is important but perhaps not as helpful in understanding attitudes as it might at first appear. The central fact about the Depression, after all, was that *most* victims were newly poor. Almost all of the studies that connect self-blame and newness to suffering were made in 1934 or before. This may have been too early to see any significant trend away from self-blame as the newness of a Depression victim's poverty faded.[29]

Indeed, as the Depression wore on, self-blame seems to have declined and been replaced by a growing view that relief was "owed" to those who received it. On many occasions groups of relief clients used the threat of force to gain better treatment.[30] A *Fortune* survey in 1935 found that 88.8 percent of the poor believed that "the government should see to it that every man who wants work has a job." The prosperous in this survey opposed the idea by a slim plurality.[31]

For all the differences in attitudes toward relief, there was near unanimity among recipients in favoring work relief over the dole. Most of the WPA workers interviewed late in the Depression made it clear, though, that, grateful as they were for work relief, they wanted to return to "real," that is private, work as soon as possible.[32]

The expressions of thankfulness for work relief appear to contrast with the resentment against relief administrators that became common among their clients. "It seems to me," a man in Michigan wrote to President Roosevelt in 1935, "that these Welfare men [administrators] drive Very good cars when they are only paying the labor class of people 30¢ and hour." Many relief clients also made the bitter charge that well-to-do relief officials were acting in a paternalistic manner toward recipients. "Why," a Los Angeles man asked about pay on work-relief projects, "should it be 'dished' out to us like we were little children, and tell us exactly what every cent should be spent for?"[33] The authors of such protests, which were frequent, as the letters in Chapter 7 indicate, may actually have had something in common with those who were thankful for the WPA but sought to return to "real" jobs as soon as possible. Both groups wanted independence and opposed paternalism. They did not like to be the recipients of gifts from the "wiser and wealthier." In sum, desire for self-reliance and independence could coexist with appreciation for work relief and even with criticism of its inadequacies.

Chapters 8 through 11 show a range of reactions to the Depression. Although the letters are divided into categories, more than one of these reactions could exist in the same individual. Moreover, as was indicated above in discussing attitudes toward relief, one might pass through stages of self-blame, desperation, and cynicism before becoming rebellious.

It is quite clear that there was a class difference between the letter writers who criticized the New Deal from a conservative or right-wing perspective and those who expressed egalitarian ideas (the latter, significantly, being far more numerous among writers of the entire sample of letters surveyed for this volume). A large proportion of the letters from the right came from people in society's upper-middle strata and were typed or written on high-quality stationery. Most had fewer grammatical and spelling errors than those calling for more equality. The egalitarian letters were often scribbled in pencil on pages torn from coarse pads.

The conservative letters usually mentioned that the author was a "taxpayer," "homeowner," "landowner," "businessman," or "stockholder." Some complained of attacks on profits and said that steep taxes would hurt their investments. It is apparent that the conservative writers were, on the whole, on an economic and educational level decidedly above that of the unemployed and poorest workers, many of whom expressed a desire for more equality and justice.

The relatively small number of apparently less-educated or poor people who expressed rightist ideas in their letters should not, perhaps, even be classified as conservatives. Most of them did not oppose government assistance programs per se but complained that the aid was being given to the wrong people: worthless foreigners, "sheeny Jews," "niggers," and "dagoes," rather than hard-working "white Americans." The fact that these people were not entirely conservative is shown by such examples as a Pennsylvania woman who wrote in 1930, "first Place the hunkies get all Show in World Poor americans has to Stand Back" but also stated, "I think the Rich People should Pay Rent for Poor People."[34] Others who were slightly above the lowest ranks of society sometimes complained of the lack of frugality among the very poor. Early in the Depression, this represented a serious split among the unemployed. Those who had obtained a few material possessions had, during the relatively prosperous twenties, tended to look down upon those who had nothing. When such holders of small amounts of property were thrown out of work, some turned against the poor rather than the rich.

As the dominant personality of the 1930s, Franklin Roosevelt became the focal point for many of the attitudes of Depression victims. Approval of the president and his policies was the most common response among the down and out, but significant numbers of the poor were unhappy with Roosevelt. A minority among this group criticized FDR for maintaining the old economic system (Chapter 12). The leading theme in letters written to Roosevelt during the 1932 campaign was, according to a study by Leila Sussman, "hostility to the 'money interest,' the utility companies, the monopolies, and the 'big boys.'" Some who wrote to the new president were not convinced that he was following the mandate of those who elected him. An eighty-eight-year-old Kansan voiced the feelings of many disappointed Roosevelt voters when he said late in 1933, "Every move that has been made was in favor of big business."

Perhaps the most common complaint about Roosevelt was that he made "every week more promises" but did not keep them. "Roosevelt's statement some time ago that no one would starve is just another broken promise," charged a Missouri postcard writer. "You promised us work," another unemployed man berated the president. "Give it to us now. We waited long enough." A Kentuckian wrote to the FERA, "You are not doing the Poor People wright the ones that haves a good Living is getting more than the ones are starving to Death."[35]

Complaints against Roosevelt were relatively scarce in 1933. For most working-class Americans, the aura of the First Hundred Days legislation of the New Deal seems to have lasted well into 1934. But in many cases the early legislation served mainly to whet the appetite for more substantial changes. By late 1934 signs of impatience were beginning to appear. "The forgotten man," wrote a Pennsylvanian in 1935, "is still forgotten. . . . The new deal and N.R.A. has only helped big business."[36]

Such criticism of President Roosevelt was, even in 1934–35, distinctly a minority position among the poor. No theme is clearer in the letters than the affection so many of the working class felt for FDR (Chapter 13). Religious terms were commonly used in praise of the president. A Florida resident proclaimed early in 1934, "President Roosevelt is certainly a Saviour to the Country." Some were ready to canonize him. "We all feel if there ever was a Saint. He is one," wrote a Wisconsin woman. "As long as Pres. Roosevelt will be our leader under Jesus Christ we feel no fear." An elderly Kansas City woman was overheard shouting, "The scriptures are being fulfilled," as she listened to an FDR speech in 1936.[37]

For a great many disinherited Americans, Franklin and Eleanor Roosevelt became parent figures. Some of Mrs. Roosevelt's correspondents addressed her as "Mother Roosevelt." As one explained, "We do not hesitate to address you as Mother, for such you are in the truest sense. Your national children have cried unto you, and you have heard and answered their cry." Unemployed people frequently felt that when all the world was against them, the Roosevelts would protect them. "Thank God we poor people have someone to call on," exclaimed an Atlanta man. In a typical 1936 letter, a sixty-year-old Arkansas woman wrote to Mrs. Roosevelt, "You as well as your esteemed husband whom we have learned to love, are the only ones we have to turn to for advise and consideration."[38]

In the eyes of many Depression victims, then, Franklin Roosevelt could do no wrong; he represented hope in the midst of despair. Early in the New Deal this belief apparently was nearly universal among poor Americans; certainly it was the dominant view of working-class letter writers in our sample.

The widespread worship of Roosevelt appears to contradict any contention that there was a potential for the growth of working-class radicalism in the 1930s. Actually, though, the adoration of FDR may add support to such an argument. Since working people generally believed that Roosevelt was their sincere friend, it was possible for millions to hail the president as their hero even though they wanted much more change than the New Deal provided. Whatever was wrong—and most workers who wrote to the White House thought much was wrong—could not be the fault of the shepherd of the poor residing at 1600 Pennsylvania Avenue. "I am sure," wrote a Seattle man, "the President, if he only knew, would order that something be done, God bless him. He is doing all he can to relieve the suffering." Such people were upset with the way the system—including the New Deal version thereof—was operating, but they were convinced that Roosevelt was also displeased with the inequities. "I love him for all he has done, and I love him for all he wanted to do and could not," wrote a Florida woman in 1936. An upstate New Yorker felt the same way. "FDR didn't do all he could," the man affirmed, "he was held back."[39]

Franklin Roosevelt thus enjoyed the best of two worlds. Many poor Americans gave credit to their president for any help they received. When it came to placing blame for their continued problems, however, most of them never pointed to the White House. "He means right" was a common response whenever a Roosevelt program failed to meet expectations.[40] The feeling many dispossessed Americans had toward Roosevelt was akin to the attitude of European peasants toward the good king, who was seen as their Protector. Local lords were often evil and ruthless, but the distant king, if only he knew, would set things right.

Americans have long been ambivalent toward strong leadership. Their democratic heritage has given them a healthy distrust of concentrated power. The basic optimism of most Americans, moreover, has led them to believe things will be "right" without strong central authority. However, when things go wrong, as obviously was the case in the 1930s, there is a tendency to blame those in positions of leadership. Many Americans accordingly turned on Herbert Hoover, blaming him for problems he had had little role in causing. If a leader is blamed for difficulties, it follows that what is needed is a new leader. Given this yearning and Franklin Roosevelt's extraordinary qualities as a leader and speaker, many Americans were prepared to follow him in almost any *progressive* direction. The adjective is crucial. One of the main reasons working-class Americans were so fond of FDR—and so willing to follow him—was that they were convinced that as he sought improvement he shared the values that became most important to them in the 1930s.

These values, uncrystallized though they surely were, are perhaps the most important theme to emerge from the letters. Working-class Americans had never quite accepted the values of acquisitive individualism and market-place economics so often associated with the middle and upper class in this country.[41] Workers' individualism had rested instead on bases other than selfishness. It was an ethical individualism, which may be contrasted to the amoral individualism of the Herbert Spencer variety, and was rooted in the notion that all people had rights. Consequently, policies and actions ought to be judged on the basis of their effects on individual people, not according to their value in the marketplace.

In the 1920s these traditional working-class values were severely strained by the materialistic appeals of an expanding marketplace economy. Advertising and installment buying helped to entice workers toward the amoral, egotistical individualism long prevalent among the owning class. But the Depression appears to have reversed the shift of workers toward the values of self-centered individualism. Throughout the letters run the themes of equity, justice, compassion, and humanitarianism. Appeals are often based upon the argument that the policy or treatment complained of is unfair. Many of the writers, in short, imply that economics should have some connection with morality. [42]

None of which is to say that any appreciable number of working-class Americans in the 1930s were socialists or were consciously anticapitalist. The values revealed in the letters were not in keeping with Smithian political economy, but few workers adopted a coherent anticapitalist ideology (although there were exceptions, as some of the letters in Chapter 11 indicate). This lack of ideology is unsurprising, and it hardly differentiated the bulk of American workers in the thirties from their counterparts in other times and places. Most "ordinary" people are *never* ideological in a way that would suit an ideologue. This does not mean, of course, that their thoughts and actions are not based upon a set of underlying assumptions and values but only that they are not conscious adherents of a systematic approach to the world.

The values American workers developed (or returned to) in the 1930s might have led more of them to adopt socialism if they had been pointed in that direction by an inspiring political spokesman. Given the compatibility of socialism with the inchoate values of many working-class Americans during the Depression, their desire for leadership to "make things right," and the remarkable affection so many of them felt for Franklin Roosevelt, it seems unlikely that the president, had he wanted (as some of his opponents charged) to bring about socialism in America, would have encountered much opposition from workers. They were anxious to be led toward justice and more equality. As one observer noted several years later, the American people in 1933 "welcomed the revolution they believed he [Roosevelt] was promoting." [43] Roosevelt was promoting no revolution, however, and he managed through his New Deal programs and his increasingly working-class oriented rhetoric to keep most workers with him, although many of them were dissatisfied with the New Deal's accomplishments, as their letters show.

The remainder of the Introduction provides a basic outline of American history in the 1930s. To put into perspective the view from below that the letters will provide, it is necessary to have some grasp of the more traditional view (from above) of the Depression years.

The economic collapse of 1929 struck a country in which income was subject to gross maldistribution. In that year the richest 20 percent of American families received 54.4 percent of the nation's family personal income. The upper 5 percent of Americans received 30 percent, and the top 1 percent enjoyed 14.7 percent of the nation's income. At the opposite end of the economic spectrum, the poorest 40 percent of American families and unattached individuals had to share 12.5 percent of their country's personal income.[44]

Such raw figures are far removed from their meaning in human terms. We may move a step closer to the human story by seeing what those fortunate enough to have jobs were being paid. Average weekly wages in manufacturing dropped from $24.76 in 1929 to $16.65 in 1933 and did not regain their 1929 level until 1940. With bread selling for seven cents a loaf, eggs for twenty-nine cents a dozen, and milk for more than ten cents a quart in 1933, such wages were barely adequate. Real earnings (in 1914 dollars) dropped by fully one-third between 1929 and 1933.[45] Yet those who made the average wage were twice lucky. First, of course, because they were employed at all, and second because their wages were average—that is, not the lowest possible. Many laborers had to settle for ten cents an hour or less. Some Connecticut sweatshop owners paid women in their employ *weekly* rates of sixty cents to one dollar for fifty-five hours of work. In 1933 an FERA field representative in North Carolina thought that $5.25 per week for a family of five was "very good."[46]

The people who were paid such wages were not the big losers of the Depression. Not even the unemployed workers lost the most, in terms of money. The reason, of course, was that, financially, they had little to lose. The huge losses were taken by certain wealthy investors who saw paper fortunes vanish in the stock-market crash. Despite all the talk in the late twenties of the widespread ownership of stock, more than 71 percent of all 1929 dividend income went to the top 1 percent of the population.[47] Most of the rich remained quite comfortable, although the extent of their deprivation was hinted at by the finding of a WPA research project that the most common previous occupations of people on urban relief rolls in 1934 were servant and chauffeur.[48]

Throughout the Depression decade, despite the myths of investors' bodies piling knee-deep after they leaped from Wall Street windows, it was generally not this sort that seriously considered suicide. Rather, it was the desperate worker, such as the unemployed Youngstown steel operative who begged for a job in 1932 saying, "If you can't do something for me, I'm going to kill myself." Similarly, a Pennsylvania man who was about to be evicted for inability to pay rent wrote to the Civil Works Administration asking, "Which would be the most human way to dispose of myself and family, as this is about the only thing I see left to do." The suicide rate increased slowly in the early Depression years, rising each year, from 14 per 100,000 in 1929 to 17.4 per 100,000 in 1932. In late 1930 a Pennsylvania man caught stealing a loaf of bread for his four hungry children was overcome by shame. He went to his cellar and hanged himself.[49]

Such tragic events were rare. Other horrible consequences of the Depression were more common. "Nobody is actually starving," President Hoover insisted. Franklin Roosevelt rarely agreed—at least in public—with his predecessor, but he did on this point. "Nobody is going to starve in this country," the new president affirmed soon after taking office. Both leaders were wrong. Death resulting directly from starvation was unusual, but that fact was of small consolation to those who did expire in that fashion. Ninety-five such cases were reported in New York City in 1931. How many more went unreported, and how many people died of diseases related to chronic malnutrition cannot be known.[50]

It can be said with assurance that sickness increased dramatically among the unemployed who were malnourished. The illness rate of families of the unemployed was 66 percent greater than that among families with a full-time worker. An American Federation of Labor representative reported early in 1933 that some workers "who have been idle for 12 to 14 months . . . could not stand the work they had done previously because of undernourishment." Many had been unemployed for longer periods. A majority among the unemployed questioned in a mid-1934 survey had been out of work for one to five years.[51]

With survival at stake, hungry people resorted to desperate remedies. Investigators found some Kentucky children were so hungry that they had begun to chew on their own hands. "We have been eating wild greens," a Kentucky miner wrote in 1932, "Such as Polk salad, Violet tops, wild onions, forget-me-not wild lettuce and such weeds as cows eat as a cow won't eat poison weeds." Such rural stopgaps, however unpleasant, were preferable to the plight of the urban hungry, many of whom were seen digging in city garbage dumps, hoping to find edible scraps. Fifty Chicagoans were observed fighting over a barrel of fresh garbage behind a restaurant.[52]

All of this was, understandably, a great shock for Americans who had been brought up on the stories of Horatio Alger. By 1937 a plurality among the poor questioned in a nationwide poll said they did *not* "think that today any young man with thrift, ability, and ambition has the opportunity to rise in the world, own his own home, and earn $5,000 a year." Other signs of a change in Americans' image of their society surfaced more rapidly. In 1931 the Soviet Union advertised in New York for six thousand skilled workers, and more than one hundred thousand Americans applied. Others pursued more traditional courses of action. Thousands went into the western mountains to search for gold. In 1935 some two hundred farm families sought a new chance by migrating to the frontier, which was now Alaska.[53]

Stories of America's plight spread worldwide. Early in 1931, people in the Cameroons collected $3.77 and sent it to New York to aid "the starving." More was needed. Some women went into one of the few fields that was still hiring in the early thirties: prostitution. Many Americans honored their national tradition of self-help by engaging in the systematic stealing of food. It sometimes became, in fact, a family affair in which children were assigned by parents to shoplift the necessary food for the entire family.[54]

Yet widespread as such looting had become by 1932, the majority of Americans seem, in the early Depression years, to have blamed themselves for their problems. Having convinced themselves that they were personally responsible for their economic success in the twenties, people had, initially at least, little choice but to accept personal responsibility for failure in the early thirties. By 1929 the American creed that held that success was open to all who were willing to work for it was ingrained in many working-class Americans. Believing that those who failed deserved to, men were often ashamed that they could no longer serve in their role as providers. So they kept to themselves, suffering in private hells, largely unaware—in any meaningful sense—of the multitudes of their fellows who were in similar situations.

If the economy was fundamentally sound—and Herbert Hoover never expressed any doubt that it was—then the Depression was a psychological, not an economic, problem. What was needed was a restoration of confidence. To achieve that end, the positive had to be emphasized. In 1930 Hoover offered Rudy Vallee a medal if he could "sing a song that would make people forget their troubles and the Depression." Hoover also launched the President's Emergency Committee on Employment (PECE). The name indicated that the situation was an emergency, not a long-term problem; the use of "employment" rather than "unemployment" in the agency's title was further positive thinking. Ultimately a somewhat more realistic name was adopted for a succeeding committee, the President's Organization for Unemployment Relief (POUR). Yet if the name was more accurate with regard to the national need, it was hardly descriptive of the organization's function. Hoover remained adamantly opposed to federal relief for the unemployed. POUR was a sounding board for suggestions from the public and, principally, a propaganda agency, issuing optimistic and soothing advertisements. As Will Rogers summed up administration policy, "There has been more 'optimism' talked and less practiced than at any time during our history."[55] One ad pictured a jobless worker and said, among other things, that the unemployed would not beg. "We're not scared, either," the ad continued. "If you think the good old U.S.A. is in a bad way more than temporarily, just try to figure out some other place you'd rather be." "I'll see it through—if *you* will!" concluded the mythical unemployed worker. Another POUR ad proclaimed: "Dollar, go forth like David!" It went on to tell readers that spending their dollars would defeat the Goliath "who wants to spread hunger and illness and despair among you."[56]

As the Depression worsened, more and more Americans came to see Herbert Hoover as that Goliath. But Hoover was not the heartless ogre that a generation and more of Democrats have depicted. He was, rather, that rarest of politicians, a man of principle. His Quaker origins left a distinct, if incomplete, imprint on Hoover. He believed firmly in individualism, but not the sort connoted by his frequently quoted term "rugged individualism." Hoover was no social Darwinist. He insisted upon equality of opportunity, and, unlike many others who used the term, he did not employ it as a mask for economic dominance by the rich. Hoover not only wanted everyone to have a chance to succeed, but he also opposed heavily concentrated wealth and believed that the unfortunate should be cared for by their communities. Another term Hoover used, "progressive individualism," was a more accurate description of his philosophy. He believed that power and decision-making should be kept close to the people. Accordingly, he wanted communities of "socially responsible individualists" to provide for the unemployed.[57] Federal relief, Hoover contended, would entail the growth of unwieldy, unresponsive, inefficient bureaucracies. It would destroy the sense of community in localities, it would strengthen the central government at the expense of individuals and local governments, and it would undermine self-reliance and hence make people dependent. Hoover was right on all counts. But his alternatives—voluntary charity, local and state relief—were wholly inadequate in the face of a crisis of unprecedented magnitude.

Still trying to restore confidence in late 1931, Hoover persuaded reluctant bankers to form a voluntary credit pool to help weaker banks. The plan's failure forced the president to take his first step away from voluntarism and agree to the creation of a government agency designed to provide loans to shore up troubled banks and businesses, the Reconstruction Finance Corporation (RFC). This represented a degree of government intervention in the economy that had no peacetime precedent.[58]

Republican prospects in 1932 were, to say the least, dim. Even those voters who were sophisticated enough to recognize that the Depression was not the personal doing of Herbert Hoover generally blamed the catastrophe on big business. Businessmen had taken credit for the prosperity decade; now they must face blame for the Depression. Republicans gladly sailed on the business yacht in the twenties; they could not easily abandon ship as the seas lapped at the decks in the early thirties. Under the circumstances, President Hoover was an almost certain loser; but so was any other Republican. To repudiate Hoover would have been to accept responsibility for the Depression, so the party faithful gave their less-than-enthusiastic endorsement for a second term that most were sure was never to be.

Glum Republicans meant cheerful Democrats, even in the midst of a depression. Out of the White House for twelve years, the Democrats were interested in nothing as much as winning. The likelihood of victory meant the struggle for the nomination would be unusually fierce. The combination of his magic surname, his leadership of the nation's most populous state, his mildly progressive record, his proven vote-getting powers, his personal victory over polio, and some shrewd political maneuvering made Governor Franklin D. Roosevelt of New York the nominee.

Roosevelt's landslide victory—the largest electoral vote margin since 1864—unquestionably represented a mandate for a "new deal," which he had promised in his acceptance speech. The vote was not really an expression of confidence in Roosevelt himself. Most of all, the large Democratic vote was simply a repudiation of Hoover. No one knew what to expect from the president-elect, but it seemed that any change had to be for the better.

Following Roosevelt's victory, the nation faced a four-month interregnum that promised to be more critical to the country's welfare than any since Lincoln had awaited the start of his presidency. The winter of 1932–33 was the most desperate of the Depression. Between 13 and 16 million people were unemployed. Funds available for relief were pitifully inadequate, but Hoover, whom Roosevelt had called a spendthrift, still refused to provide meaningful federal assistance. It was not a time for much hope.

Roosevelt's inauguration and the rapid action that followed it began to provide some hope. Aside from the banking collapse that had accelerated during the interregnum, the most immediate problem confronting the new administration was that of providing relief for the millions of depression victims for whom all resources—personal, family, local, and state—had run out. Needless to say, it was a difficult problem.

In the early months of the Depression, the question of providing for the poor continued to be viewed in the way that had become traditional in the United States, at least among comfortable folk. The basic assumption was that most poverty was self-inflicted. Indolence, improvidence, and intemperance were widely seen as the main causes of financial difficulties. There were, to be sure, some unfortunates who were genuinely unable to care for themselves: the blind, the crippled, elderly widows, and orphans. Most Americans professed a belief that such worthy poor should be helped. They also believed that in order to prevent the more numerous "unworthy poor" from obtaining assistance, charity should be extremely difficult to qualify for and should be handled entirely on the local level. If such precautions were not taken, many feared, relief would undermine self-reliance and create a large, permanent class of dependent people. Above all, adequate, easy-to-obtain public relief must never be made available, lest it upset the natural workings of the free enterprise system by discouraging workers from taking jobs at market-determined wage rates.[59]

In the early 1930s, prevailing opinion still held that any genuine relief needs in a community could and should be met by the voluntary benevolence of local citizens of means. As long as the administration and major business leaders continued to insist that prosperity was "just around the corner," traditional remedies seemed sufficient. "Our people," Hoover declared at the end of 1931, "are providing against distress from unemployment in the true American fashion." The president was whistling in the dark. So was the United States Chamber of Commerce when it asserted, "The spontaneous generosity of our people has never failed."[60]

Already in the Hoover years the problems of unemployment and destitution were unprecedented in America, and the customary means of dealing with them were plainly inadequate. By 1932 only about 25 percent of those without jobs were receiving any relief whatsoever. Those who did get on the rolls could hardly be considered particularly fortunate. In New York City, one of the better-providing localities, families on relief were given an average of $2.39 each week. Still, both businessmen and administration officials remained reluctant to admit that there was a problem, much less to do anything to deal with it effectively. Many businesses demonstrated their belief that people should be their brothers' keepers, leaving the care of the unemployed to the brothers of the destitute. Companies started schemes whereby employees could give (or, sometimes, were forced to give) part of their meager wages to help the unemployed. The main virtue of such methods of attacking the problem was that they cost employers nothing.

By 1932, however, attitudes toward the unemployment crisis were beginning to change, mainly because suffering had become so widespread that it was now more difficult to contend that the problem was the fault of the victim. Relief, moreover, was becoming a political necessity because need for it was spreading far beyond the usual poverty strata. As increasing numbers of middle-class Americans (many of whom could be expected to vote in November) demanded help, federal relief became more likely.[61]

Soon after taking office, Roosevelt proposed the creation of a Federal Emergency Relief Administration (FERA), which would make grants to the states. Under the energetic administration of Harry Hopkins, a gifted social worker who had headed New York's relief program, the FERA dispensed money to the states with extraordinary speed. Neither Hopkins nor Roosevelt liked the idea of direct relief. Like Hoover, these New Dealers feared that the dole would destroy self-reliance and create a permanent class of paupers. They were right. But in the desperate spring of 1933 there was no choice. Federally funded state doles kept the poor physically alive, a prerequisite to restoring self-reliance.

If relief was necessary, however, work relief—the creation of public service jobs for the unemployed—was clearly preferable to the dole. A person's skills and self-respect might be maintained if he worked, while both were likely casualties of direct relief. Thus Title II of the National Industrial Recovery Act called for the establishment of a Public Works Administration (PWA). The organization, placed under the direction of Secretary of the Interior Harold Ickes, was intended to stimulate recovery both through payments for its own projects and through the multiplier effects of the funds thus pumped into the economy.

Ickes favored both of these laudable objectives. His primary concern, though, was to see to it that the public's money was well spent. This meant not only constant (and highly successful) vigilance against corruption but also careful study of each project's value and how it could be completed most efficiently. All of this was highly commendable, and numerous monuments to the PWA's activities remain around the nation. But solid buildings constructed at bargain prices were not the chief need in 1933. Jobs and economic stimulation were, and here Ickes's diligence was counterproductive. The deliberate pace of spending by the PWA failed to provide a sufficient stimulus for the economy, and much of the money spent went to engineers, architects, construction companies, and materials producers. The PWA did not do enough to remember the "forgotten man."

The president was in no position to forget him. The likelihood of revolution may have been overestimated, but administration officials did consider it a possibility if relief were not provided. In any case, disaster at the polls surely awaited any president who, like Hoover, failed to provide some degree of assistance. This certainty was not lost on a politician as astute as Franklin Roosevelt, and relief expenditures rose rapidly. The FERA alone spent about 1 billion dollars a year over the next three years, which amounted to approximately 2 percent of national income, and government expenditures in this field increased greatly in 1935 and 1936. But even the earlier FERA figure takes on more meaning when one recognizes that, even after the "welfare explosion" of the 1960s, federal welfare costs represented less than 0.7 percent of national income, about one-third of the share that went for relief in 1933–34. Such massive expenditures were, of course, acceptable to a majority of Americans only because of the scale of suffering. Most people now believed that relief payments were justified, and many feared that they might soon need them.

Almost all potential recipients favored work relief over the dole, and work is what Roosevelt gave them in the winter of 1933–34. Harry Hopkins wanted a works program that, unlike the PWA, would spend quickly and spend mostly on ordinary workers' wages rather than expensive materials and equipment and high-salaried personnel. Roosevelt agreed to set up a program, the Civil Works Administration (CWA), to provide jobs and tide the unemployed over the winter of 1933–34. The CWA was strikingly successful in its objective of putting many people to work quickly. Hopkins, for the time being, virtually transformed the FERA into the CWA. Incredibly, in a few months, the organization put into operation 400,000 projects with more than 4,000,000 workers. Then it was disbanded. Roosevelt apparently thought that work and income were less necessary in the spring than the winter. He worried constantly, moreover, about the large deficits caused by the expensive work program. Most important in his decision to terminate the CWA, however, was the virulent criticism of the program from the right. Businessmen feared competition from the government, even though the CWA projects were confined to areas into which no private business would venture. Southern planters had a more serious complaint: the pitiful wages paid black CWA workers were actually more than twice the going rate for field hands. Roosevelt still thought he could get along with business; he needed the South; his reelection campaign was more than two years off.

So CWA was sacrificed. Eventually, though, the president would have to decide, as the labor song put it, which side he was on.[62]

Roosevelt made that choice in 1935. Pressure from his working-class constituency led the president to turn sharply to the left with his "second New Deal" of that year. The pressure included the remarkable popularity of Louisiana Senator Huey Long and his "Share Our Wealth" proposals, of Father Charles Coughlin's radio sermons calling for "social justice," and of Dr. Francis Townsend's Old Age Revolving Pension plan, which promised $200 each month to every citizen over sixty years of age.

Roosevelt's eventual endorsement of the Wagner Act (the National Labor Relations Act), his call for new taxes on the wealthy, and his signing of the Social Security Act all flowed from his decision to catch up with his followers who were demanding more justice and equality. Another aspect of the turn in administration policy in 1935 was an Emergency Relief Appropriation of 4.8 billion dollars. The amount was breathtaking, equaling approximately 10 percent of the national income of the previous year. Much of the huge sum went to the new Works Progress Administration (WPA), headed by Harry Hopkins. For the remainder of the Depression, relief policies and controversies centered around the WPA.

Relief policy changed dramatically under the impact of the Depression and New Deal. Thanks to the climb of suffering up the social ladder, relief had become far more widespread, somewhat less inadequate, a bit easier to obtain, and not quite so degrading. Yet it still did not nearly meet the needs of the unemployed. The WPA, at its peak in 1936 (cutbacks in WPA rolls began early in that year and increased sharply after election day), gave jobs to only about one-fourth of those counted as unemployed.

Despite the WPA's shortcomings, the accomplishments of the agency were impressive. By 1940 the organization had constructed or rebuilt more than 200,000 buildings and bridges and some 600,000 miles of roads. More important, it had helped millions of unskilled laborers (as well as a significant number of middle-class people) to survive the Depression with a modicum of self-respect.[63]

One more point about relief deserves mention. The system grew, as we have seen, when the economic crisis reached up into the middle strata and became politically dangerous. The value of relief in calming potentially rebellious Depression victims was not lost on political leaders. Nor were all relief recipients unaware of this function. "You know a hungry man is dangerous but a hungry man with a family is twice dangerous to any community," said a young WPA worker. "I don't know whether other people ever thought of it or not but, to me, WPA employment certainly has had its moral effect upon the people and to my way of thinking has kept many a good man from turning thief or bank robber." Or, he might have added to bring his thought in line with what likely was on the minds of "other people," from turning into socialists or revolutionaries. An Ohio WPA employee believed that the program was "absolutely necessary to the man in need. Without it," he said, "there would be countrywide destitution and consequent social upset."[64]

To what extent relief was motivated by a desire to relieve suffering and to what degree by the need to defuse discontent, it is impossible to say with certainty. Much circumstantial evidence exists for assigning the latter factor a heavy weight. Perhaps most significant in this regard was the rapid reduction of relief that followed Roosevelt's 1936 electoral victory. This diminution was due in part to a general improvement in business conditions and to the president's distaste for both budget deficits and relief. Yet the problem of unemployment was far from solved. The relief cuts took place with between 7 and 8 million workers without jobs, an unemployment rate of approximately 15 percent.

The effects of the cuts in relief were devastating. Those who could not get on WPA rolls were thrown back on the resources of the states and localities, resources that had already proved to be wholly inadequate. Novel measures were tried by some hard-pressed industrial states. Probably most revealing of the effects of the premature cutbacks in federal assistance was New Jersey's decision to issue, in lieu of unavailable relief payments, licenses to beg.[65]

Seen in this light, relief might also be viewed as a wedge that separated the poor from the almost poor by causing the latter to see themselves as supporting lazy welfare recipients. And yet, although there may be some truth to such an impression, the notion that it was somehow unfortunate that the New Deal provided relief for the distressed, since without this subsistence the working class might have risen in revolution, is unacceptable. This argument is based on a view of society as something other than the sum of the individuals who compose it. Such an outlook allows one to conclude that letting the unemployed starve is a way to improve the lives of the masses. It is a belief that is easier to hold if one is a comfortable professor thirty or more years after the fact than if one happens to be among the down and out during the crisis.[66]

Relief may have been the most pressing need when FDR took office, but massive problems abounded in many areas. The rapid-fire legislation of the famous First Hundred Days of the New Deal represented an attempt to begin to treat the many maladies of the American economy.

One of the most chronically ill sectors of that economy was agriculture. For many American farmers, hard times did not commence in 1929; conditions just grew worse at the end of that year. Agriculture had been depressed throughout the "prosperity decade." In addition to their economic problems, rural Americans suffered psychological dislocation. Seeing themselves as the backbone of the nation, farmers were alarmed at the apparent decline in their status in American society. The values for which they stood seemed everywhere under attack in modern, urbanizing America.[67]

The farm family hit by depression had over its city counterpart the advantage of being able to grow its own food. Still, the position of millions of farm "owners" who were mortgaged to the hilt was precarious. The net income of American farmers had reached 9.1 billion dollars in 1919. It declined during the following decade, falling to 6.2 billion dollars in 1929. As bad as farm conditions were in the twenties, though, they became far worse after depression struck the rest of the economy. Farmers' net income collapsed to 2 billion dollars in 1932, less than one-third of the already depressed level of 1929. Annual income per farm had fallen to about $300 by 1932, scarcely more than 20 percent of what it had been in 1919.[68]

The basic problem was one of overproduction, not in the sense that there was more food and fiber than the nation and the world could use but that there was more than a buying market could support. The agricultural depression of the twenties gave rise to many schemes designed to increase farm income. When Roosevelt was elected, advocates of different agricultural plans sought his approval. Master politician that he was, the new president insisted that a farm program be agreed upon beforehand by leaders of major interest groups. In this way, he could take credit for any success but could shift blame for failure to others. Such a plan might be inconsistent economically, but it would make much political sense.

The Agricultural Adjustment bill that emerged in the spring of 1933 incorporated bits and pieces of most of the various farm proposals then afloat. The basic concept, however, was clear: farm prices would be raised by government-subsidized scarcity. The principal means by which this was to be accomplished was government-organized payments to farmers who agreed to take acreage out of production. The payments were to be funded by a tax on the processing of food products.

When the Agricultural Adjustment Act became law in mid-May, the production that it sought to limit was already well underway. The only solution that Agricultural Adjustment Administration (AAA) leaders could see was to plow under crops and—to prevent a hog glut—to slaughter 6 million baby pigs and two hundred thousand sows. To many ordinary Americans it seemed like insanity to destroy food while millions in America and hundreds of millions around the world were hungry. Such critics, the experts pointed out, just did not understand economics. (On the other hand, some of the AAA leaders had a less than complete knowledge of farming. One was reported to have asked what a proposed regulation would do for macaroni growers.) Depression America faced the paradox of hunger and want existing in a land of plenty. The New Dealers' solution seemed to many observers, in this case at least, to be to destroy the plenty. Actually, however, the plenty was not wasted. The Surplus Relief Corporation canned the slaughtered pigs and distributed them to the needy.

The AAA suffered from a number of defects. The use of payments to keep land out of production was helpful to large landowners (who were represented by the Farm Bureau Federation, which was one of the main architects of the AAA). The effects on tenant farmers and sharecroppers were less beneficial. They owned no land and so could receive no direct payment. Provisions that required passing benefits on to tenants were often ignored. Their land, moreover, was frequently designated by owners for removal from production, thus cutting off the meager livelihood of the tenant. Finally, since the payments were for reducing acreage, not production, many owners simply stopped using their poorer fields and employed more intensive methods on the better land, maintaining production at the same time they were paid to reduce it.

Where Roosevelt and Agriculture Secretary Henry Wallace failed, however, nature succeeded. The massive drought that began in 1934 reduced production and raised farm prices far more efficiently than the AAA alone could have. Indeed, the drought and consequent dust bowl became so serious that by 1935 the United States was importing large amounts of wheat. This seemed to throw the wisdom of crop curtailment into question, but large growers were pleased with their higher incomes. The less fortunate continued to live in miserable poverty in the South, or to become the pathetic "Okies" and "Arkies" who fled to California in search of the promised land, a promise that was rarely fulfilled.[69]

Many of the southern tenants and sharecroppers left in poverty were black. It may at first seem baffling, in view of this continuing poverty (which was as bad for blacks in northern cities), that one of the most striking political shifts of the 1930s was the movement of a majority of black Americans from the party of Lincoln to that of Roosevelt. The switch took place not with the onset of the Depression but after 1932. In that year, FDR won less than one-quarter of the votes in the black wards of such cities as Chicago and Cleveland. Four years later his totals were up to 49 percent in Chicago and 62 percent in Cleveland. Plainly it was Roosevelt and the New Deal, not the economic collapse itself, that led to the political change among blacks. Yet Roosevelt never even proposed any legislation aimed specifically at aiding blacks or easing racial injustice. The president offered no assistance to congressional liberals attempting to pass a federal antilynching bill. Nor was segregation avoided in New Deal programs. Civilian Conservation Corps camps, for example, were completely segregated.

Policy toward blacks, to be sure, confronted Roosevelt with serious difficulties. On the one hand he had to try to maintain southern support. On the other, he sincerely wanted to help all Americans, he was under pressure from his wife and other racial liberals, and the black vote in northern states with large electoral votes was becoming important. Faced with such conflicting pressures, Roosevelt naturally tried to steer a middle course. He defended his failure to seek legislation designed specifically to help blacks by asserting that if he antagonized southern Democrats, none of his programs would get through Congress. This, he said, would hurt blacks as well as whites. Moreover, FDR contended, black people would benefit most from legislation aimed at helping the poor since a greater percentage of blacks than whites were poor.

There was a certain logic to this approach, particularly when the effects of the New Deal's loss of southern support in the late thirties are considered. And Roosevelt obviously treated blacks more fairly than had previous presidents. Although it was not a new departure for a president to consult with prominent blacks from time to time, FDR enlarged and formalized the practice. In making several blacks officials of the United States government, he took a step that was largely symbolic but nonetheless important.

Yet here the nature of New Deal relations with blacks becomes apparent. With few exceptions, black appointees in New Deal agencies were hired as "racial advisers," "advisers on Negro affairs," or heads of "divisions of Negroes." To call Roosevelt's appointees a "Black Cabinet" is to exaggerate greatly the distance he had traveled. His black advisers were more a group of salesmen who could help Roosevelt win and keep black support. For all the new recognition the Roosevelt administration accorded blacks, it was still prepared to compromise them away when it came to the important social insurance and wages and hours bills, both of which excluded the domestic- and farm-laborer jobs predominantly held by minorities.

Through all the continuing problems of injustice, though, Franklin Roosevelt was able to convey to blacks the same sense of caring that he transmitted to down-and-out whites. And the New Deal did provide benefits for blacks. Official policy in relief programs was that there was to be no racial discrimination. As several of the letters in Chapter 4 make clear, this did not prevent many local relief administrators from mistreating blacks. But the mere enunciation of a policy of equality was a great advance. In addition, referendums required by the AAA to determine policy provided many southern blacks with their first experience of voting. And the Farm Security Administration in the late thirties helped a significant number of blacks to buy and improve farms.

Whatever later critics have said about the failures of the New Deal on racial matters (and the omissions were large), the shift in black political allegiance demonstrated that blacks themselves saw the half a loaf being offered by FDR as far better than the breadless rhetoric of the Republicans. As one southern black said of his neighbors in the late thirties, "They's talked more politics since Mistuh Roosevelt been in than ever befo'. I been here twenty years, but since WPA, the Negro sho' has started talkin' politics."[70] The deck, most assuredly, was still stacked against blacks, but President Roosevelt was dealing it in a new and better—if not particularly bold—way.

Labor unions fared poorly in the relatively prosperous 1920s, and the decline in union membership was accelerated by the early Depression. By 1933 the number of Americans holding union cards was only 40 percent of what it had been in 1920. The launching of the New Deal reversed the decline by kindling a new spirit among workers. Particularly important in this regard was Section 7(a) of the National Industrial Recovery Act, which appeared to protect the rights of workers to organize. With the exception of a few industries in which workers used it effectively, however, the hope that 7(a) had raised was gone by early 1934.

But the new spirit among workers survived, and in 1934 nearly 1.5 million workers participated in some 1,800 strikes. In several places—most notably San Francisco, Minneapolis, and Toledo—the conflict approached open warfare. In several of the struggles unemployed workers joined picket lines. This was highly unusual, particularly during a depression. The jobless traditionally had been considered to be strikebreakers.

The new attitudes among workers that were evident in 1934 could not safely be ignored in Washington. The labor turbulence was one of the important motivators for the Second New Deal. In May 1935, President Roosevelt belatedly endorsed the Wagner Act, which prohibited unfair practices by employers who sought to prevent unionization. It also provided for federal supervision of elections to determine whether employees wanted to be represented by collective bargaining agents. It is important to note that this did not oblige workers to join unions. It simply made the federal government, often in the past an ally of employers, an active neutral in labor disputes. This was such an advance that the Wagner Act may well have been the most important law passed in the 1930s. Workers were now free to organize themselves, if they would and if they could.

If Roosevelt could not afford to disregard the new spirit and desire for organization among unskilled workers, those phenomena were practically ignored by many labor leaders themselves. The American Federation of Labor showed little interest in organizing the huge numbers of workers in the mass production industries. Unskilled American workers in 1934 and 1935 seemed to be a movement in search of a leader. Although he was in many ways an unlikely candidate, John L. Lewis, president of the United Mine Workers, became that leader.

Rarely one to miss the main chance, Lewis saw the opportunity to organize the widespread rank-and-file discontent. When his attempts at a serious campaign aimed at unionizing the mass-production industries were rebuffed by the AFL hierarchy, Lewis and other industrial unionists formed the CIO, an organization that did not call forth the worker actions of the thirties but responded to them. Young and rebellious workers, many of them motivated by the egalitarian values evident in some of the letters reproduced in this volume, were waiting for an organization like the CIO. They flocked into it as soon as it was formed. Such workers were not prepared to await instructions from their putative leaders. Thus, at the beginning of 1936, rubber workers at three factories in Akron, Ohio, went on strike without direction from the CIO. What made their strike notable was that, instead of picketing outside the plants, the workers occupied them.

This new and efficient tactic—the "sit-down" strike—spread rapidly. The best-laid plans of John L. Lewis could not keep up with the enthusiasm of the workers. He had been concentrating the CIO's efforts on organizing the steel industry. Automobile workers, however, would not wait. By the end of 1936 a spontaneous sit-down strike against General Motors had spread from Atlanta to the corporation's main facilities at Flint, Michigan. Six weeks later, GM surrendered, accepting the United Auto Workers as bargaining agent.

The CIO now appeared on the way toward a complete organization of the nation's mass-production industries. The United States Steel Corporation, long a bastion of antiunionism, reached an agreement with the CIO Steel Workers' Organizing Committee two weeks after GM lost its battle with the UAW. Other large employers fell quickly into line, but the gains slowed in the spring of 1937, with smaller steel companies leading the resistance. The effects of the "recession" of 1937–38 and growing public opposition to the sit-down tactic enabled several major companies to hold out against unionization until World War II.[71]

The word "union" was given a new meaning by the CIO. No longer did it connote overweight bureaucrats with gold watch chains who made deals with owners and lived off workers' dues, giving little in return. The exclusiveness of Gompers-style unionism ended. Most CIO unions organized workers without regard to race, creed, nationality, or sex. The new spirit among American workers resulted in part from the Wagner Act, in part from Roosevelt's new class-oriented politics, and in part from the launching of the CIO. But at base, it was the result of the ethical values of justice, equity, and compassion evident not only in workers' actions but also in their answers to questions on polls and in their statements in letters such as those that follow.

This book makes no attempt to retell the entire history of the Depression era. The Introduction and the brief headnotes preceding each chapter are intended to place the letters in perspective. Otherwise the people who experienced the Depression are allowed to speak for themselves. Editing has been restricted to a small number of deletions of portions of letters that seemed insufficiently interesting to justify complete reproduction. Spelling, syntax, grammar, and capitalization have been preserved exactly as written, in order to convey the full flavor of the letters. To assure the privacy of the writers, their names have been replaced by initials. In those cases where the writer made a specific request in the letter that his privacy be protected, even initials have been omitted. Division of the letters into topical categories is a matter of convenience. The categories, based upon divisions within the nation and upon the themes discussed earlier, often overlap. Many of the letters could as easily have been assigned to other chapters as to the ones in which they appear.

The underlying assumption upon which this book is based is that "ordinary" people are not merely acted upon by history. They are also actors and, to an extent, playwrights, producers, and directors as well. Too often the down and out of the 1930s have been seen as passive victims. Unquestionably, some were. The letters reproduced in this collection, however, show that many Depression sufferers were active in attempting to deal with their plight, to solve their problems. Many Depression era Americans were, in short, down but not yet out. The degree to which the human spirit was able to survive in the face of economic collapse is clear in the words of those on whom the economy fell. What follows, then, is essentially a volume written by those forgotten Americans.

PART I

The Early Depression

Hoover is my Shepherd, I am in want,
He maketh me to lie down on park benches,
He leadeth me by still factories,
He restoreth my doubt in the
Republican Party.
He guided me in the path of the
Unemployed for his party's sake,
Yea, though I walk through the alley
    of soup kitchens,
I am hungry.
I do not fear evil, for thou art against me;
Thy Cabinet and thy Senate, they do discomfort me;
Thou didst prepare a reduction in my wages;
In the presence of my creditors thou annointed
    my income with taxes,
So my expense overruneth my income.
Surely poverty and hard times will follow me
All the days of the Republican administration.
And I shall dwell in a rented house forever.
Amen.

E. J. Sullivan, "The 1932nd Psalm"

Chapter 1. Reactions to Hoover and Economic Breakdown

We have done all we can do;
There is nothing more to be done.

Herbert Hoover, 4 March 1933.

The letters contained in this chapter were addressed to Herbert Hoover's special committees set up to deal with the economic crisis, the President's Emergency Committee on Employment (PECE) and the President's Organization for Unemployment Relief (POUR). Unlike his successor, Hoover never managed to establish rapport with working-class Americans. Victims of the Depression rarely looked to him as a father figure. Accordingly, this chapter has a larger number of communications from relatively well-to-do citizens than will most of the later chapters. These are included to show the attitudes of some of those who remained basically unscathed by the Depression. Many such fortunate people continued to believe in the early thirties that those who failed must be lazy, incompetent, or stupid.

Patience remained a cardinal virtue for many in the early years of the Depression. Things would get better if everyone would remain calm, some of the well-to-do implied. Some suggested that "depressing statements" about unemployment and hunger should not be broadcast. Although President Hoover could not keep depressing stories off the radio waves, he did his part to hide the bad news by refusing to allow official unemployment statistics to be collected.

Those hard hit by the Depression could not ignore it. Some pointed to what they saw as the causes of economic collapse but continued to support Hoover. Others were less generous in their views of the president and his class. The last several letters in this chapter are examples of differing degrees of worker discontent in the Hoover years. Some of them appear to have been inspired by leftist organizations, but others are plainly the spontaneous expressions of "ordinary" workers who had become disillusioned with the economic system and the captains of industry at its helm.

One thing that is striking about all of the letters to the Hoover administration is the lack of warmth or affection for the president. Even those who supported Hoover seem to have admired, rather than loved, him. Others had, understandably, concluded that "Engineers may be intelligent but poor Presidents." Feelings toward Franklin D. Roosevelt, as later letters unmistakably show, were completely different.

1. The American people are wonderful!

Fremont, O.
Dec. 21 - 1930.

President Hoover
White House
Washington, D.C.
Hon. Sir –

I am fifty years old. For many years I have been a house-to-house canvaser, Through good times and bad. After Canvasing Akron, Ohio, Canton, Ohio and Fremont, Ohio, as well as Detroit, Mich, I say <u>The American People are wonderful!</u>

During the past 9 months I have encountered poverty, worry and patience. The people endure hard times without evidence of rancor or disloyalty. Many men try daily for employment. The hard times have served to emphasize the loyalty, the patience, the Stoic-like qualities of American citizenry. I <u>wish</u> they could get employment. Their wives and children pray for it. <u>Justice</u> cries for it. The Heart of Humanity must heed.

Sincerely,
L. J. B. [male]

---

2. There is not five per cent of the poverty, distress, and general unemployment that many of your enemies would have us believe

Contractor and Builder Real Estate Insurance Mortgages
W. H. H.
Annapolis, Maryland
September 10, 1931

President Herbert Hoover
Washington, D.C.
My dear Mr. Hoover,

It is my purpose to write you a short letter and to cheer you along with your trying undertakings. During the war I had a brief interview with you when I was fuel administrator at Annapolis, and although I well remember you, yet it may be that I am not even a memory to you. However, I was so favorably impressed that I worked for you when you were elected President, although I appear to have been born a democrat.

In these days of unrest and general dissatisfaction it is absolutely impossible for a man in your position to get a clear and impartial view of the general conditions of things in America today. But, of this fact I am very positive, that there is not five per cent of the poverty, distress, and general unemployment that many of your enemies would have us believe. It is true, that there is much unrest, but this unrest is largely caused,—by the excessive prosperity and general debauchery through which the country has traveled since the period of the war. The result being that in three cases out of four, the unemployed is looking for a very light job at a very heavy pay, and with the privilege of being provided with an automobile if he is required to walk more than four or five blocks a day.

National Relief Director, Walter S. Gifford, and his committee are entirely unnecessary at this time, as it has a tendency to cause communities to neglect any temporary relief to any of their people, with the thought of passing the burden on to the National Committee. I am also of opinion that the suggested five billion dollar loan, that the Hearst papers have been agitating, is an impractical, foolish and unnecessary burden and obligation that they would place upon the shoulders of future posterity to pay off.

One of the days, when I am in Washington, I shall hope to greet you in person for two or three minutes, and during the interval believe me to be one of your well wishers in this ocean of conflict.

Yours Sincerely,
W. H. H. [male]

---

3. President Hoover is not responsible for any of our problems

J. W. B.
Minneapolis
November 9, 1931

Hon. Walter Newton*
White House,
Washington, D.C.
My dear Mr. Newton:

I listened to the President's Relief Program for more than an hour last night. It was a good program.

The Sunday papers were full of encouraging information about almost

---

*Mr. Newton was secretary to President Hoover.

every line of activity. The advance in wheat was particularly stressed, as was the advance in the price of silver. Stocks and bonds, both foreign and domestic, were shown as having enjoyed very substantial advance over the quoted prices of the week previous. Sunday's papers made in the main pleasant reading.

In the evening, the radio programs brought out a lot of most depressing statements.

If the information contained in the papers is true, and I believe it is, as most statements are supported by statistical records, it seems to me we are not justified in broadcasting statements to the effect that six million or more people of the United States are actually starving or will starve before the winter is over, unless those who have contribute generously to the needs of those who have not.

I am not opposed to contributions for the benefit of those in need. My thought is that the President has been doing everything humanly possible to promote right thinking by the minds of the American people. The broadcasting of such a program as we listened to last night, cannot help but have a depressing effect, or of offsetting some of the things which we claim we have accomplished.

The organization responsible for the President's Relief Program is not soliciting funds. A great many of the campaigns for funds in the larger centers have been completed or will be before the end of the present week.

I was impressed last night with the fact that all reference to unemployment emphasized the suffering and deprivations we might expect to experience during the winter months. If conditions are improving, would it not be well, if these programs are to be continued, to have at least a number of the people on the program speak of the improvement that has been made, the improvement that is being made, and leaving to others the responsibility of telling of the depression that still exists in certain industries and in certain sections of the country?

If the employers of labor throughout the country would reduce the standard day's work, temporarily at least, twenty-five percent, thereby providing work for those who are at present unemployed, the necessity of providing for the maintenance of additional soup houses and shelter would be eliminated.

I am not unmindful of the problems President Hoover has been called upon to solve. They are not only national, but international. He has been criticised by many—men in high places and men in low places. I have failed to see where any of them have offered a constructive solution of any of the problems that confront us.

President Hoover is not responsible for any of our problems. Criticism comes largely from those who are responsible; and his critics will be the first to try to take the credit unto themselves as soon as we get out of our present predicament.

This letter comes from a Democrat who usually votes the Republican ticket, and it may or may not be of interest to you. However that may be, I am, with best regards,

Very truly yours,

J. B. [male]

---

4. They do not need men to work any more

Amarillo

Texas

November   1930

Colonel Arthur Woods

Chirman U.S.   Comm.

Dear sir:

I thought I would write and ask you if the Government can advise a person of some new foreign country or Some <u>big Island</u> away out in the ocean where a fellow can go and build up a home.

This United States is getting or has got to many poor laboring people in it, for the good of everybody and from now now on the schools and Colleges in these United States will be turning loose on a Glutted labor market about Fifteen milion more young common labor Pick and shovle men besides they do not need men to work any more they have machinery to do the heavy work that is fine if we could find Something else to do, but there is nothing else to do a man can not work for less than fifty cents per hour Eight hours per day and pay for his room and board.

You may say it does not cost a man four dollars a day but you must under stand there is a sunday in each week and a lot of hollodays. that a company will not let a man work.

We have an awful fine Government in this U.S. if we can keep good honest men at the head of it. but dishonest in the men at the head of this government would ruin it in a very short time.

The President of this U.S. has a big job and I am for President Hoover reguardless.

Yours truly,

G. B. [male]

5. The rich dont care so long as they have full and plenty

[Pottstown, Pa.]
October 30, 1930

[President Herbert Hoover
The White House
Washington, D.C.]
Dear Sir:

I am persuaded to write you, concerning aid to unemployment. I hope this movement will be speeded up so people in Pottstown will feel and know the results before Cold weather comes upon us, the struggling starving working class under nourished Men. women. and children. It really is alarming that this so called prosperous Nation that we must suffer on acct of a few men seeking power and rule and have laws pass to suit themselves. . . . I am one of the men out of work but the rich dont care so long as they have full and plenty. . . .

I hope relief will be coming soon and some action not Just paper talk. Oh the People have been so much belied that you cannot believe anything only what you can see. I hope that Wall St will never have the power again to cause such a panic upon the people money tied up hoarded up Is a crime. I hope the guilty gang will be punished before they die. I say this whole panic was brought on by dishonest group which I hope will be punished. . . .

[Anonymous]

6. Why does every thing have exceptional value except the human being

[Vinland, N.J.]
November 18, 1930

[Herbert Hoover
Washington D.C.]

. . . Could we not have employment and food to Eat. and this for our Children Why Should we hafto [illegible] now and Have foodless days and [illegible] days. and our children have Schoolless days and Shoeless days and the land full of plenty and Banks bursting with money. Why does Every Thing have Exceptional Value. Except the Human being—why are we reduced to poverty and starving and anxiety and Sorrow So quickly under your administration as Chief Executor Can not you find a quicker way of Executing us than to Starve us to death. . . . Why not End the Depression have you not a Heart. . . . Yet we are served from the Source of Life by setch an unjust System. . . . Why Isnt there an limitation to you people planning to get It all and Starve the rest of use. . . . Yet you have cut us of with plenty before our eyes—for your Selves. Yet You Can not use It. The people are desperate and this I have written, only typical of the masses of your Subjects. how can we be Law abiding citizens and Educate our children and be Happy Content with nothing to do nothing to Eat. when your System has Every Thing under control and cant use It. nor will you give any thing a way. why take more than you need. why make Laws. and allow Industry to take It all. why Isnt the Law fixed so Its Just as Just for one or the others then Industry couldnt take it all. and make us all victims of your Special arrangement. of things. . . . I am an Ignorant man and you are Supposed to have great Brains yet I appeal to you In behalf of thousands In your dominion who would be good americans Citizins If you would make It Possible. . . .

[Anonymous]

---

7. You men must answer for degraded selfishness

[Los Angeles, Calif.
September 1, 1931]

[Mr. Walter S. Gifford
Director, POUR
Washington, D.C.]

Surely it is a most heart-rendering life of poverty cast upon capable workers by unintelligent + cold blooded ruling of our Native Country. Engineers may be intelligent but poor Presidents. . . . Death looks better + you money-grubbers who have it all + want the earth besides would be happy if we did die + we poor old poverty [illegible] + most of our conditions you men must answer for degraded selfishness. . . . Yeah—its for you big fellow to scratch your head + smile but I hope to God your back bone will be scratching your stomachs from emptiness before you die + Gods Vengenance will be a cruel deal to all of you guilty. . . . Shame on all of you money-grubbers who laugh now—but may you + your families have torture from God—if your guilty of betraying us.

M. T. [female]

8. Now is the time for all rich men to come to the aid of their country

Denver, Colo.
[November 1930]

Col. Arthur Woods,
Dear Sir:

I am writing you as a laboring man to let you know what I think of the way this situation is being handled. I understand a railroad company is now raising a fund for the un-employed from the men. They are donating nothing but part of their time, which don't cost them a cent.

Why don't the big corporations dig down and donate a little? It's always the poor devil that has to fork over. Of course some of the companys are donating a certain per cent of what the employes raise and that's fine. It is what they all should do. Of course they couldn't pay high dividends if they donated actual money and I suppose that's what they are worrying about more than the un-employed. If they would only open up their shops and factories and put these men to work that would give people money to spen and create a market, but no, the big bugs horde their money away and it's never touched to help the under-dog. A working man puts away a little, sticks to his job and the first thing he knows he's got to donate to releive a situation he did not create. The big moneyed men created it by juggling with the market. But of course all they have to do is think up some scheme whereby they can make us take care of the un-employed. The poor guy furnishes the money, they distribute it.

They preach to the small guy, get out and spend. Well, all our money put together wouldn't come up to some capitalist's bank-roll. So why not preach to the big guy to spend some of his millions? If they would only keep their shops and factories open none of us would have to give up part of our earnings.

The first thing that should be done is stop immigration. let the other countries take care of their own un-employed. Of course the big corporations wouldn't like this either for then they couldn't get any cheap labor, but they should be kept out. Arthur Brisbane* doesn't like this either, he says immigration enlarges the market. It also Makes that many more men after the same job.

There was a peice in the Post about how the movie industry had prosprd

*Arthur Brisbane was a newspaper editor (New York *Evening Journal*, Chicago *Herald and Examiner*) noted for his editorial writing.

in spite of the depression but in another issue you read where they are laying off stars and extras. If they are prospering why don't they keep these people on the job? But that's it the big boy tightens up because every body else does. Now is the time for him to show his gratitude to those that helped him in time of prosperity by keeping them on the job.

It seems that the big companies should be preached to more than the little fellow as they control thousands of jobs. A few odd jobs won't help the situation much with thousands of men out of jobs.

People that are working are those that can spend money, which creates a market, which creates business, that makes times better. People out of work tighten up, spread gloom to others, thus scaring those that have money and of course then they tighten up too.

I wish you success in your endeavor and hope that the situation will be relieved before the winter is over.

Yours For Better Times
A Laboring Man

Now is the time for all RICH MEN to come to the aid of their country.

---

9. It's the same old "bunkum" handed out every depression

Madison, N.J.
Sept. 27, 1931.
7:30 P.M.

Mr. Walter Gifford,
New York City.
Dear Sir:

Just listened in on your radio address.

I can't believe that your intelligence allows you to believe that what you said tonight will be swallowed by the rank and file of American working men. Certainly their intelligence tells them that it's the same old "bunkum" handed out every depression.

You said, "This emergency is only temporary and therefore requires temporary relief." It's going to be the longest temporary relief you ever saw.

And before this thing is over, it's going to be "National Government" relief and the working men are to be insured against unemployment and want.

You say wages have, and are being reduced only to correspond to reduced cost of living. Why haven't you reduced telephone rates?* Ha! ha! this is

---

*Mr. Gifford was the head of A. T. & T. in addition to being director of POUR.

only one instance of hundreds I could tell you of tonight. Light and fuel have not dropped in price—poor man's necessities.

President Hoover called your crowd together a few months ago and you all faithfully promised to keep wages up. Papers were out in heavy type. How you all made such promises, and it was only same old story. Not even worth a scrap of paper. You capitalists are up against it this time. And this good old U.S.A. is going to get down to the real facts, that this Government is really meant for a rule by the people, of the people, for the people.

C. M.

Check

P.S. If I could listen to your talk over the radio you might be game enough to read this letter.

Double check.

Mr. Secretary: Dare you give this to the boss.

Triple check! As I have a lot of "Hoover Time" on my hands, would like to improve it. Please let me know where I can get some Socialist literature.

---

10. This is a radical letter but the time is here to be radical

Detroit, Mich.
September 29, 1931

Mr. Walter Gifford

Dear Sir:

You and Pres. Hoover shows at times about the same degree of intelligence as Andy [of the "Amos & Andy" radio show] does. The other night Andy was going to send a fellow a letter to find out his address.

You have told us to spend to end the slump, but you did not tell us what to use for money, after being out of work for two years you tell us this, Pres. Hoover on the other hand tells the working man to build homes, and in face of the fact nearly every working man has had his home taken off him, "some more intelligence." This is a radical letter but the time is here to be radical. when an average of two a day has to take their own life right in the City of Detroit because they can not see their way out. right in the city where one of the worlds riches men lives who made last year 259 000 000 dollars. where hundreds of peoples are starving to death. . . . Mr. Gifford why not come clean. and stop bluffing us tell us the truth. remember you have the all seeing eye of God over you. Tell us the reason of the depression is the greed of Bankers and Industrialist who are taking too great of amount of profits. . . . The other day our Pres. Hoover came to Detroit and kidded the soldier boys out of their bonus. Pres Hoover a millionaire worth about 12 000 000 dollars drawing a salary of 75 000 per year from the government asking some boys to forgo their bonus some of them have not 12 dollars of their own "Some more nerve."

Am I right when I say you and he shows the same degree of intelligence as Andy.

J. B. [male]
(unemployed tool & die designer)

[The following was written on the front of the letter by a POUR official: "no use answering"]

---

11. Oh for but one statesman, as fearless as Abraham Lincoln, the amancipator who died for us

[Oil City, Penna.
December 15, 1930]

Col Arthur Woods
Director, Presidents Committee
Dear Sir:

. . . I have none of these things [that the rich have], what do they care how much we suffer, how much the health of our children is menaced. Now I happen to know there is something can be done about it and Oil City needs to be awakened up to that fact and compelled to act.

Now that our income is but $15.60 a week (their are five of us My husband Three little children and myself). My husband who is a world war Veteran and saw active service in the trenches, became desperate and applied for Compensation or a pension from the Government and was turned down and that started me thinking. . . . [There should be] enough to pay all world war veterans a pension,* dysabeled or not dysabeled and there by relieve a lot of suffering, and banish resentment that causes Rebellions and Bolshevism. Oh why is it that it is allways a bunch of overley rich, selfish, dumb, ignorant money hogs that persist in being Senitors, legislatures, representitives Where would they and their possessions be if it were not for the Common Soldier, the common laborer that is compelled to work for a

---

*In 1924 Congress had agreed to pay World War veterans a bonus in 1945. During the Depression the demand grew for the immediate payment of that bonus. The pressure reached its peak in the summer of 1932 when some 20,000 veterans took part in a "Bonus Expeditionary Force" that converged on Washington. Although the Bonus Army was hardly revolutionary, General Douglas MacArthur drove the veterans out of Washington. The job of removing the peaceful campers was accomplished with tear gas, bayonets, and six tanks.

starvation wage. for I tell you again the hog of a Landlord gets his there is not enough left for the necessaries if a man has three or more children. Not so many years ago in Russia all the sufferings of poverty (and you can never feel them you are on the other side of the fence but try to understand) conceived a child, that child was brought forth in agony, and its name was Bolshevism. I am on the other side of the fence from you, you are not in a position to see, but I, I can see and feel and understand. I have lived and suffered too. I know, and right now our good old U.S.A. is sitting on a Seething Volcano. In the Public Schools our little children stand at salute and recite a "rig ma role" in which is mentioned "Justice to all" What a lie, what a naked lie, when honest, law abiding citizens, decendents of Revilutionary heros, Civil War heros, and World war heros are denied the priviledge of owning their own homes, that foundation of good citizenship, good morals, and the very foundation of good government the world over. Is all that our Soldiers of all wars fought bled and died for to be sacrificed to a God awful hideious Rebellion? in which all our Citizens will be involved, because of the dumb bungling of rich politicians? Oh for a few Statesmen, oh for but one statesman, as fearless as Abraham Lincoln, the amancipator who died for us. and who said, you can fool some of the people some of the time, But you can't fool all of the people all of the time. Heres hoping you have read this to the end and think it over. I wish you a Mery Christmas and a Happy New Year.

Very Truly Yours

Mrs M. E. B.

PART II

Conditions of Life in the Thirties

Out of the depths I cry to thee,
O Lord!
Lord, hear my voice!
Let thy ears be attentive
to the voice of my supplications!
Psalms 130: 1–2.

Chapter 2. Proud But Frightened: Middle-Class Hardship

We did not dare to breathe a prayer,
Or to give our anguish scope;
Something was dead in each of us,
And what was dead was Hope.

Oscar Wilde, *The Ballad of Reading Gaol*

The ravages of the Depression did not hit all Americans with the same force. Some were untouched by it; a few even profited. The ill effects were so widespread, however, that they were not confined to the very poor. Many middle-class Americans, steeped in the values of *Poor Richard's Almanac* and Horatio Alger, suddenly found themselves either unemployed or with greatly reduced incomes. Some of their reactions are contained in the letters of this chapter.

Statements made by middle-class people hit by economic hardship are especially revealing of the psychological impact of the Depression. They seem to have been proud people, deeply embarrassed by their plight and the need to seek help. Several of them pleaded that their requests be kept confidential.

The work ethic was clearly a large part of the background of many of these people. They often emphasized that they had "never as yet begged," that they had "worked many a day when . . . almost unable to stand up." An erosion of the work ethic was sometimes hinted at, though, as when the writer of the latter statement added that it was "all to no avail."

Middle-class (as well as many working-class) writers insisted that they did not want charity. In seeking assistance they made it plain that they wanted to *borrow* money. Such letter writers sometimes offered prized family possessions as security for the loans they sought. Also like their working-class counterparts, many middle-class Americans turned to the Roosevelts as a last hope, the way one might turn to a parent. In addition to this parental image, a close association of FDR and God appears frequently in the letters. Many of the writers repeated the assumption that Roosevelt must not know of the conditions facing them, for "if only the President could know he would help."

Perhaps the greatest of the middle-class worries of the thirties was that of losing the family home. The Home Owners' Loan Corporation, launched in 1933, was seen by many as their salvation. For some it was, but for others it was a huge disappointment. Like other alphabet agencies, HOLC demonstrated that the New Deal could sometimes create hopes and then destroy them. In fact, HOLC provided only a temporary salvation for many. The thousands of homes it did save notwithstanding, by 1938 over 100,000 HOLC mortgages had been foreclosed.[1]

In the letters that follow, some of the splits between middle-class victims and their poorer counterparts are evident, but so, too, is the fact that the problems facing the newly poor were becoming more similar to those of the chronically poor.

The last four letters in the chapter are from people who are apparently quite poor but who express the same shame at asking for help and the same desire that their letters be kept confidential that are characteristic of the middle-class letters.

---

12. To have this baby come to a home full of worry and despair, with no money for things it needs, is not fair

Eureka, Calif.
June 14, 1934

Mrs. F. D. Roosevelt
Washington, D. C.
Dear Mrs. Roosevelt:

I know you are overburdened with requests for help and if my plea cannot be recognized, I'll understand it is because you have so many others, all of them worthy.

But I am not asking for myself alone. It is as a potential mother and as one woman to another.

My husband and I are a young couple of very simple, almost poor families. We married eight years ago on the proverbial shoe-string but with a wealth of love. We both wanted more than anything else to establish a home and maintain that home in a charming, quiet manner. I had a job in the County Court House before I married and my husband was, and is, a surveyor. I kept my job as it seemed the best and only way for us to pay for a home as quickly as we could. His work was not always permanent,-as surveyors jobs seldom are, but we managed to build our home and furnish it comfortably. Perhaps we were foolish to put all our money into it but we felt it was not only a pleasure but a saving for the future.

Then came the depression. My work has continued and my salary alone has just been sufficient to make our monthly payments on the house and keep our bills paid. But with the exception of two and one-half months work with the U.S. Coast and Geodetic Survey under the C.W.A, my husband has not had work since August, 1932.

My salary could continue to keep us going, but—I am to have a baby. We wanted one before but felt we should have more assurance for the future before we deliberately took such a responsibility. But now that it has happened, I won't give it up! I'm willing to undergo any hardship for myself and I can get a leave of absence from my job for a year. But can't you, won't you do something so my husband can have a job, at least during that year? I realize there is going to be a lot of expense and we have absolutely nothing but our home which still carries a mortgage of $2000. We can't lose that because our baby will need it. And I can't wait until the depression is over to have a baby. I will be 31 in October and I'll soon be too old.

We had such high hopes in the early spring that the Coast and Geodetic work would continue. Tommy, my husband, had a good position there, and we were so happy. We thought surely our dreams of a family could come true. Then the work ended and like "The best laid plans of mice and men" our hopes were crushed again. But now Fate has taken it into her own hands and left us to work it out somehow. I'm happy, of course, but Tommy is nearly out of his head. He has tried every conceivable prospect but you must know how even pick and shovel jobs do not exist.

If the Coast and Geodetic work could continue or if he could get a job with the Bureau of Public Roads, - anything in the surveying line. A year is all I ask and after that I can go back to work and we can work out our own salvation. But to have this baby come to a home full of worry and despair, with no money for things it needs, is not fair. It needs and deserves a happy start in life.

As I said before, if it were only ourselves, or if there were something we could do about it, we would never ask for help. We have always stood on our own feet and been proud and happy. But you are a mother and you'll understand this crisis.

Tommy is competent and dependable. He has a surveyor's license and was level man for the U.S. Coast and Geodetic work in this (Humboldt) county. He will go away from home for work, if necessary, but, dear Mrs. Roosevelt, will you see if you can arrange for a job for him? It sounds impossible, I know, but I am at a point where I ask the impossible. I have to be selfish now.

I shall hope and pray for a reply and tell myself that you are the busiest woman in America, if I don't receive it. I am going to continue to work as long as I can and then- an interval of waiting. God grant it will be serene and untroubled for my baby's sake.

Very sincerely yours,
Mrs. M. H. A.
Eureka,
Humboldt County,
California

13. I have always put up a good fight, and worked many a day when I was almost unable to stand up, but all to no avail

St. Louis, Mo.,
10/23/33

Hon. Franklin D. Roosevelt,
Chief Executive:-

After listening to another of your very interesting talks over the Radio last night, as I have never missed any, I am taking the liberty of writing you, and I will try to keep it as brief as possible.

Am the father of five good Christian children, and my wife has been, and still is an invalid most of the time for the past twelve years; being afflicted with a very sore limb, being caused from vericose ulcers.

I have always been able to provide fairly well for my family, but in the past three years my salary has been on a constant decline, but still I am thankful that I have a position.

The points that I am trying to bring out are these: I owe a few little minor bills that have accumulated in the past three years, through no fault of mine. These people keep hounding me night and day. Through this, I got back with other matters. Even to the [illegible], and this is the reason for me writing you; Winter coming on, no coal in our coal bin, and the children needing warm clothes to go to school. Two children in Grammer School, and two in High School. Cannot even give my wife the necessary medical attention she should have.

I have a loan company that I borrowed some money from, and who have more back now than was borrowed, who keep on Garnisheeing my pay when I fall behind.

Is there some way or some person who I can go to that can help me through my difficulty. I have never as yet begged, but I must and will be very candid, that I would appreciate some kind of help for just a short period of time, so that I can get caught up a little and back on my feet right again. I have always put up a good fight, and worked many a day when I was almost unable to stand up; but all to no avail. I am 50 years old, and never missed an unnecessary day from work, until just forced to do so.

Thanking you in advance for any help, advice or information given me, I remain, your humble servant,

[Initials omitted because of
writer's request] St. Louis, Mo.
My one request is, to please keep this correspondence confidential.

14. I assure you I am worthy of any help you render

Miami, Fla.
December 14, 1934

Mrs. Franklin D. Roosevelt
Washington, D.C.
Dear Madam—.

I am a widow with a son fourteen years of age and am trying to support him and myself and keep him in school on a very small sum which I make.

I feel worthy of asking you about this: I am greatly in need of a Coat. If you have one which you have laid aside from last season would appreciate it so much if you would send it to me. I will pay postage if you see fit to send it. I wear size 36 or 38.

Please treat this confidentially and I shall do likewise in case you reply.

I assure you I am worthy of any help you render.

Sincerely—
[Initials omitted because of
writer's request]

15. Our pride isn't all gone

Lawndale, California,
Feb. 1—34.

Most Honorable President:

I am writing you this morning in all faiths, that if I can get word to you of our horrible plight you will not pass it by unnoticed.

I am a mother of seven children, and utterly heart broken, in that they are hungry, have only 65¢ in money, The father is in L.A. trying to find something to do,—provisions all gone—at this writing—no meat, milk—sugar —in fact, about enough flour for bread two meals—and thats all, I have two children in High School—and our pride isn't all gone, our story is this—and if we have a chance we can care for ourselves and be happy.

We have a boy 17 yrs. old who is capable of holding a good position as a musician, is an excellent French Horn player, I have been told by good musicians he is a professional now. There is a job he could have had a while ago in the C.W.A. program of music that would help us out. but this being handled thru county we could not take advantage of it, having not been here a year. . . . O, President, my heart is breaking, as I see him go from home with half enough to eat, and go all day with out a bite of lunch, to be sure he could <u>beg</u> his lunch but he's to proud to beg as long as he can help it, and I have spent the day yesterday praying God to help me bear this, and as I tried to prepare their very scarce breakfast, [illegible] that came if only the President could know he would help you to help your selves, and on this impulse I try to tell you. . . . O, what a burden and how helpless I am, how proud I am of my children, and how dark a future under this condition.

Their father is 62 yrs, old—a preacher a good carpenter—a saw-filer—but Industry won't hire a man This age, scarcely, even if they are strong in body, and he has no church to preach in—so—

O, surely there's a place for us in the world. . . .

I humbly pray God's Divine blessing on you, for you have tried every way to help the people.

Very Sincerely,
Mrs. I. H.

---

16. I would have killed myself if I would have lost my house

Montvale, N.J.
Aug 28, 1934

Dear Mrs. Roosevelt,

Thank you very much for helping me to keep my house. If it wasn't for you I know I would have lost it. I hope and pray that Mr. Roosevelt will keep his position a long time. You have saved my life. I would have killed myself if I would have lost my house. I will never forget you and will always pray for you and your family. I went to the Home Loan and they said everything would be allright. Forgive me if I caused you any trouble. I remain.

yours truly,
Mrs. J. G.

17. I am sure the president, if only he knew, would order that something be done, God bless him

Seattle, Wash.
Dec. 12—1934

Federal Emergency Relief
Administration
1734 New York Ave N.W.
Washington D.C.
Gentlemen:

When the Home Owners Loan Corporation first opened in Seattle, I made an application for a loan, the mortgage was for $2,000.00 on a 6 room house and nearly an acre of land, during the last two years conditions have been so adverse with me that I have been unable to make any payments on the interest neither have I been able to pay the taxes, the mortgages at first agreed to take the Government bonds, but when certain repairs were included, the total amount the Government would loan was not enough to pay the mortgagee all his money in fact it would show a loss of nearly $400.00 after all acrued interest together with all taxes and repairs, so the mortgagee refused to take the bonds, and consequently my loan was rejected although I was one of the first to apply. I took it up with the repair department, to let me do the painting and repair the roof myself and in that way give the extra money to the mortgagee but just when it seemed I was about to get my loan through the Government stopped all loans, and since the mortgagee has been hot on my trail demanding me to give him a deed or he will foreclose at once.

Gentlemen, this is all I have in the world my home and family. I have four boys and a little girl all in school this is an Ideal place to raise my family to be good american citizens, we have enough good ground to raise lots of garden stuff and this goes a long way toward keeping the table, we are now forced on relief and it seems that everything comes at once, if they are allowed to take away my little home I don't know what I'll do, I understand the Government is planning to supply homes for those who have none, it would be 100 times better in my particular case if the Government would make it possible for me to keep my own little home.

I always have been able to give my family a decent living until economic conditions got so bad I was unable to make it go any longer.

I am inclosing the last letter I received from the mortgagee.

I sincerely believe if the Government will help me save my place, it wont be long before I will again be on my feet, I think, the <u>worry</u> and wear and tear for fear that the mortgagee would try and foreclose on me has kind of gotten me down a little, I have not been well for two or three weeks, but I'm sure if I can secure help from the Government at this time of my distress, it wont be long till I will again be on my feet.

I sincerely <u>hope</u> and <u>pray</u> you will come to my aid and help me save my home for my family, if I should loose it I don't know what I'll do as I have <u>no other place to go</u>, if I can save it, I will be able to raise my family to be <u>good useful citizens</u>.

My place is worth about $3500.00 but to me it is my <u>home</u>. where I have a lovely happy family, good loving wife, who is thrifty, energetic, and who makes a home what it should be, we teach our children to love God, go to Sunday school and train them to live to be <u>proper Americans</u> who love their country, and if needs be give their lives for it.

I believe God will see us through some way but it has been the hardest thing I have had to go through, this maybe His way so I'm writing to you <u>asking and praying</u> that you will do something to save our little home.

I am sure the President, if he only knew, would order that something be done, God Bless him. he is doing all he can to relieve the suffering and I am sure his name will go down in history among the other <u>great men</u> of our country.

> Respectfully Yours
> A. G. [male]
> Seattle
> Wash

---

18. I have no money, no home and no wheres to go

> Phila., Pa.
> November, 26, 1934

Honorable Franklin D. Roosevelt.
Washington, D. C.
Dear Mr. President:

I am forced to write to you because we find ourselves in <u>a very serious condition</u>. For the last three or four years we have had depression and <u>suffered</u> with my <u>family</u> and little children <u>severely</u>. Now Since the Home Owners Loan Corporation opened up, I have been going there in order to save my home, because there has been unemployment in my house for more than three years. You can imagine that I and my family have suffered from lack of water supply in my house for more than two years. Last winter I did not have coal and the pipes burst in my house and therefore could not make heat in the house. Now winter is here again and we are suffering of cold, no water in the house, and we are facing to be forced out of the house, because I have no money to move or pay so much money as they want when after making settlement I am mother of little children, am sick and losing my health, and we are eight people in the family, and where can I go when I don't have money because no one is working in my house. The Home Loan Corporation wants $42. a month rent or else we will have to be on the street. I am living in this house for about ten years and when times were good we would put our last cent in the house and now I have no money, no home and no wheres to go. I beg of you to please help me and my family and little children for the sake of a sick mother and suffering family to give this your immediate attention so we will not be forced to move or put out in the street.

Waiting and Hoping that you will act quickly.

Thanking you very much I remain

Mrs. E. L.

---

19. He is worse off then the real poor

[Cincinnati, Ohio
April 16, 1932]

Department of Labor
Presidents Organization
Washington D.C.

. . . tell me what kind of help can this man [unemployed homeowner] get he is worse off then the real poor, you will help the poor whose has spent all his money in good times now he is the one who gets first aid but the little home owner can get nothing and doesnt know what to become of him . . .

[Anonymous]

20. It is very humiliating for me to have to write you

Chicago Ill 4/3—35

Mrs F.D. Roosevelt
Washington D.C.
Dear Mrs Roosevelt:—

Please pardon the liberty I am taking in writing you this note. Like thousands of others have lost and used up what we have saved, have been forced to go on relief. Have been compelled to store the small amt of things we had, and live in one room which is detrimental to our health. and unless we can raise our storage chg. Amt $28 by 4/10 the things may be sold for storage while not so valuable to any one else there are things that Cannot be replaced. I would like to borrow the amt $28 so I can pay the chg. and get a More healthful place to live. We are American born citizens and have always been self-supporting. It is very humiliating for me to have to write you Asking you again to pardon the privilege I am taking. I am hoping I may hear from you without publicity by ret. post.

Very Respectfully
Mrs. [Initials omitted because of
writer's request]

21. Somehow we must manage—but without charity

Troy, N.Y.
Jan. 2, 1935.

Dear Mrs. Roosevelt,

About a month ago I wrote you asking if you would buy some baby clothes for me with the understanding that I was to repay you as soon as my husband got enough work. Several weeks later I received a reply to apply to a Welfare Association so I might receive the aid I needed. Do you remember?

Please Mrs. Roosevelt, I do not want charity, only a chance from someone who will trust me until we can get enough money to repay the amount spent for the things I need. As a proof that I really am sincere, I am sending you two of my dearest possessions to keep as security, a ring my husband gave me before we were married, and a ring my mother used to wear. Perhaps the actual value of them is not high, but they are worth a lot to me. If you will consider buying the baby clothes, please keep them (rings) until I send you the money you spent. It is very hard to face bearing a baby we cannot afford to have, and the fact that it is due to arrive soon, and still there is no money for the hospital or clothing, does not make it any easier. I Have decided to stay home, keeping my 7 year old daughter from school to help with the smaller children when my husband has work. The oldest little girl is sick now, and has never been strong, so I would not depend on her. The 7 year old one is a good willing little worker and somehow we must manage —but without charity.

If you still feel you cannot trust me, it is allright and I can only say I donot blame you, but if you decide my word is worth anything with so small a security, here is a list of what I will need-but I will need it very soon.

2 shirts, silk and wool. size 2
3 pr. stockings, silk and wool, 4 1/2 or 4
3 straight flannel bands
2 slips—outing flannel
2 muslim dresses
1 sweater
1 wool bonnet
2 pr. wool booties
2 doz. diapers 30 × 30—or 27 × 27
1 large blanket (baby) about 45" or 50"
3 outing flannel nightgaowns

If you will get these for me I would rather no one knew about it. I promise to repay the cost of the layette as soon as possible. We will all be very grateful to you, and I will be more than happy.

Sincerely yours,
Mrs. H. E. C.

---

22. These pass few years have been a dark struggle

Jamestown N.J.
Nov. 1st 1935.

Mrs Franklin Roosevelt
Dear Madam:—

Perhaps you will think it a strange thing by me writing to you, but I shall endeavor to make it plain before I have finished my letter.

First of all have been interested in all the things you've been doing since our president's wife and admire your courage in your place. But as I was deeply in prayer to God a short time ago praying that I might receive the nessacry needs in life for my body.

As my husband has had a battle to work to earn enough to keep us with shelter + food and a little clothing which has been put on his own body to keep him so he could work. these pass few years have been a dark struggle we lost our home and all through it. But yet my faith looks to God our Maker he will guide and keep us to the end. But as it is coming nearer toward colder weather I have nothing for my body to keep me warm and can't see where I will be able to get it out of my husbands small earnings as we have debts to pay as I have cost him so much through sickness in the pass few years. And I was impressed through prayer for God to put some one on my heart that might want to lend a helping hand. In some way   I haven't had a new coat in 8 years and my coat is beyond wearing any-more under clothes dresses shoes and such things is needed so bad by me   I am a rather stout woman weigh 189 lbs 5 ft 7 in. high age 49 years   I get when I have size 48 to 50 bust in dresses coat I believe I must be a least 52 <u>in</u> shoes I wear size 5. perhaps you might have some things you want me to have   I shall greatly appreciate it and will know it is an answer to prayer   I am a Christian and striving everyday I live to please God. and do his will please don't accept this letter as begging but as I have meant it to be to you   May Gods' riches blessing go with it and I will be waiting to hear from you.

Mrs M. W.
Jamestown
N.J.

I shall keep praying For the prayer of a righteous man availeth much. God hears and answers prayer.

---

23. I got faith in you and the Lord together

Fort Worth Texas
Nov. 9. 1934

dear Mr Roosevelt i am riting to you for help if you please will help us we are Bying a home from Mr Stuckert and Company and we have got so we can not keep up the Paymet and Now they want to take the Place away from us and we have 8 Children to take Care of and no Body working but my husband and he is getting surch a Little Pay for his work and we have a very sick Child and the man want to Put us out and we have no money to move on . . . and i am asking you for help and dont let them take our Place away from us pleas sir Becaus when we was working hard to keep our Payment up and soon we all got out of work he want to take the home away from us and dont want to give us a Chance Because i had work to hard to Loss all of that money i have payed on this home and if you Pleas dont Let them take it away from us please sir Because if you are a Child of God you will help us out in our [illegible] and i thought it was against the Law to take folks homes now since this N.R.A. come out and Please Mr Roosevelt dont Let them take our home away from us Please sir Because i I have spent all of my money on this home and now they want to take it away from us and I was told to rite to you for help and i would get it and i got faith in you and the Lord together that you will help us in our trouble and answer soon Pleas sir

from Mr. and Mrs. G. M.

fort worth Texas

Chapter 3. The Grass Roots:
Rural Depression

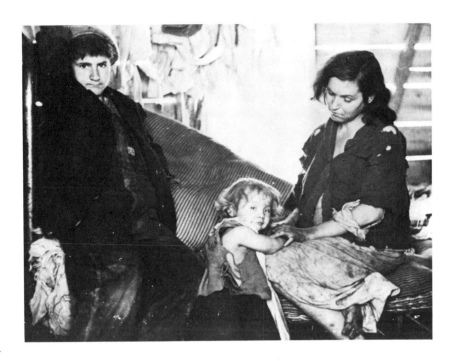

Seven cent cotton and forty cent meat
How in the world can a poor man eat?
Poor getting poorer all around here,
Kids coming regular every year.
Fatten our hogs, take 'em to town,
All we get is six cents a pound.
Very next day we have to buy it back,
Forty cents a pound in a paper sack.

Bob Miller in *Hard Hitting Songs for Hard-Hit People*

Rural and small town people in the 1930s were, of course, steeped in the American values of individualism, self-reliance, hard work, and thrift. The hold of such values, as well as the bleak conditions of life, are evident in some of the letters contained in this chapter. Writers said that they sought not relief but work.

The letters that follow show many of the problems that were frequently the lot of the rural poor in the thirties. The notes written by Arkansas tenant farmers to Norman Thomas, for example, underline in bold strokes the conditions landlords often placed upon tenants and sharecroppers. In turning to Thomas for help, these Arkansans were viewing the Socialist leader in much the same light as that in which so many poor Americans saw the Roosevelts: he was a possible source of assistance. The Southern Tenant Farmers' Union would attempt to organize such oppressed people so that they could help themselves.[1]

Although most rural Americans clung to their traditions and pride, the Depression forced many to set aside the former and swallow the latter. As we have already seen, requests to the first family for financial assistance were common. Even more poignant, though, were the letters to Eleanor Roosevelt asking for old clothes, one of which we have already seen. Thousands of such appeals reached the White House in the mid-thirties.[2] They came from urban as well as rural residents, but several representative requests from small town correspondents are included in the present chapter.

---

24. Dont you know its aful to have to get out and no place to have a roof over your sick child and nothing to eat

Winnsburo, La
Oct. 29, 1935

Mrs. F. D. Roosevelt
Dear Ladie

I read your letter telling me to write to the relif office for help I did they wrote me that they was puting people off the relif now instead of takin them on and I dont want on the relif if I can help it I want to work for my livin but the last thing we have is gone my cow that I ask you to send me some money to save her for my little children to have milk has bin taken and we only ge $17.50 on our debt for her we picked cotton at 40¢ per 100 lbs till it was all gone now there isnt one thing here that we can do to get bread to eat my sick child is still livin and takin medicine but the Dr says he cannot keep leting us have medicine unless we pay him some for he is in debt for it and the man that has let us have a house and land to work wont let us stay in the house if we cant get a mill plow the land with and we cannot get a mill and cant get a house and dont you know its aful to have to get out and no place to have a roof over your sick child and nothing to eat I cant tell all my troubles there isnt any use we only have a few days to stay here in the house now wont you please send me some money I am sure you can three hundred dollars would get us a mill some corn and other things we need my children hasent gone to school a day and if we cant get some help they wont please send me some money and please dont write me like you did before my Husban is in bad condishion and if you write me a letter like you did before it will hurt him so much so wont you please send it and say nothing about it I live 15 miles from my postoffice have no way to go no place and cant stay here many more days so please help me soon the man that the place belongs to wants his land worked and he is nice and kind and will wait on us a little longer I hope I wont be disappointed my troubles is great I has to get help from you in time to get to stay here for dont know any place we can go so please hury and asking you again to please not write anything about me asking you for help again wishing you much pleasher

Mrs. C. D. C.

Winnsburo, La

---

25. I have laid many a night & cried my self to sleep when I think of what I have to work with

April 1935

Dear Friend,

Mrs. Roosevelt

Just a few lines in regard to the letter I had wrote to you a short time ago I was wondering if you had received it depression has put us in debt so deep that we are almost forced to ask for money in some way I am trying to win a contest of $3,500.00 but I would be satisfied if I could only get $350.00 that woulnt cover our bills would you please write a letter to Ernie Miller, Manager, Department Da—18C. H.Q. Building, Cincinnati, Ohio & ask him to please give me a prize I am telling the truth in the very depth of my heart how bad we are in need of money that is why I am begging to win this contest. Oh how I wish you could come to my home today & see what I have to keep house with we have an 8 room bunglelow that we paid $950 for it & it is going to ruin if we cant fix it up there is no roof on it & the sheeting is wearing out on account of the roofing being so bad & the wood work inside is bad because the varnish is wore off I have nothing for on the floors except you might say rags left of the linoleum & we have no mattresses for our beds only things laid together for a bed. my dishes are nearly all broken. we have 4 boys. I am a Diabetic patient I am feeling pretty good but I do not have the money to get the medicine I should have no one knows what these hard times mean to one unless you have once gone through with it our family seems broken up the kiddies are not happy because they do not have one toy to play with & I have laid many a night & cried my self to sleep when I think of what I have to work with. the town we live in is small & there are no factory of an kind to get work from. I suppose you think I am writing this just to get a pile of money but I am telling you the truth. I thought maby if you would write a letter to Prize Manager for which I gave you the address & ask him kindly to give me a prize he would do it quicker if for you because I suppose he would think I was only a sucker but I want to be honest all answers must be sent in this month if he would give me the full amount $3,500.00 I would repair my home & pay my debts, Doctor Bills, Store Bills, Gas etc & the rest I would take & buy some land that I could raise the things we need to eat. If you will be so kind to ask the manager to help me out I hope your reward will be Heaven some day my Husband & I have both given our votes for Mr. Roosevelt & Mr. Earle* & I want to thank them both for what they are doing to get the world back to how it should be I know there task is great but I believe if they succeed in trying they will win

I will close hoping to hear a return

Yours Respectfully
Mrs. C. C.
Summerville, Pa.

---

26. Can you fix for me some way so my family wil not purish

Aug. 6, 1934.
Newcomb, Tenn.

Mr. J. Will Taylor†

I am enclosing you a few lines for instructions if you pleas I am here with 5 five children and a wife and under the new act of law I cant get a days work

*George H. Earle, elected in 1934 as the first Democratic governor of Pennsylvania in 44 years.
†United States Congressman (Republican, Tennessee).

at eny thing at all I havt had a days work for over two 2 years I am a disable body man and cant get a days work at all. I am a ruptured man my family is barfooted and naked and an suferns and we all are a goin to purish if I cannot get some help some way I cant get eny ade at all and if I could get it in Scot County where it is from me I could not go and get it for it is about 20 miles to the clostly rail rode station from where I live in the county. I have got no horse no autmobel and no nothing to ride can you pleas if posible fix for me to get some help some way can you fix for me some way so my family will not purish.

So hoping to here from you soon from

N. P. [male]
Newcomb, Tenn.

---

27. I hate to see Xmas come this time

Sulphur Springs, Texas
December 11, 1934.

President Roosevelt,
Washington, D. C.
Dear President:

I am in debt needing help the worst in the world. I own my own little home and a few live stock. Nine (9) head of red white face cattle and a span of mules. I have them all mortgaged to a man and he is fixing to foreclose me.

I have done all I could to pay the note and have failed on everything I've tried. I fell short on my crop this time and he didn't allow me even one nickle out of it to feed myself while I was gathering it and now winter is here and I have a wife and three (3) little children, haven't got clothes enough to hardly keep them from freezing. My house got burned up three years ago and I'm living in just a hole of a house and we are in a suffering condition. My little children talking about Santa Claus and I hate to see Xmas come this time because I know it will be one of the dullest Xmas they ever witnessed.

I have tried to compromise with the man that I am in debt to and he wont except nothing but the money or my stock and I can't borrow the money and I need my stock so I am asking you for help of some kind please.

So I remain,

Your humble servant,
N. S. [male]
Sulphur Springs, Texas.

P.S. That man won't even agree for me to have my stock fed.

28. We are on relief but the people here want give us any thang

Parsons, Kansas
Nov-12-1935

To the President of the U.S.A.
Washing D. C.
Dear President   I am writing you to let you know we are a family in Need.
and are not getting the proper attention. I am a widow left without any
thang. I have a boy who was hurt in school he is cripple.

We are left with support of any kind   we are on the relief but the people
here want give us any thang. we cant get any fuel   Nothing a long food line
they wont give us any consideration at all. Just give us a little money not
enough to buy food. some weeks we dont have anythang to get food. my
children need every thang to wear. Money is so short I would appreciate all
the help I can get   I have four children three boys and on girl and we havnt
a home

[Anonymous]
Parsons Kansas

29. Time have been so hard on us

Knoxville, Ill.
March 29 1934

Mrs. Franklin Rosevelt
Dear Madam:

I now drop a few lines to ask you a few questions as I can not find out any
place else.
Now as my daughter die and left 3 little girls 4 years ago and as time have
been so hard on us and as I have been told by folks we should have a pension
for to help support the girls and as I have try to find out here and I cannot. I
have been told to write to you and ask you about it. Now I do not care to part
with Un little one and as last year was a very hard year on us and we are a
family of 9 and as my husband has been work on the ceed. Projest but it sure
is very hard to keep 9 and 12 dollars other for me to see if I could not get a
pension to help care for the 3 girls.
for I am glad to keep them at home if I can only have a very   Now I have to
school them little one they need clothes and things and as I can not them

they are in the 9th grade 5th and 3th grade and now in the time I like to be able to keep them going right along. would like to hear from you to see if they are entitled to a pension. I also have 2 boys in the 8th no I have quite abit to care for.

I will close before this reach you all right and before you can under stand this all right

from Mrs. N. A.
Knoxville Ill.

P.S. As we were try to buy us a small. Place and as we wer out of work and as the chinch bug and dry weather kill all of our crop now we have to move if we can find aplace we do not know where we go so please let me here right back as was time is out April 4. We try to get 5 or 10 acre so we can raise most of our livig.

Answer soon.

and oblige me.
Mrs. A.

---

30. I have not got any work are no where to put my thing

[April 5, 1934]

Mr Norma Tohmas

Dear Sir

in regard to condition I am in I have Not got any work are No where to put My thing   I have got My house hold setting in a wood shed and the rain is runing ever thing I have got   I thought I would write you and see if you help me get Me a tent are some place to take my wife and thing

Your E. W. [male]
[Tyronza, Arkansas]

---

31. He got half of every thing

April 6, 1934

Dear Mr Norman Tohmas

there is a man Live clost he get $4.50. Every 2 weeks he has to trade at Brown Store and Brown Charge him 50¢ for letting him traid there   I live on Brown place he Says I haft to move For he going to tear this Old house there no place I can find to move to   I ask him for a garden he Said no Mr Spirun   Shear crop for him he him he got half of Every thing he rais the paople that get orders Just haft to trade at Sertin Stores and they our

Charge for their products there are me and my to Babys and mother and her little Boy   no one Elce would turn Brown in So I thought I would

Miss L. B.
Leachville, Ark.

---

32. If you would send me some of the clothes that is of no longer use to you

Waterburg, Vt.
Jan 19 1934

Dear Mrs. Roosevelt:

I am write you to ask you if you would send me some of the clothes that is of no longer use to you

I have a family of nine children   It would be if grate helf of you would send me some clothes witch I could fix over for them.

I would be very grateful

I remain

Your respectfully
Mrs. A. M.
Waterburg Vermont

---

33. For the first time of my lifetime I am asking a favor

Goff Kansas
May 10-1935

Mrs Franklin D. Roosevelt:

My Dear Friend:

For the first time of my lifetime I am asking a favor and this one I am needing very badly and I am coming to you for help.

Among your friends do you know of one who is discarding a spring coat for a new one. If so could you beg the old one for me. I wear a size 40 to 42 I have not had a spring coat for six years and last Sunday when getting ready to go to church I see my winter coat had several very thin places in the back that is very noticeable My clothes are very plain so I could wear only something plain. we were hit very hard by the drought and every penny we can save goes for feed to put in crop.

Hoping for a favorable reply.

Your friend Mrs. J. T.
Goff. Ks

34. He cannot work for the clothes because he has not got any clothes to work in

Martinsburg, W. Va.
January 16, 1935

Dear Mr. Neely:*

I am writing to you to see if you can help me of what I am writing you. My family needs some clothes for they are about naked i have four boys going to school and this makes the second week they have stay home for they do not have any clothes or shoes to wear.

I wrote to Mr. Hopkins a few weeks ago about the matters and I have got no clothes yet. Mr. Hopkins write to Charleston W. Va. and they wrote to me to see the Administrater here. And I seen the vistor and she said they made there own rules and they said I had to work for the clothes befor I could get them or my son and he cannot work for the clothes because he has not got any clothes to work in. And I have got one little boy he has not had any shoes on this winter. I notify the school board about my children staying home from school and the school lady sent me to Mrs. Thorn who is on the board on the relief office and the Administrator here said that Mr. Hopkins letter did not amount to anything.

They are 11 of us in the family and i do not make money enough to buy them clothes for I only make $7.20 a week a 96 hours a month. I do not refuse to work for the clothes but my family and myself need the clothes bad before I can work for them and will you please try and help me.

Your truly,
J. T. C. [male]

35. We have had lot of bad luck

November 25, 1935

Dear Mrs. Roosevelt:

I will take the most pleasure in writing to you. I am writing to see if you have any cloths that you could give me. I live in the country and I haven't got enough maoney to buy for my family and I need a coat if you have an old coat or swetar you can give me   I will be glad to get them. We have had lot of

*Matthew M. Neely, United States Senator (Democrat, West Virginia).

bad luck. We are on one of the rehabilitation farms and we have made some food this year. We have just been on it one year and we are still going to stay on it   I think it is grand and I appreciate every thing the president has done for us. If you have a picture of yourself and Mr. Roosevelt please send me one for I sure do want one. I am wishing the president the best of health and good luck and also you. if you have any thing you can give me please sent it to me.

> Sincerely
> Mrs. J. N. T.
> Athens, Ga

---

36. Oh don't think that it is not with a effort I ask you

[June 1936]

Dear Mrs. Rosevelt:

I am coming to you for help   please do not think this does not cause a great feeling of shame to me to have to ask for old clothing. I am a Luthern Sunday School teacher. we are very poor. I know we must not let our clothes keep us from church (neither do I), but some times I feel so badly when I see all the others dressed so nice. I don't care for swell clothes, But you know one feels awful in old clothes worn shiney and thread bare. I think your clothes would fit me by your picture. Please do not think me unworthy. I am so badly in need of a summer coat and under things and dresses. oh don't think that it is not with a effort I ask you to please send me anything you may have on hand in that line which you do not care to wear yourself. Not a great lot only a few please. I never thot the time would come when I would find it nessary to do this   oh please help me. May God bless you and Mr. Rosevelt. If you think me unworthy don't send anything. But think! think! hard put yourself in my place. we mothers always put what little we have to spend on our children. I to am a mother. I haven't had a new coat in 16 years so please don't think me unworthy   I do not wish my children to feel ashamed. regardless of what you do please do not put my name and letter up for people to laugh at.

Just do what you honestly think is best that is all that is required of any of us. Please help me. Thanks in advance.

> Yours Truely
> [Initials omitted because
> of writer's request]
> Aurelia Iowa

Chapter 4. A Worse Depression:
Black Americans in the 1930s

I been down so long, being down do not worry me no more,
I been down so long, being down do not worry me no more,
I'm goin' pack my suitcase, an' cross the way you know, I'll go.
Afro-American folksong.

Letters written by black Americans during the Depression show both the similarities and differences between their problems and those of their white countrymen. Like many whites, black letter writers wanted no one to know that they had written; but their reason was not, in most cases, the shame that whites attached to seeking assistance. Instead, it was fear of reprisals by local whites against complaining blacks. Blacks expected to be jailed, killed, beaten, or run out of their homes if their letters were discovered.

Remarkably, in spite of the requests for confidentiality, many of the letters blacks addressed to the Roosevelts were referred to local relief agencies: to precisely the people against whom the allegations of discrimination had been made.

A significant similarity between black and white Depression victims was their love for the president. Most of the letters written by blacks show the same reverence for Roosevelt that was common in letters from white workers. The writers thanked the president because, as one put it, "You has prepare Money enough to give every one a Decent living." Like whites, many blacks blamed lower officials, rather than Roosevelt, for the inadequacy of relief funds. Other letters from blacks indicate an adherence to the work ethic and a desire for loans rather than charity. Thus it appears that the so-called middle-class values discussed in chapter 2 were shared by some poor blacks, even in the South.

The bulk of the letters that can be clearly identified as having been written by blacks* seem to have come from the South. This in no way indicates that Roosevelt's popularity among blacks was confined to that region. The shift in black voting allegiances demonstrated that the admiration for FDR was widespread in black communities throughout other parts of the nation. One of the letters, written by a black woman in Iowa just after the 1936 campaign, says that the author hoped that the president would give recognition to blacks by mentioning in a radio broadcast that their votes were valuable to him.

One reason why Roosevelt never made such a broadcast is apparent in the last two letters of the chapter which were written by southern whites. The final letter, from a poor Georgia woman, is a good example of the success upper-class whites in the South had achieved in splitting the poor along racial lines.

*Additional letters written by blacks appear in other chapters where they seem appropriate.

37. These white people will kill all the Negroes in Marion

Marion Ark
Feb 3, 1935

Pres Roosevelt
of Washington DC

Dear sir if every eny body need you we poor peoples need you here at marion   we are all sufing mody bad   the drauf [drought] come and cut off the corn and white peoples took all the cotton and wont give us a day work at in the marion cort House mrs miller and mrs nomen and mr mace ant doing nottien for the poor negores at all   wont give them no work and just robing the Govement and mr abry Kooser is roobing all the negroes one the farm   he wont furnish the peoples untell the last of april and the wont furnish nothen but a little somtom to eat and dont car how large your family is he just you 2 sack of flour and one sack of meal and 8 lbs of lard for weeks if you got 13 in family that is what he give   dont even gave a rag of clothen and shoes. and all of his peoples that is got large family has made from 11 to 17 bales of cotton and come out in deat over 300 hirndraw dellers in dat.

you aught send a man around one his farm just talk with his negores and see how they is suffen and that money all the otheres white men has pay thay negroes he did not gives his negroes but 5 dollers and mad them sine on the second day of this month and told all that dident sine to give him his house and move   please send a man here one orbry Kooser plase at marion ark and dont send the letter back here he will have every negro on his place put in jail   please come here at marion ark and helpe the poor negrous and stop them peoples at the cort house frome Robing the govment dont send this back here do these white peoples will kill all the negroes in marion   some of us have been here one this man place fore 10 to 17 years   and all over 3 hundrew dollars in deat yet

[Anonymous]

38. Cant sign my name Mr President they will beat me up and run me away from here and this is my home

Reidsville. Ga Oct 19th 1935

Hon. Franklin D. Roosevelt.
President of U.S.
Washington D.C.
Dear Mr. President

Would you please direct the people in charge of the releaf work in Georgia to issue the provisions + other supplies to our suffering colored people. I am sorry to worrie you with this Mr. President but hard as it is to believe the releaf officials here are using up most every thing that you send for them self + their friends. they give out the releaf supplies here on Wednesday of this week and give us black folks, each one, nothing but a few cans of pickle meet and to white folks they give blankets, bolts of cloth and things like that.

I dont want to take to mutch of your time Mr president but will give you just one example of how the releaf is work down here   the witto Nancy Hendrics own lands, stock holder in the Bank in this town and she is being supplied with Blankets cloth and gets a supply of cans goods regular   this is only one case but I could tell you many.

Please help us mr President because we cant help our self and we know you is the president and a good Christian man   we is praying for you. Yours truly   cant sign my name Mr President   they will beat me up and run me away from here and this is my home

[Anonymous]

39. Som gets a little and som gets none

March 9th 1936 Dry Branch, Ga.

Mr. Franklin D. rusevelt President of the united States of america
Dear President

I am writing you a few words abot the condishioned of the poor oled aged collard people how thear are sufring they are on the county an onley gets 2.50 per month and 1.50 out of that for house rent and sum of them cant hardley get about and when the govenment senes cars loads of food som gets a little and som gets none and thats the way it is about the clothes some gets some and some gets none and if you do have Ennie pensions sent to the poor oled aged colard people pleas send them checkes if you dont they will never get a pennie of it this From

[Anonymous]

---

40. They give all the worke to white people and give us nothing

[Picayune, Mississippi
September 3, 1935]

Dear Sir   I am ritening you a few Lines to Let you no how they are treating we colored people on this releaf   I went up to our home Vister and rep lied for some Thing   to do an Some Thing to eat and She told me that she has nothing for me at all and to they give all the worke to White people and give us nothing an Sir I wont you to no how we are treated here

So please help us if you can

[Anonymous]

---

41. I am to old to be turned out of doors

7/31/34
West Point Ga
East 7th St

Dear Mr President I dont no Just How to rite to you But I want to ask Your Help   I am a old Citizen of West Point and I am about 75 or 6 years old and Have Labored Hard all My days until depression Came on and I Had No Job in three years and I Have a Little Home I Bought when times was good and I managed to Pay my state and County tax But they Claim I owe about 15 fifteen dol City tax and going to sell my Little Home for that and will you Please sir Help me out the government Can Have a Lean on the Little House until I Get some way to Pay Back Please Sir do what you Can for me I am to old to be turned out of doors   I tried to get a Job on the CWA But they wanted younger men   Ive Never gave the City any troube Have always stood in fear of god and ben Law abiding and Ben a Hard Worker all my days and Is able and Can work   Now if I get any thing to do   its Just about a quarter of an ace [acre] and a 2 room House and it Need Fixing Bad aint No account Much But I toil so Hard to get it I dont want to Loose it so Please Sir Help me I am and old Colored Man and seems like they Just want to take my Place I aint got Nothing and Cant get Nothing if ever a Poor Person Need Help I do   Pleas Sir Let Me Hear from you at once I Havent got but a few

days to get the Money up   they Supose to sell it some time in Aug I dont
No the excat day

> Yours and oblige your
> Humble Servent
> D. A. [male]
> West Point Ga

---

42. All I want is a chance and I well prove to the world that I can come up the hill in stead of goin down

> Buncombe County Jail—
> Asheville N. C.
> Feb. 1.19.34

President hoover Dear Sir

well you Pleas help Poor me i am a Colored woman 34 years old have 4 Children 3 Girls 1 Boy   I have work awFuly hard Every Senice i 9 years old. Did not Get to Go to School But very little—But I have all ways held my Job never Ben turn off unless Sickness I was Born in a little town By the name of Laurens S. C. I Came to ashevill N C 10 years aGo and I had very good Luck For awhile My husband wasen So well but he work on Just the Same he Got hurt in the world War at the Camp/wheller Makon Ga he and I Done all that we Could to Rear our 4 Children up RiGht. well he took Real Sick and Died. Well i nely went Crazy when the Dr told me that they Could Not Save him and BeGain to Drink   I tried to Drink it off and Got in Jail why I Drank Every thing aney one would give me   I [illegible] I was Sick and worred nely to Deth   I have tried and tried to Get a Job But they are Scarse the City Releaf takes Care of my Children at Present   Dear President Pleas —give me a Job. and I well Do my Best all I want is a Chance and I well Prove to the world that I can Come up the hill in Stead of goin Down I Relize it was wrong to Drink and I am Sorry that I Ever tourch it But I was Cold and hunGry a menie Day that no one Knew But God and I is had Plenty of Friend when my husband was—livinG and we all ways help others as Mutch as we Could. now my health is not So Good   my hart is Bad and I haven Got aney Job no whear harley to Stay   I had to all most give furnitur a way Because I Could not Pay the house Rent   I Pray that you well Give Me Some thing to Do I Dont Care what I sure well thank god and you   then I well Get me Some Clouse an Shoes an go to Church Every Sunday I have made up in my mind to Stop DrinkinG and if god for Give me and you give me a Job I never. never. tourch it aGain   Pleas answer Soon i well Get out on the 18 of Feb. and haven Got aney money an no home no Job So I Pray you well tell Poor me what to Do may god tourch your hart that you well underStand Every thinG and help me I Feel Just like the whole world is aGainst Me Sometime I am not a Bad—woman Just worred Crazy   Pleas Give me a trial—

yours truly
Mrs. M. R.
Buncombe County Jail
Ashevill N C.

---

43. The government has probale enough money to feed all Negro and poor white

[Camp Hill, Alabama
April 22, 1935]

Mr Roosevelt the President of the unite State   I want to Explain the condition of the poor farmer and the unemployed people. Mr Roosevelt I know that the government has ProBale enough Money to Feed all Negro and Poor White and to Day they are suffering For Food and clothes   We know that you has perpare Money enough to give every one a Decent living But to Day the relief offices and other who has a plenty to live on is getting this money and slaving the Poor People.

[Anonymous]

---

44. I have not got any thing for security but my honor

Tupelo. Miss
Feb. 4th 1935

Mr President and Wife

Im about to ask you A Question that I hate to trouble you with. but Ive tried hard to get by With out any assistance but Ive Nearly got to road end, I Just Cant make my way as I will explain. Now Mr President I owe Several different people that are compeling me to pay them   They are Sending Squires an colectors To me every Week   I hate not to pay them but I Just can not   Ive a Job. but owing from 8 to 12 different ones It make it difficult To pay be Sides the fuel food House rent That has to be paid each week an fuel each Time it is ordered then Mr prisident the food is a Necessity We have to have that to keep going on our Jobs. every thing is very high in

Tupelo but Im thankful To have a Job. Making Something but not nearly enough To pay those Bills I owe. Im not Writing Just because I can write for I have tried to borrow from the white people here and they say they have not got any money   So I cannot get help from them as I used to. Now I am asking you please to help Me. Ive a little child 4 years a mother 62 years an She has ben Sick for 15 or 18 years   Ive got along all right till the middle of last year up till now. It has ben hard for 7 or 8 month doctor Bills Groceries coal Bill   I do not ask for Money for foolish thing an I do not ask you to give it to me. I am only asking a loan   an I will pay you as you desire Me to   by the week or by the month only as you say. but please mr president keep This confidential as I would loose my Job. you See Mr President I can pay one person easier Than a lots of people. These Bill has got a head of me when I didnt have any work an they are demanding their pay   please if It will not Trouble you to much help me   I will appreciste it More than Any Thing. My bill Totals $150.00 that is for The Thing That I have Necessaraly needed not one bit of foolishness for I Tries to put every cent to good use please help me in the Name of the lord an I will pay you back. I have not got any thing for Security but my honor   if you will Trust me   Thank you

A Colored Friend down in Tupelo Miss
G. T. [female]
General delivery

P.S. please answer direct to me

---

45. And treates the colored peoples so bad that they cant help from crying at times

Washington D.C.
Portsmouth   Sep 26, 1935
and Norflet V.A.

Mr Presentdent its Certainly a strange thing the way we colored peoples is treated here this government money was sent down here for these peoples where is in knead and the poor widows Where is here going from place to place trying to get work and cant get Nothing to do and hungry and what they does with the Money we cant tell some thimes

we makes as much as a quarter aday in the field and some thing will have to be done or else the peoples will perish and freeze this winter because when we cant make no money to pay the doctors bills far sickness and house rent they usually Just turn us out doors and we is pitiful Object here in this world of sorry trying to do the best we can every thing is so high we isnt able harly to get a good meal and pay for it and we knead clothes and shoes and and they have at the city a plenty clothes and quilts and the peoples certain kneads do kned those clothes shoes we is treat some bad and treates the colored peoples so bad that they cant help from crying at times when they go to them and ask for work and they turn we colored peoples of in such way   the object is these peoples that did have work like washing and irning these white peoples is doing there own work and there fore that knocks the colored out of work and it isnt enough work in the field to depend on and these peoples isnt going to let us stay here in their houses with not pay they promist to give grocers every week but they fail to do that by some means. we is Just in a place we dont know what to do but I hope you will make it better for we poor colored peoples   Some of we colored peoples is so ragged we is asham to get out among the peoples like some Folks and its getting cold no wood and cold and if we dont get something to do in order so we can have some money we will Freeze to death doing the winter some of these peoples here where we rents houses from if a person cant pay house rent some of them will take the window out and take the doors of so please do what you can for we peoples please

[Anonymous]

---

46. Mississippi is made her own laws an dont treat her destuted as her pres. has laid the plans for us

May 1936

Hattiesburg Miss

Mr Presedent Sir We are starving in Hattiesburg we poor White's + Negros too i wish you could See the poor hungry an naket half clad's at the relief office an is turned away With tears in their eys Mississippi is made her own laws an dont treat her destuted as her Pres. has laid the plans for us to live if the legislators would do as our good Pres. has Said What few days we have here we could be happy in our last old days both old white + Colard

Cencerely looking for our old age pension's an will thank you they has made us Sighn for $ 3 <u>00</u> a Month Cant live at that

[Anonymous]

47. Do the government insist on Jim Crow on the W. P. A. projects?

Chicago Illi
Mar 9, 1936

Mr. Hopkins:
Dear Sir:
We Are law biding Citizens and legal Voter's of the United States. We would like to know do the government insist on Jim Crow on the W. P. A. projects? We are working at 56th And So parkway and Collored are working at 51th and So Parkway, and the white to their self in Washington park located at 57 And Cottage grove Ave. We Are all on the Same project Number 2262. The white Are to their Self and the Collored to their Self. the men Are Kicking About this very much. Will You take Care of this particular Matter at Once?   (yours Truly)

[Anonymous]

48. The white + colored is haveing a hard time here

Memphis Ten
Mar. 30, 36

To the President Roosevelt we Poor People here in Memphis are having a hard way to go No work to do   If our Invester gatters wood See to us getting Fuel Clothes + Food   we wood be in a better shape than what we are in. what hand full of Food do get From the relief we have to go up to the auditorium + work For it so Our worker says that we wont get Nothin else to eat on the relief because She is going See that we will be Cut of this comming Wednesday April the 1   The most of us did not get no Wood or Coal this Winter + no cloths eather + hard words if we ask for enny Please turn us a helping Hand even Salt meat they dont give it to us + that we do get it wont last a week   4 in a Faimly dont get enough to last 4 + 5 days   Most of the times we dont have Nothing to eat   The White + Colored is haveing a hard time here it Ought to be Some to look after this it was a hard Winter here + they did give us wood or Coal. Please dont For get

Memphis
Tenn.

not 1 Faimly cut of the relief But all of us.

49. The way they are treating the darkies here is a shame

Vicksburg Miss
9-22-35

President Theo. D. Rosevelt. U.S.A.

Gentlemen: I think you Should invistigate this matter your Self. The way they are treating the Darkies here is A Shame. They wont give them food nor Cloths nor Work to do When they Ask for Any thing they drive them away as they were dogs. They wont even let them talk to the head man here. you Aught to See that Some men get this job that will give this Relief to whom it was Sent here for. you can prevent all brutle treatment of the Darkies here if you will. And its more than 200 Darkies in groups Standing on the Road each day. begging for food and Cloths. And the Relief working women. They tell them there is no job for them to hunt. And the Head men of the Office will help them to drive the Poor darkies as they were dogs. And I gets in My care and Rides from one end of the County to the other to See how the Darkies are treated. All of the Darkies in the Flooded District are in a Suffering condition I know Personally. And please Invistigate The Matter at once. The Darkies in Flooded District are not able to pay they Taxes and they wont let them make enough to pay them. And I Judge the Relief Workers are taking all of the Poor Darkies Money and buying fine Cars.

[Anonymous]

50. They are helping white but are not me poor colored man

October 27, 1935.
Marietta. Ga

The President Roosevelt: —

You honor sir and your royalty. Majesty. This is the one of the most honable Colored workers of America who has been faithful and true law abiding Citizens of this Cob County & the City of Marietta, Ga   Your honor sir I am down now is very feeble and isnt able to work for my living   Ive been keep up by the releif but now have fail   They haven't help me any in a month I am very poor and needing Condition I am not able to support my self so dear sir you honor I begging you please sir for food and raimont dear sir. I am very much in need now   They are helping white but are not me poor Colored man my whife has been going there times after times but refused give her anything to eat. So I am hoping through your highness and good natured and kindness that I succeed. So dear sir I am Thanking you in Advance and your benevolence will never be for gotten here after For I know have the power to Correct such matters if you will.

Those of the Community Chest and the state of Releif and the food Administration and distributors.

Your honorable
President Roosevelt.
Colored
Cob Co. Marietta. Ga.

---

51. We will have to face the winter naked, hungry

Huntsville Ala.
November 12, 1935

Mr. Woodworth
Dear Sir:

I wont to know why it is we people in Huntsville are working and cant get any money or food. We white and colored people we are on a starvation. It is any way on earth you can help us we are really in need. We han't got but one check in three months. We will have to face the winter naked, hungry + nothing to go up on not even fuel to burn. we can't live + work off of nothing.

We can't get any credit to get any food or any thing families of six + seven can't get food for their kids. The kids are hungry.

I will close
From
Huntsville

---

52. We hope all will get some, some get and the other dont

Selma Alabama
Sept. 1935

Dear Mr. President:

Please, please dont let our checks be stop they say that they have close up. We can't even get by now, what shall we do.

Please when they open Work for us the Women let us have a fire our legs are acking now where they work us all the cold Winter And we did not have a fire. please send us some more good meat. for we Cant get Any it is so high. School os open   We haven't got Any clotheing for our chridren and our self. Some got dresses and some did not. what shall we do. it is getting cold And we havent got no Coal + no wood   we just can get a little food. Please see about us and when you send Any cover to Any thing We hope all Will get Some, Some get and the other dont, some get a raise And some get a cut. We thank you for All you are doing. Thank you.

The Colored
Women.

---

53. Hope that sometime . . . you will mention what the value of the coloured votes has been to you if you think they are worth it

Burlington, Iowa
Nov. 4-36

President + Mrs. Roosevelt
Dear Ones:——

Congratulating you first on your success in staying in the "White House." for which I am well pleased.

I want to write just briefly about my work in the campaign.

First let me say most everyone takes for granted "Coloured" voters are Republican   we owe that party a debt.

I worked day and night proving to the U.S.A. voters that phrase is not true. I think this election will convince all, because the Negro of today are more educated. Of course when there are more in one locality it is easier for them to prove their ability to fill worth while positions.

I wasn't working in this campaign to fill an office. I was working for the betterment of this community in which I live, and the men I worked so hard for I feel are real men that will back me up and show a few of my race folk here a little consideration.

I struggle here trying to educate my boy (19 yrs.) and girl (17 yrs.) and trying to keep this locality a haven for them so to speak.

I worked without pay so as to prove to the people here I wasn't working for a personal cause.

I'm not on relief. My husband is a Railroad chef, I worked at odd jobs since where I live my vocation isn't patronized very much. Would like to obtain Ia. licinse but do not feel I can afford spending that much right now right on the verge of winter.

Hope that sometime during your future talks over the radio you will mention what the value of the coloured votes has been to you if you think they are worth it.

Trust that this letter will reach your hands.

Happiness and Success to Both of You.

Sincerely

Mrs. I. H.

---

54. All we ask is that you please remove this Negro sewing-room from our midst at once

July 10, 1936

Mr. Harry L. Hopkins
Washington, D. C.
Dear Sir:

We, the residents of N. Spring Street, Concord, N. C. are all ardent supporters of President Roosevelt and the New Deal and have been loyal Democrats for a long time, and in behalf of this same White neighborhood on N. Spring Street, we are asking you to remove a negro sewing-room that was put in our midst this week.

This is supposed to be a Government project, and it is at least a mile from the negro settlement. It is being conducted in a negro woman's home, in which she occupies part of the house, and there are 39 negro women attending the school. This negro owns five houses and lots, her own car, and also teaches a negro school, which is a project also. The two adjacent homes she owns on this street both have sewing-rooms in them. To make one of the houses available she had the sheriff of Cabarrus County evict a White family from the house, BECAUSE she said she could get more money from the Government. Now we believe in these projects and think you've done a wonderful work, but do you think that she deserves this position she has and the rent she is receiving from our Government?

I wish to refer you to the Sheriff of Cabbarus County, Mr. Ray C. Hoover, and also to the Mayor of this city, Mr. W. A. Wilkinson.

Before closing let me state this negro has no dependents at all, and we would certainly appreciate you looking into this matter and removing this thorn at once. It is needless to say that this is one thing that the Southern people do not approve. If she were needy and deserving it would be an entirely different matter, but she doesn't need this income from the Government. Mr. Hopkins, we don't care how much the Government gives her, although we have plenty of other deserving people that need help, ALL we ask is that you please remove this NEGRO sewing-room from our midst at once.

> Respectfully and sincerely,
> Citizens and Residents of
> N. Spring St.,
> Concord, N.C.
> Cabarrus County

---

55. Negroes being worked ever where instead of white men it dont look like that is rite

> [Canton, Georgia
> July 22, 1935]

[President Franklin D. Roosevelt:]

dear Sur as you are the president of our State it looks like you could do Something to help out the poor white people the negroes can get work where the poor white man canot and his family are one Starvation The negroes are in post offices getting $1000 dollars a month and white families Suffering and it is not write just look at it your Self if it was your family in Canton Ga there is a negro working in the post office and white men cant get a job to feed his family and a white woman up holding for just Such as that and negroes being worked ever where instead of white men it dont look like that is rite and is not rite and lay off white men where there is a large family and keep men with big farms and just a man and wife and both at work unless there are something done the poor people will pursh to death will you please help the poor people out this relief work is not helping the poor out just make $300 a week them that uses the pick and Shovel and the ofice men and woman gets the rest there is to many in office for the poor working man to get any pay. rote by a woman that has a large family and is on Sufference

> [Anonymous]

Chapter 5. To Be Old, Sick, and Poor

There is no experience in an industrial neighborhood more poignant and heart-breaking than those connected with old age.
Jane Addams

Many older Americans had worked hard all their lives, expecting to reap some benefits when they reached their last years. Such people were understandably bitter when the Depression prevented them from enjoying what they believed they had coming to them. Desperation forced many of the aged to seek help; the traditional status of society's elders justified a demand for government assistance.

A significant portion of the American population above the age of sixty was attracted to the Townsend Plan. The passage of the Social Security Act in 1935 satisfied some, but by no means all, of the older people who had called for assistance.

Sickness, like age, was made more difficult by the Depression. As one of the letters below suggests, poverty could *cause* illness as well as make it harder to conquer.[1] The loss of one's job or home could trigger psychological and physical disorders.

Depression era doctors and pharmacists appear to have been more understanding than many of their modern counterparts when patients were unable to pay their bills. Still, credit was not unlimited and one of the greatest fears of the aged and the sick was that poverty would prevent them from obtaining necessary treatment and medication.

The Social Security Act notwithstanding, the old who were also sick and poor seem to have been justified in numbering themselves among the forgotten men and women of the Depression.

---

56. What are we to do since the calamity has swept our all away?

Lincoln Nebraska.
May 19/ 34.

Mrs Franklin D. Roosevelt
Washington, D. C.
Dear Mrs Roosevelt;

Will you be kind enough to read the following as it deals with a very important subject which you are very much interested in as well as my self.

In the Presidents inaugral adress delivered from the capitol steps the afternoon of his inauguration he made mention of The Forgotten Man, and I with thousands of others am wondering if the folk who was borned here in America some 60 or 70 years a go are this Forgotten Man, the President had in mind, if we are this Forgotten Man then we are still Forgotten.

We who have tried to be diligent in our support of this most wonderful nation of ours boath social and other wise, we in our younger days tried to do our duty without complaining.

We have helped to pay pensions to veterans of some three wars, we have raised the present young generation and have tried to train them to honor and support this our home country.

And now a great calamity has come upon us and seamingly no cause of our own it has swept away what little savings we had accumulated and we are left in a condition that is imposible for us to correct, for two very prominent reasons if no more.

First we have grown to what is termed Old Age, this befalls every man.

Second as we put fourth every effort in our various business lines trying to rectify and reestablish our selves we are confronted on every hand with the young generation, taking our places, this of corse is what we have looked forward to in training our children. But with the extra ordinary crisese which left us helpless and placed us in the position that our fathers did not have to contend with.

Seamingly every body has been assisted but we the Forgotten Man, and since we for 60 years or more have tried to carry the load without complaining, we have paid others pensions we have educated and trained the youth, now as we are Old and down and out of no reason of our own, would it be asking to much of our Goverment and the young generation to do by us as we have tried our best to do by them even without complaint.

We have been honorable citizens all along our journey, calamity and old age has forced its self upon us please donot send us to the Poor Farm but instead allow us the small pension of $40.00 per month and we will do as we have done in the past (not complain)

I personly Know of Widows who are no older than I am who own their own homes and draw $45,00 per month pension, these ladies were born this side of the civil war the same as I, therefore they never experianced war trouble.

Please donot think of us who are asking this assistsnce as Old Broken down dishonorable cotizens, but we are of those borned in this country and have done our bit in making this country, we are folk in all walks of life and businesse.

For example I am an architect and builder I am not and old broken down illiterate dishonorable man although I am 69 years old, but as I put forth every effort to regain my prestage in business I am confronted on every side by the young generation taking my place, yes this is also the case even in the effort of the government with its recovery plan, even though I am qualifyed to suprentend any class of construction but the young man has captured this place also,

What are we to do since the calamity has swept our all away,? We are just asking to be remembered with a small part as we have done to others $40,00 a month is all we are asking.

Mrs. Roosevelt I am asking a personal favor of you as it seems to be the only means through which I may be able to reach the President, some evening very soon, as you and Mr. Roosevelt are having dinner together privately will you ask him to read this. and we American citizens will ever remember your kindness.

> Yours very truly.
> R. A. [male]

---

57. There is nothing sadder than old people who have struggled hard all their lives . . . to be forgotten

> [Akron, Ohio
> February 1936]

My Dear Mrs Roosevelt.

I thought I would write a letter hoping you would find time to read it, and if you thought it was worth while answering it, I would be glad of any advise you would care to give me. A few weeks ago, I heard your talk over the air, on the subject of the Old age pension, and I got to thinking what a blessing it would be to my mother, if it was possible for her to receive that pension, if the bill should pass. My mother has been in this country since April 1914 but she has never made herself a American Citizen, as she was sixty years old when she came here, and now she is eighty.

Mother come out to this country nineteen years ago [from Scotland]. . . .

I thought as long as I lived there was no need to worry about her being taken care of, but I never dreamed of a depression like we have had well it has changed the whole course of our lives we have suffered, and no one knowes but our own family, I have two children one nineteen, graduated from high school last June, and the girl graduates this coming June, and we have had the awfullest time trying to get the bare necessary things in life.

I am in no position to do the right thing for mother, I cant give her anything but her living but I thought if it was possible for her to get that pension it would be like a gift from heaven, as in all the years she has been in this country she has never had a dollar of her own.

I wish she could get it her days may not be long on this earth, and if she just had a little money coming once in a while, to make her feel independent of her family, I at least would know that if anything happened to me she could get a living, and not have to go back to the rest of her family, because she says she would rather go to a poor house, than live with any of the others.

Mrs Roosevelt you might think I have lots of nerve writing to you when you have so much to attend to but I could not help admiring you for the splended way you talked about the old people of this nation   I feel sorry for all of them, they seem to be forgotten, and most young people think they have had there day and should be glad to die. but this is not my idea, I think that their last few years should be made as plesent for them as it is possible, I know that if it was in my power to make my mother happy by giving her what she justly deservs, I would gladly do so. Well whither my mother ever gets anything or not, I hope all the other old people that is intilted to it gets it soon, because there is nothing sadder than old people who have struggled hard all there lives to give there family a start in life, then to be forgotten, when they them self need it most.

I will finish now but befor I do I want to thank you Mrs Roosevelt and also Mr Roosevelt for the good both of you are doing for this country you have gave people new hope and every real American has faith in you and may you both be spared to carry on the good work and lead this nation on to victory.

Yours Respectfully,
Mrs J. S.
Akron, Ohio.

---

58. If I could have a small pinsion each month so we would not starve

Mancelona, Mich
Aug 6 1934

Dear Mrs Roosevelt:

I am writing to you to ask you to help me and my old Father to live I am in a farm which he owns and has planted or farmed all he was able to do we havnt any stock nothing to feed them untill his corn is through growing we have a fuw chickens   this is what I would like to ask of you and the President if I could have a small pinsion each month so we would not starve my father is seventy six to old to work at the Antriim Co furnace   I cant go away and leave him alone to look for work and to stay here in such poverty I am so disturbed trying to know what to do I could write more of this but I think both you and the big boss meaning our President will understand: Thank you   address—

Mrs. E. R.
Mancelona
Michigan

---

59. I helped so many out but it seems now that I am in the grattes trouble no=body will help me

ElKader   Iowa   Sep the
11
1934.

Mr. FranKlin Roosevelt
Dear President Roosevelt
I am in a terrible perdicament So I thought of you to send my plea of trouble to you because I drempt the other night that I Should write to you thinking that may=be I could get Some help from you as long as no one els will help me out I am an old woman Seventy two years old and an invalid that is the worst of it I can't get around at all. I bin Sitting in a chair for years already if I am not in bed I can't walk alone atall So that makes it pretty hard fore me to be put out of my home the one I worked so hard for over forty-Six years, So please help me Some way or I will half to Sine my last bit away if I could only raise thirteen Hundred Dollars than I could Stay in my home Oh. So please help me Mr. Roosevelt and answer right away or els it will be to late if I ever get onto my feet I Sure will try and pay you bacK. I helped So many out but it Seems now that I am in the grattes trouble no=body will help me So please Mr. Roosevelt help me Sincerly Mrs. A. M. U.

---

60. I only wish President Roosvelt only node what of cind of a shape the old pele were in

[November 1934]
excuse Bad hand rite and Bad paper   please Dont let this go to the West Basket in till read
   Mrs roosevelt
      president wife   i though i would Drop you a few lins Mrs roosvelt you Seem to Bee a kind harted women from the reeden of the papers i would like to talk to to let you know how things is goning heir   my husBen is 68

years old and is in Bad helth   he was on the relefe an they taken hom of
we have a home   we have lived on for 23 years   we have a morg on it and i
Dont no where we will hapt to heve it are not

Mrs roosevelt i only wish president roosvelt only node what of Cind of a
Shape the old pele were in   those that have Clilden Cant give them Close
and food Such as the old peole need   Mrs roosevelt we reed in the papers a
Baut the old age peachen   are there eny thing to it   if So let me no by
return Mail   hoopen Mrs roosevelt the old puple have lots of faith in are
President   a Baut the old age penshen rite me and let me no   i have a
mother 84 years old and She is enduled

from Mrs. B. G.
Farmiaso Ark

---

61. I cant get out if I tried to get piece of bread wich of times need

Jan 30th

Wash. DC
Mr. Hopkins
Dear Sir—I [M. M.] of 2221–7St NW Is sick and In a cold House and has
sent to my case worker several times for a little coal and has not received
any yet—The House Is so cold It keeps me Ill with the rhumatism and
grippe I also have a bad leg—so I cant get out if I tried to get piece of bread
wich of times need—I will thank you so kindy if you see that get some coal
  please oblige

M. M. [female]
2221—7 St NW

---

62. I think that women is more sympathetic than men for the old and distressed people

Sept 7—1934.
Webbville Ky

Mrs Roosevelt:
I am riting you in regard to my Condition and the Reason that I am riting you
is that I think that Women is more Sympathetic than men for the old and distressed people. if there is any Way or any thing that you Could do or say that

would help me a little in my last days I would be Verry thankful. I have all-most lived out my three score and ten and have bin in ill health for 2 years not able to Work any—I have no income at all I have a wife and tow Children looking to me for suport—

I was on the federal relief a part of last Winter and by fraud or some reason I was Cut off in March not noing the Cause* and I think if there is any one that acutal needs help I am one of them We are destitute of food and raiment With no income no relation able to help me. Just on the mercies of the people and I have two statements from two doctors in the Commitees office at the County Seat Shoeing my disability

Mrs Roosevelt you have a talk with the president and see if there is any Way for me   I red your speech in the paper in regard to old age pension I sure would be glad if it does become a law to give all old aged people that are in distress a living in their last days as for my Self I would be glad to get it for a short time that I Will not need it long my time is a bout up if you could give me any advise that would help me in any Way I sure Would appreciate it and Stand by any Candidate that Stands for the old age pension.

Respect yours
J. C. G. [male]

---

63. The Atlantic calls from our shores that there is plenty of room for us

Beverly Mass. Dec. 4 1934

Dear Madame:

I read your touching letter about the old friend you had neglected and how she had fallen upon evil times and how you had worried that you had not helped her.

Now is your opportunity to retrive your mistake.

There are thousands of aged women in this great and rich country who are facing poor house or suicide, it is not their fault that they are poor not that they are too old to work.

The suicide rate is now, one in every 27 minutes, by far there is no doubt that it will be 27 suicides in one minutes. Now there are a lot of us will choose suicide in preference to being herded into the poorhouse. The Atlantic calls from our shores that there is plenty of room for us.

*The Civil Works Administration was phased out rapidly in the spring of 1934.

I have faithfully studied all the plans of relief offered but this great array of aged are not considered.

But if the Townsend Plan were put into effect all classes and ages would be benefitted.

Therefore we ask you in the name of Humanity to use your influence for it.

If you do not you will have the pleasant reccolection that you have condemned us to death of humilation.

I am eighty years old neither a ranten nor a red, my pedigree is as good as yours, my people have always been loyal to our country.

Very Truly yours for the Townsend Plan.

Mrs. F. E. G.

Beverly Mass.

---

64. I am one that need it and need it bad

Atlanta, GA

10-6-34

Dear Mrs. Roosevelt

I am writing you a few lines in regards for a Pension as I have only heard of it. Will you pleas tell me something coning it whether or not if you will send me a list to sign or how to put in for a Pension I am a Widow Lady no one to depend on I am loosing my home I will have no where to stay and not able at the present time to do any work on account of my health. I tried to get my home in the Home loan but they failed to get it in because I dident have anyone to go my seceurety. if their is any way for me to get on the Pension list Please advise me as early as you can for I am one that need it and need it bad I have worked hard all my life put all my earnings in a home and now having to give it up and no where to stay it almost break my heart I will have to get out in a very short while hope you can help me. some way in helping me get on a pension list I was told about the pension papers but I failed to get one to send in so I though you would advise me what to do or how to get on Please let me hear from you real soon

Yours Resp

Mrs. N. M. A.

Atlanta GA

65. It is hard to be old and not have anything

[Petersburg, North Dakota
March 21, 1934]

[Dear Mrs. Roosevelt:]

you must excuse me for writing to you but I have heard that you would like the pension for old people to be set at $30 a month. Mrs. Roosevelt I would be very thankful if you could force that through. I see that you have us old folks in mind that have not a thing.

I am living in North Dakota and we have just gotten through the old age pension bill. It will be $12.50 a month (twelve dollars and fifty cents), so when one is going to pay house rent and have a little for clothes and some to eat, why it isn't much.

I am so glad to get that much but we are not able to get any before the first of May and that is a long time to wait, for we hasn't anything.

I am now 72 years old and have never had anything. I have always been poor and have always worked hard, so now I am not able to do any more. I am all worn out but am able to be around and I thank God that I have no pains. It is hard to be old and not have anything. I do not own as much as one cent to my name, so I know God would bless you, if you could help us to get more money for pension, so we would have enough to eat.

I am sure Mrs. Roosevelt you will try all you can to help us old folks.

The President has done a great deal to help all the working people and I am sure he will help you too with this pension.

I enclose Mr. + Mrs. Roosevelt in my prayers, God bless you both and may you live long on this earth to be of help to all the needy.

God bless you always. From a poor Norwegian wife in North Dakota.

Mrs. A. A.
Petersburg N. D.

66. I have worked hard all of my life and bad luck has overtaken me in my old days

Kevil, Ky.
12/1/1934

Honerable Alben W. Barclay.*
Kind friend:-

I am riting you in reguard my financial condition. I have lost all of my belogins. I have worked hard all of my life and bad luck has overtaken me in my old days and i wanted to see if you could help me get a little Releaf so i can get me a team and to make a crop this next year the drought ruined me this year you know that i need it or i would not ask for it. i out to have a place that i could make a liven without havein to farm. i rote Mr. Hopkins in reguard to my case i will be 72 years old my next birthday and i am the father of 21 children 14 boys and 7 girls i have 3 boys & 2 girls and wife at home. i have always worked for you in all of the campaigns you ever had and done everything i could now if you can help me any way it will be appreciated. So i remain

Your friend as ever,
B. F. T. [male]
Kevil, Ky.

67. Please oh please mr. president don't say no

Baxley, Georgia
December 19, 1934

Mr. President:
I am obliged to ask of you a lending and helping hand because I know of no one on earth to do me any good but our own President—I have prayed to my God and he has shown me a through a vision to ask your President whom I have given knowledge to, to be chosen as the United States President—he can help.
Mr. President my father and mother's home will be taken away from them the first of January if I can't get up $50.00. My father is 83 years of age and

*Alben W. Barkley, United States Senator (Democrat, Kentucky).

my mother is 64 years of age, and I am all the dependents they have. I am a poor girl my salary is $3.00 per week and I have to feed myself out of that. I just can't raise it—I have no way and on my salary I can't borrow any on it, for my wages is so small—can you help me some—please oh please Mr. President don't say no—looking and wishing for a hearing from you, truly worried

Signed

A. M. H. [female]

---

68. They are so wealthy . . . have swell homes and cars and we havent anything

Connersville, Indiana

[no date, 1934]

Dear Mr. Roosevelt:

I hardly know how to start this letter to you and maby I shoulden bother you with it but I just want you to know the dirty trick I had served me. Several business men have advised me to write to you.

I had been employed as clerk at E. J. Schlichte Company this city for seven years 5 months until the N.R.A. went into effect. They let me out said they coulden pay me $14.00 a week. When I first started to work there they paid me $12.50 then cut me to $9.00 then to $8.00 for the last year we worked every other week that was at the rate of $4.00 a week we could hardly live but with help kept our humble home together. Oh how hard they worked us had to do two peoples work. I was as tired of an evening lots of times, I went wright to bed. but was glad to do it as I needed the money so bad. I am a widow have a son 18 years old. Also have my mother with me she is 77 years old. My husband was an ex soldier served 18 months in France he came home sick and never was able to work again, I worked all the time trying to keep our home together we had an alful hard time. last Dec 10th he died, poor thing, just two days before he died he said Xmas was coming and we didn't have anything. he didn't even have any warm clothes —we tried so hard to get a pension for him but never could get it through— until the day after he died I rec a letter saying as soon as a rating was set he would be notified—but of it was too late, had he only lived a few more days it would have made him feel so good because he worried about us so.

I had no insirance because I coulden keep it up. When the N.R.A. Went into effect, I was so happy I had planned to lay in some coal and pay on some bills I owe, I guess I was too happy. On August 4th that was the week I was off they come to my house in the evening and told me they would have to let me go because they would have to pay me $14.00 a week and they coulden do it she said business was so bad they were going to get a manigar she said they didnt have a thing in the world against me and diden want any hard feelings, Mr. Roosevelt what hurt me so the other woman they kept is married. Her husband has steady work She also has a daughter working they own their own home have a car. Early in the summer she told me they had their coal laid in for the winter, and they kept her and let me go. They also knew that I didn't have a cent coming in. She had been there longer than I had, so I suppose that is why they kept her. They didn't give me any notice. Mr. Roosevelt, it almost killed me. I cried all day Friday and Saturday. Sunday my nerves gave away and I fell to the floor. Dr. Said was too much of a shock for me. I had a complete collapse nervis breakdown. I was in bed five weeks almost died was alful sick. I am up and around now but alful nervis and week. Dr. said I wont be able to work for 4 months. Was the worst shock I ever had. Mr. Roosevelt they never came to see me that hurt me terrible. I talked to the Priest about it as he came everyday to see me while I was so bad, and he said they were ashamed that was the reason. Mr. Roosevelt, they are so wealthy, have two groceries stores and dry goods dept. also own half share in the Ice Co all have swell homes and cars and we havent anything only what we have given to us my sister and brother help us a little but cant a whole lot my son only had one more year high school but coulden go back, as he diden have clothes or books. I wanted him to finish school so bad because he isnt a bit strong. I have an N.R.A. sticker in our window and several people have told me they would sure take that down, because the N.R.A. diden do anything for me lost my job they said, but I told them wasent the wish of our good President nor Mr. Johnson either it was just the dirty people I worked for they knew they could get by with it. I wish I could talk with you and tell you how dirty they are. When the N.R.A. went into effect how they cussed and wasent going to do it—they talked it over and decided they had better or they would be boy cod. They said they bet they would never vote the Democrat ticket again isent that alful and they were all raised Democrats their Father is dead and the Boys and one Sister runs the business, and are they dirty.

Mr. Roosevelt, I don't think they are doing right by keeping that married woman if she is going to work then let him go because there are so many men out of work. I think there should be a law to that effect. I thought it was to be that way that if the Husband worked then the woman coulden. the people here are sure sore about the way they did me and several have quit trading there. one Business man siad they ought to be maid to pay me my salary for one year also my Dr. bill. I am not able to work now and it is all their fault. I wish you would take the Blue Eagle away from them because they are not doing their part, Mr. Roosevelt what I am going to aske of you, will you give me a widows pension. I just have to have some help, it will mean so much to me and so little to the Government if we could only keep our home no matter how humble its home. We only pay $12.00 a month rent and I would be so happy if you can do this for me. Some one told me the other day that they are worried the way they did me and are afraid they will get some word from the Government but I don't know if that is true or not because they arent afraid to do anything. Please, Mr. Roosevelt, give me a widow's pension. I am deserving of it as I have had and am having an alful hard time, I feel like I would go insane if I didnt get some help before long. My poor mother is down sick in bed just from worry. Please Mr. Roosevelt, I am asking you again to help me. I will remember you in my prayers as I always do say without prayer we are lost. Please pardon me for bothering you.

Hoping you will write to me.

I am yours very sincerely,

Mrs. B. H.

Connersville, Indiana

P.S. Please do not mention my name to them should you write them. Since I started this letter to you I am back in bed again some other trouble has come up. Dr. said is caused from being on my feet so much. As soon as I get a little stronger and my nerves better I will have to be operated on. I am so worried I am beging you from the bottom of my heart for help. Please give me a widows' pension it will make me so happy to know I will have a little income. God bless you.

---

69. I will loose my credit + good standing I so much prized

Weldon, N Car.

Jan. 21—1935

My dear Mrs Roosevelt.

I am a great admirer of you and President Roosevelt. I feel we are so fortunate to have you in the white house. I have always supported you and shall in the future. I have often read your addresses + heard you speak some over the radio and I find you so much in sympathy with the (worthy needy) I know it is hard to realize how one can suffer financially when you never know what it is to want for any thing money can buy. But I am prayerfully appealing to you for a loan gift or any way we can manage it. I am desperate over my situation I cannot go on getting in debt for food milk coal and many other little necessary things. I feel I must be relieved in some way soon. I just cant stand to think I owe so much. No way at present to pay it. I will loose my credit + good standing I so much prized. I am a Widow 57 years old. three in my family. my income is not sufficient to pay my board + household expences   I have drawn on my insurance until I will loose it if I dont pay the interest and part premiums.

Last summer I had a critical operation. was in the hospital + bed eight weeks. I got so far behind I just cant catch up. I am not able to do my work. and cant get any one to help me because I cant pay them. Please let me have $600.00 dollars just to pay my back debts   maby I could catch up. I have a home but I dont want to mortgage my home. I am trying to rent part of it as an apt. to get something out of it. if you will just please let me have it. I will try to pay you back little at the time. I am a good honest truthful woman of a good high class family, but none are able to help me. Please dont make my name public in any way. I just feel you will help me. please <u>do</u> send me a check or money order. I feel I cant go on. So please help me I am desperate. I know you have appeals often + hard to know which is worthy but please help me. and dont let it be anything but a private affair with us   if you could only know how I feel. I am most frantic with depression. Please let me hear from you. many thanks. —much Grattitude,

[Initials omitted because of
writer's request]
Weldon. N. Car.

---

70. The dear good Lord gave plenty for us all. Some people wants it all

Little Rock, Ark.
Jan. 10, 1935.

Dear Senator:*

I am writing to you in regard to conditions in Ark. The people that is on Transient Beaureau are starving to death $2.50 per week is for a family of two going filthy and dirty will not give clothing to anyone then have to beg for it I my self I asked for a syrine I have to take an infection for my bowels to move have ever sinc my Babe was born over 32 years ago was torn and

*Hattie Carraway, United States Senator (Democrat, Arkansas).

wasant attended to right a terrible affliction through no fault of my own but have kept well with good attention to my self they tell me they do not give syringes I lost my money when the Banks closed havent anything & millions of others have done the same* & am getting along in years but if the Old Age pension is given am eligible to it praise the Lord every thing turns out all right in the name of Christ Jesus will you please look into this the money was approperted for the people but they are not getting it herded in dirty rooms. I came from a good family & have pride. Am nervous can hardly write this letter my husband is in hospital if he was to pass away would not have anything to put him away. My head aches to look at the conditions of the world. The dear good Lord gave plenty for us all. Some people wants it all. The dear Senator will you please look into this horrible crime visited upon the world.

Thank you.

> Mrs. J. W.
> Little Rock, Ark.

---

71. God told me to write to you

> [Long Beach, Calif.
> December 13, 1934]

Dear Mrs Roosevelt

May I have one Line from you to Remember your good Work   I have a Birth Day Dec 17 Born Dec 17 1869 in Knoxville Tennessee   I have Been Very Sick August 1933 operated on for Cancer the Left Breast Removed   I cannot work Very much   have 2 small houses but I Cannot Pay the Taxes this year while they are only 52 Dollars but I Cannot I have 2 Children but they are Not able to help me   Will be Bad Birth Day and Christmas on All the Paper I have God Gave us The President   None but him Could Do What has been Done. Please Dont Pass this anywhere Else I Dont tell any of my Friends my Circumstances   I just want one word from you   God Told me to write you

> Cincerly,
> [Initials omitted because of
> writer's request]

*Although the still prosperous were fond of accusing the down and out of having failed to be thrifty during prosperity, many of the latter had saved diligently only to see their nest eggs vanish in the bank failures of the early Depression. One of the decade's favorite cartoons showed a prudent squirrel asking a man on a park bench, "But why didn't you save some money for the future, when times were good?" "I did," the victim replies.

72. He need plain necesities and I hav'nt one cent

Chi Ill
Nov/21/34

Mrs Rosvelt.

My sister in Christ—Pleas read this letter. My only boy is <u>sick</u> very sick. He is about to <u>die</u> with Heart trouble Enlargment. We are on Charity from 739 Winchester. We have been cut from 4.00 per wk to 3.00. Now Mrs Rosvelt I would work at any thing to save him if I was not so weak I Cant work. He used to be so happy and singing and going to church. Now he cant even sing again for 1 yr they say until his heart is normal   Since my only daughter left He is all I have left. He is 19 yrs old   Such a lovely Boy. He need Plain necesities and I hav'nt one cent. Could you help me a little to make his life a little happier. He had Pneumonia in June and is left very weak. Oh Mrs Rosvelt you realize [illegible] you go in one valley of Death. When a child is born you do so hate to give them up. I am not asking a thing for my self But I am trying to keep my poor Boy hear as long as I can. Now dont matter how little is is wont you Assist me a little I love my boy so very much. Jesus says ask + you shall receive. Please help ans my Prayer

I Pray for Pres Rosvelt + you to be covered with Blood of Christ every Day.

I live at . . . Chicago Ill

P.S. Please Pray for him.

[Anonymous]

Chapter 6. The Forgotten Children

It was an enormously hard life. . . .
But there was also a sense of great
satisfaction in being a child with
valuable work to do and, being able to
do it well, to function in this world.
Margot Hentoff in *New York Review of Books*

"O ut of the mouths of babes and sucklings," Jesus said, "thou hast brought perfect praise."[1] As with most proverbs, there is much truth in this one. Children are often able to see things more clearly than their elders, and they tend to be less reticent in expressing their thoughts and feelings. Thus it is possible to gain another, and especially illuminating, perspective on the problems of the down and out by examining a selection of letters written by children in the 1930s.

Like the old, children faced special problems in the Great Depression. The troubles of children and adults were rooted in basically the same causes, but unemployment and economic decline affected young and old in dissimilar ways. Each generation shares certain experiences. The children of the thirties lived through the same economic hardship as their parents did, but it meant different things to the new generation.

Perhaps the most important difference between the effects of the Depression on adults and children was that the latter were largely free from the self-blame and shame that were so common, at least initially, among their parents. Obviously, economic problems are not the fault of a child. He could rest assured that *he* had not failed. Whether the blame was individual or collective, it fell on members of the older generation. Adults might have botched things up, or Dad might have failed, but few children felt any personal guilt. The Depression's greatest psychological problem, then, was nearly absent in the young.[2]

Many Americans seem to have seen children as a burden during the thirties. It was the first decade in the history of the Republic in which the number of children under ten in the population declined. Indeed, the nation had fewer children under ten in 1940 than it had had twenty years earlier. The birth rate remained below its 1930 level until 1942. From 1932 through 1940, the rate of live births per thousand women aged fifteen to forty-four years was below twenty. At no other time in American history before 1965 was this the case.[3]

Children were obliged to mature rapidly during the economic crisis. This rapid maturation is evident in several of the letters that follow. The concerns of ten- to thirteen-year-olds in the 1930s were often with paying bills, avoiding eviction, and providing clothes for the family. Some, such as the writer of the last letter in the chapter, were even able to put fundamental economic questions in simple terms.

73. We have no one to give us a Christmas presents

Warren, Ohio
Dec. 22, 1935

Dear President Roosevelt,

Please help us   my mother is sick three year and was in the hospital three month and she came out but she is not better and my Father is peralised and can not work and we are poor and the Cumunity fun gives us six dollars an we are six people four children three boy 15, 13, 12, an one gril 10, and to parents. We have no one to give us a Christmas presents. and if you want to buy a Christmas present please buy us a stove to do our cooking and to make good bread.

Please excuse me for not writing it so well because the little girl 10 year old is writing.

Merry Christmas
[Anonymous]

74. My friends at school have skates and laugh because I dont have some

Blacksburg S.C.
January 19. [1934]

Dear Mrs. Roosevelt,

Mrs. Roosevelt will you send me and my sister, Ruth, a pair of ball bearing roller skates? Our friends have skates and we are not able to buy them. We sure will thank you if you will.

yours trully,
L. L. [female]

P.S. I am twelve years old and in the sixth grade at Blacksburg Grammar school. My friends at school have skates and laugh because I dont have some.

your's trully
L.

75. All the time he's crying because he can't find work

[February, 1936]

Mr. and Mrs. Roosevelt.
Wash. D. C.
Dear Mr. President:

I'm a boy of 12 years. I want to tell you about my family   My father hasn't worked for 5 months   He went plenty times to relief, he filled out application. They won't give us anything. I don't know why. Please you do something. We haven't paid 4 months rent, Everyday the landlord rings the door bell, we don't open the door for him. We are afraid that will be put out, been put out before, and don't want to happen again. We haven't paid the gas bill, and the electric bill, haven't paid grocery bill for 3 months. My brother goes to Lane Tech. High School. he's eighteen years old, hasn't gone to school for 2 weeks because he got no carfare. I have a sister she's twenty years, she can't find work. My father he staying home. All the time he's crying because he can't find work. I told him why are you crying daddy, and daddy said why shouldn't I cry when there is nothing in the house. I feel sorry for him. That night I couldn't sleep. The next morning I wrote this letter to you. in my room. Were American citizens and were born in Chicago, Ill. and I don't know why they don't help us Please answer right away because we need it. will starve Thank you.

God bless you.

[Anonymous]
Chicago, Ill.

76. I do hope that President Roosevelt can make those big money guys loosen up the money

Moorhead, Minn.
March 26, 1934

Dear Mrs Franklin D. Roosevelt

I have been very interested in you because I read in the papers how much you are doing for the poor children and crippled children. I want to thank you for doing so much good for those little children cause I know how tough it is now.

I am thirteen years old and am going to school with my twin brother, and little sister May who is eleven years old.

As daddy has been having kind of hard luck and is trying to get a letter through to President Roosevelt. I had to quit music lessons about two years ago as we had to sell the piano daddy bought me, too get clothes and stuff to eat.

Daddy used to teach school about twenty-five years ago. Mamma has been making all the old clothes over for us for the last two years   I do hope that President Roosevelt can make those big money guys loosen up the money so daddy can get some carpenter work. I am going to send you a picture of my twin brother and I taken about three years ago. I would like if you would write to me when you have time.

H. S. [female]

---

77. I have no shoe and we are suffin

St Louse   Mo
Feb 1, 1936

Dear mrs Rossevelt   my mother can not read nor write and she have to take care of five in family   I have no shoe and we are suffin   sometime we is with no frie and I am bare foot. and she said that she does get a entes mama said I can not help myself and I told my mother I read a new paper where in nobody should not starve and I told her that was going to write to that good man and rember that was you. Mrs Roosvilt Age 13 and hoping to get a answer from you soon . . . Saint louis Mo   Mama went to the re-leafe to get some help. and they refuse to give it to her and we are poor my mother is all our support. She is on the W.P.A.

[Anonymous]

---

78. Some time we don't have eni thing but we live, but you no it so hard to get cloth

March 29–1935

Dear Mrs. Roosevelt: I am writing you a little letter this morning. Are you glad it spring I am. For so manny poor people can raise some more to eat, you no what I am writing this letter for Mother said Mrs Roosevelt is just a God mother to the world and I though mabe you had some old clothes you no

Mother is a good sewer and all the little girls are getting Easter dresses And I though that you had some you no papa could wear Mr. Roosevelt shirts and cloth I no. My papa like Mr. Roosevelt and Mother said Mr. Roosevelt carry his worries with a smile you no he is always happy. You no we are not living on the relief we live on a little farm. papa did have a job and got laid on 5 yr ago so we save and got two horses and 2 cows and a hog so we can all the food stuff we can ever thing to eat some time we don't have eni thing but we live, But you no it so hard to get cloth. So I though mabe you had some. You no what you though was no good Mother can make over for me I am 11 yr old. I wish I could see you I no I would like you both. And shoes Mother wears 6 or 6-1/2. And papa wear 9. we have no car or no phone or radio papa he would like to have a radio but he said there is other thing he need more. papa is worried about his seed oats. And one horse is not very good. But ever one has't to worrie, I am send this litter with the pennie I get to take to Sunday school Mother give me one so it took 3 week. Cause Mother would think I better not ask for things from the first Lady. But Mother said you was an angle for doing so much for the poor. And I though that would be all rite this is some paper my teather gave for Xmas. My add is

C. V. B. [female]
Rushsyhania, Ohio

---

79. How can a bank take our money

Cleveland, Ohio
Nov 7, 1934

[Dear President Roosevelt:]

. . . What I would like to know is this: how can a bank take our money and get by while an old couple have to let their houses go. . . .

N. K. [male]
age 13

PART III

Reactions to the Depression

*Hunger and hurt are the great begetters of
brotherhood:
Humiliation has gotten much love:
Danger I say is the nobler father and mother.*

Archibald MacLeish, "Speech to Those Who Say Comrade"

*By learning the sufferings and burdens of men,
I became aware as never before of the life-power
that has survived the forces of darkness, the power
which, though never completely victorious, is
continuously conquering. The very fact that we are
still here carrying on the contest against the hosts
of annihilation proves that on the whole the battle
has gone for humanity.*

Helen Keller, *Out of the Dark*

Chapter 7. Attitudes toward Relief

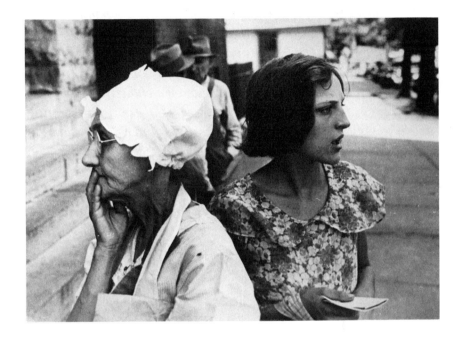

*But what we do want is a chanst to make an
honest living like what we was raised.*

One of the down and out

. . . Beings thus imperfect are nature's failures, and are re-
called by her laws when found to be such. Along with the rest they
are put upon trial. If they are sufficiently complete to live, they do
live, and it is well they should live. If they are not sufficiently com-
plete to live, they die, and it is best they should die. . . .
. . . there is unquestionably harm done when sympathy is
shown, without any regard to ultimate results. . . . Only
when . . . it suspends some particular department of life the
relationship between constitution and conditions, does it work
pure evil. Then, however, it defeats its own end. Instead of di-
minishing suffering, it eventually increases it. It favors the mul-
tiplication of those worst fitted for existence, and, by consequence,
hinders the multiplication of those best fitted for existence—
leaving, as it does, less room for them. It tends to fill the world
with those to whom life will bring most pain, and tends to
keep out of it those to whom life will bring most pleasure. It
inflicts positive misery, and prevents positive happiness.
Herbert Spencer, *Social Statics*

The letters that follow include a wide range of opinions on relief. Starting with a rather typical criticism of boondogglers, the selection continues through letters from poorer people who share the view that many relief recipients are lazy and intemperate. Some of the letters demonstrate the preference of almost everyone for work relief over the dole. Others show the prevalence of complaints about injustices in the distribution of relief. These letters shade into the sort that see relief as a right and become demanding in tone and content. The chapter closes with a series of communications that attack relief bureaucrats who ride in fine cars and do not understand the problems of the poor.

---

80. Merely making loafers out of individuals who don't want to work

New York City
May 25th 1936

Mr. Harrl L. Hopkins
Federal Emergency Relief Administration
Washington, D. C.
Dear Sir:

It seems worth while to call your attention to what is going on in near by Hoboken relative to "relief". And it can be said with certainty that Newark is typical of what can be done all over the U S A if the present Administration has but the guts. True relief is approved by the people of the U S A but merely making loafers out of individuals who don't want to work is definitely to the detriment of the country and is disasterous to the taxpayers of the country. If the situation as it now exists is not soon changed the voters of the country will give the present administration a thorough cleanout next November.

Yours truly,
[Signature illegible]

81. Keep out of so much sin and the terrible things idleness leads to

[Arkansas
March 1936]

Dear President.

In the past several months more than one time it has come to me that I should write you about this relief that is so widely and fast spreading all over these unitedstates, Mr Roosevelt I mant to ask you to please stop it, there is plenty of people today on relief who have plenty, just want to idle about not work think its fine for some poor working man to keep them, there are hundreds and hundreds of folks who should bee making there own liveing and could get work if yhey wanted it, but it is comeing to the point where no one wants to work, avery one is fighting and strugling to get on relief.

And Mr Roosevelt, I do believe if you could reaaly see the ruin it is doing you would I know stop it, the idleness it is causing, the sin it is causing and all sorts of mean things. penty of richfamilys here with a half dozen or more niger familys liveing on their farms one to run at their call they furnish them ahouse and manage to get them on relief for food and clothes. this relief is realy geting thigs in abad condition. there is plenty here in my sight both black and white on relief, Iam sick most all time cant hire one to do a thing have to struggle along somehow. dont aven raise agarden or a thing to help theirselves just go around braging about the goverment keeping them, and more and more getting on every day, people seperating and men being put in pen for their awful crimes and there families put on relief, screening and fixing all the houses they have never had a screen before and wouldnt have now if they had to earn them. nigers and all.

Mr Roosevelt I realy believe if you could see aven what I do everyday you would change your mind and put this relief out of sight, and let men and wimen go to work and keep out of so much sin and the terrible things idleness leads to, Mr President I dont think God intends or wants us few slaves to keep up the idle world, Do you? keep themin idleness and sin, for God is a just God he says so in his Holy word. and this is not just. there is work for every one in this land if they would get out and do it, God has furnished plenty of land and every for every one of us to havesomething to do besides loaf and get into all sorts of trouble and sin.

The taxes are getting so heavy on us few who are trying to get along it takes all we can make to pay our tax. my last word is Please put the relief offthe map and make folks go to work.

Mr Roosevelt, Ihope you read this letter and feel that it is really sincere,

And Yours Truly,

A poor Southern Ark Woman.

---

82. If my husban new this he would kill me

Nov 27 1935

Nashville ten

To the Govner Mr Roosvelt   Just want to tell you a few words   Lisen half the men you have Put to work taken there maney When they get Paid an spends it for whiskey some dont Com home with a Peny as have a wife an 4 an 5 Children not a Bite to eat an no money to Pay Rent some Com home an give there wife 7 an 8 dol take the rest an go get whiskey my husban does the same way an i am tired of it Couldent you have there checks mailed to there home an we Could have a much Bettr living you Can help us Wimen in that way Please do want tell my name but wish you would Pass that law to send there Check to there home

an oblige to you

Just a Friend

P S if my husban new this he would Kill me

---

83. It makes us feel like an American citizen to earn our own living

Battle Creek Mich.

April 5, 1936

President Roosevelt:

Please continue this W.P.A. program. It makes us feel like an American citizen to earn our own living. Being on the dole or relief roll makes us lazy and the funds are not enough to live decent on. We are thankful for what we receive though.

So we as W.P.A. workers in Battle Creek Michigan, appeal to you as our Great Leader to continue this great cause for Better citizens in Battle Creek Michigan.

Your Faithful,

W.P.A. workers

of Battle Creek

84. Some has been layed off that I no has nothing

[April 1936]

Dear Mr Roosevelt

i will write you a few lines in regard of the work which is being done by the relief men there is Some of the relief men not getting to work Some has been layed off that i no has nothing to live on Some hasent no milk are eggs are nothing to do with and there is men Still working is farming bottom land and got as much as Six are 8 head of milk cows and Some that has got a living with out the relief work and they are working ever day and those men that isent working has got large family to and nothing to live on So i think this Should be Seen after as those family cannot live with out Some help So please See after this. those men were working on the Van + Schofield road

as ever

a friend

85. I cant make any thing at that rate

[Macon, Georgia
September 9, 1935]

Mr president   dear sir Just a few lines to let you here from me   They have cut us down to 17-1/2 cent and hrs and I cant make any thing at that rate   They pay us every 2 weeks and then some time we dont have enought food to last. They have change up work so I will close to the president

[Anonymous]

86. I am willing to work but I dont seem able to get food, work or encouragement of any kind

Newport, Ore.
Jan. 11, 1935.

To the Hon. Chas. McNary,
Senator from Oregon.
My dear Sir:

I am sorry to have to intrude at this time regarding my own personal welfare but you seem to be my last place to appeal to. I am in need of relief. And

I am willing to work but I dont seem able to get food, work or encouragement of any kind. I am by occupation Lineman, age 56. I went to the County seat and I was given a work order for 12 dollers. Next time I was given 6 doller order. I worked both these out this week I was given an order of 5 dollars and told I was not able to work and I could not get food, seems as tho I should appeal to some one who wrote to her. I am a married man with a wife to surport. I was never a beggar and I want to know exactly why men past 50 years cannot get help. I have been in this County allmost a year. Year in April. Came here from Jackson Co., Medford, Ore. I have been starved untill I am certainly weak. There is others in the county in the same fix we are in. We have no surplus strength to fight sickness off and would be up against it for proper medical aid. I am asking you to personally notify the proper officials there on the Relief Committee or the President his self as to this plea as it is a matter of starvation to others besides my own individual case. If the relief bodys here have been unfair I am well convince of that the President will see to it. We have relief. If you will kindly help me to get this to him.

Mr. & Mrs. A. K.
Newport, Ore.

---

87. The ones that nearly starve some widow woman and old people that realy needs it they turn them down

Elizabethton, Tenn
Sept. 7, 1935

Mrs Franklin. D Roosevelt
Dear Mrs Roosevelt
Am writing you a few lines in regard to the money thats put out for the poor that cant help their selves Now there is some that lives better then they ever did, while it looks like the ones that Nearly starve some widow woman and old people that realy needs it they turn them down Now you are the Lady of our nation and do you think the people should be done this way when there is away provided for the poor dont you think there is something wrong some where that should be looked in to some poor men that Just gets one day while others get 3 or 4 and some cant even get a day there ought to be responsible people look after these Needy people before winter if they dont there will be lots of Suffering Now there is realy people getting off of this relief a that can get along with out and others that has no way on earth to get Any thing cant get work or food it seems they have the

ones they want to give to now if you dont think this is true Just send Some Detective here to investigate   as sure as you live this money thats being put out for the poor is not put where it should be

Very Respct

[Anonymous]

---

88. I have to steal coal from the railroad to keep us warm

January 23th, 1935

Hon. M. M. Neely, U. S. Senator, Senate Office Building,
Washington, District of Columbia
Dear Sir:

I am riting you this letter to tell you they wont give me no work on the relief and my children have not got no shoes and clothing to go to school with and we havent got enough of bed clothes to keep us warm and I told them this and still they wont give me no work we have to take old coats to cover up with. I have to steal coal from the Railroad to keep us warm the man where we did live made us move and we owed him one hundred and $40.00 dollars and my wife went to work in the mill to help us along and then the man sude her for my rent and tached her wages and now she has to pay $4.00 dollars every 2 week and we owe twenty dollars here where we live now our rent is $10.00 dollars a month for this house she has to pay the $4.00 dollar if we dont have a thing to eat my wife has those broken vaines in her legs and 2 of them them bursted in ulser sores and she cant hardly rest at night ore worke either my wife dont make enough to pay those both rents without my help and eat to we owe Docter Bill and dont have no money to get her legs tended to for her we owe store bill and cant get no credit realy my wife ant able to suport me and 4 children and school them and pay those two rents without my help. I have bin out ther several tim and they tell me your wife is working in mill I have got no clothes to wear myself I would and served in the World War and I dont see why I cant get a few days work relief people are keeping people who own their own property and also some people who has property to rent and they are working them on the Relief. One of the women envester who goes around to see who need help why her own husband works rite in the mill wher my wife works and thiy have only one child. I think this relief place her is not given people who needs they are helping people who dont need it. I think you all oute to come here and you will find out for they are lots of people would tell you just what

I am telling you here. I wish you would send this letter to them as same as you send me.

> Your very truly,
> Mr. G. W. K.
> Martinsburg, W. Va.

For we rely need help are I wouldnt send this letter.

---

89. We who need help are the ones who are not getting it

> Brooklyn, N. Y.
> May 22, 1936

President Franklin D. Roosevelt,
White House,
Washington, D. C.
Honorable Sir:

Having been one of the unfortunates who have been dropped from the W. P. A., I am taking this opportunity to write you why your program is failing in its mission to do good to those who need assistance.

When you took office it was your goodness of heart to help those who could not help themselves, but since 1933 we who need help are the ones who are not getting it, and those who do not are holding down positions not one but two on the W. P. A. rolls. There are cases right here in Brooklyn where not only the husband has a good job, but the wife also is holding one down, where the poor fellow who has all he can do with a small salary is trying to take care of four or more, and yet that is the fellow that is dropped and he is expected to go on relief, whereas the fellow with a non-relief rating remains working. It is now all those with communistic feelings who are rioting we too should because of the way we have been mistreated. That is why I have written to you to clean up the bad spots otherwise, I am afraid reelection will not be forthcoming because they will blame you and Not Harry Hopkins.

> [Anonymous]

90. Several men here are holding down two jobs which isn't right and letting another family go hungry

[October 29, 1935]

[Harry Hopkins
Federal Relief Administrator]
[Dear Mr. Hopkins:]

This letter I am sending is of great importants and hope you will look into the matter. These WPA men are working as high as three weeks without a pay and we are sitting here now waiting for our checks without nothing in this house to eat and a child sick with the measles and can't even buy a bottle of milk or bread for her to eat. I have worked a month now and only got one check for two days at 4.36 and a $6.00 grocery order is all we have had this month for six to live on. This has been going on for a long time and we poor people can't put up with it much longer, if several of these men such as Zuercher and Gravenkemper were gotten out things would go better. Several men here are holding down two jobs which isn't right and letting another family go hungry.

This money you have gotten for people without jobs isn't being used right. They are even working the men in the pouring down rain which isn't right.

. . . I know it isn't your fault so please do something or get somebody who will do something.

I was very glad to go on this work and is a awful nice thing but we can't sit here and starve waiting on our money when it isn't necessary.

I know you dont know about little things like this and you can't help it. For instance there is a family of 10 near us and he never has been put on W.P.A.

Sure hope you can do something and will be very much appreciated.

Yours Respectfully
A WPA Worker

91. I only wants a common living to exist without starving and freezing to death

December. 11—1935

to the President,

Executive Mansion, Washington, D. C.

Your Excellency—President of the United States,

this is to inform you to let you know how we are suffering as workers on the P. W. A. project here in Chicago. We are suppose to get $ 55.00. a month, and you knows at it best, $ 55.00 a month is too small amount for a man and his family to live on without any other help, when he have to pay just as small as $ 12.50 at the lowest rent, and buy coal, food, clothes, medicine or doctor bill and other expenses, on this small amount of money a month. Now I know that you are a man of a family too, and you knows the expenses of a family in this high price of living, and I knows and think that you feels our care, and means right. And you will do what is right if you knows the suffering of the people.

Now dont think that I want to live over my means, or want to live like a rich man, I only wants a common living to exist without starving and freezing to death. $ 55.00. a month not only too small for a family, but we are [not] even getting $ 55.00. a month, because we dont get two pays a month, it be three and four weeks before we get one pay, and when we do gets it we owe all of it and more besides. And the landlords and the groceryman runs us down for that, and if we continue to get paid like this, it will be that lots of us to be set out on the streets, and will have a hard way to get anywhere to stay.

If you dont believe what tell you is true, just have this investagated, and if the truth is known you will see that this is true.

Now dont think that I am a red, I am not and would not be one, I am only suffering, not only me myself, but my family, and lot others, Christmas will soon be here and we will have nothing for our family.

I am not trying to make trouble, and am not going to sign my name to this letter because it might make it hard for myself. Just investagated what I say.

[Anonymous]

92. Please try to make wages a little more equal

Forest 2-24-1936

Dear President Roosevelt

You speak about the good neighbor Idea and Mr Farley speaks about the Humane Treatment the Poor are receiving. Do you think it is Humane to load a lot of old infirm men in steel bottom Trucks no protection from the storms or cold send them 25 miles into the County and Place them in charge of Tyrants and Slave driver bosses. with no place to hang their coat or leave their dinner pails only a snow bank and serve them dinner in a frozen state also in a snow bank. then if some have the misfortune to get sick and are sick 5 days cut them off from W.P.A. and Releife for a month just becaus they happen to get sick. is that Humane. Is it right to give Hasbeen Republicans all of the jobs as Timekeepers and Bosses whose cellars are full and who have Farms. cows. Pigs. chickens. and full and Plenty to live on leave us Democrats out in the Cold. you pay them $65.00 $75.00 $90.00 and on up you give us a starvation $48.00 and use us like dogs. you would be arested if you treated a dog or any other Dumb animal that way. then Mr Farley has the nerve to stand up and tell how Humane we are being treated. you can remedy this by cutting The Bosses Pay and giveing us a little more so we can live as well as them. there is no reason they should be paid over $10.00 a month more than we are dont consider them skilled workmen becaus they are not. out of every 1000. White collor jobs how many Democrats will you find no more than 10 do you think us poor fools cannot see and understand what is going on oh yes we can and dont blame us if we have to prove it when the time comes.

Yes we realize you are Trying to do your best and how you are being kept from doing it but we dont think you know what the men in charge of this W.P.A. and Releife are doing Will you try to change the Programe a little so there will not be so much dissatisfaction and Starvation and Unequalization.

A Poor Icecycle

Dear President Roosevelt

Dont think when you read this letter that we are against you we are not we are for you 100 of percent. We the Poor People the Laboring class us men in the Overalls we know how hard you have worked and you sure helped us when we needed help we will not turn against you now when you need our help you are going to be our next President we are sure of that. But please try to make wages a little more equal

93. He say 1 dollar a day is a nuf to pay any man

Suffolk Va
Oct 11th 1935

[Mr. Harry Hopkins]

Dear sir i am one of your labor But i Dont think the town treat any of us that Work on these Jobs as thhy should. We Dont get the Price you Promas su and Dont get that untill thay get ready 17¢ an hour and fare like Dogs to get that Pleas Sir Send some one here to see hou We Poor Men ar fareing Just Hardly can get a living i get curst at on the Job and fired if I say any thing and the City Manager Dont Treat us right He say 1 Dollar a Day is a Nuf to Pay any Man

Please send some one to our relief We are Not treated fare

yours trully
a labor of
Suffolk Va

94. I think people need to get to gether. And feel as a body

Hackensack. NJ.
Nov. 12. 1935

Dear Mr. Hopkins,

I take pleasure to write a letter. I dont know if you have any thing to do with the Matter or not. But I want to ask you question about the PWA. projects: why do the men have to waite so long For their little money. after they have made it: I think it is ashame. the way these poor men. have go around in the rain and try to get their money. I think they are makeing small enough wages. after all every two week: is nothing to talk about. when you have paid house rent and buy food and colthes. children and everything is sky high. The poor people feel is very much. I saw a very good piece in the morning paper. that you had put. if was not for the good Lord. sending us such good weather. I dont know what the poor people would do? Because you dont have buy no coal. that is a saveng. The conditions are bad enough in this State. I think the people need to get to gether. and feel as a body, There is much hatred toward one another. But I hope some day things will be a little better. it is hard to send you children to school. with hardly any-thing to eat. and not the warmer kind of colthes. I have three little children and I can hardly feed them right: Because. dont have the right kind of thing: I have one sickly child and he need milk I can buy the milk for him because my Husband wages are to small. I think this country ought to look after her own. people. unstead the country Her people are in-need: There are many poor in the world that need help. I hope day condition will be better. I think is ashame that the men made the money 1 week ago. and to run in the rain after it   this is unsted be on Relief But they dont want no more Relief But after all the men work and get the money. How do they except to suport a family:

I hope this matter will be take care of

from a Mother.

---

95. We are poor people but we are human

Rising Sun   Md.
Jan 13   1936

To our President

Whom it May Concern

We are writing you in regards to a Sewer System project which is going on in Rising Sun. Md. In which we men are working. We want to know why it is that we are not getting the Proper WP.A. wages. It seems to us that the wages was set at 45 Cents an hour for 30 hrs a wk and they here are Making us work for 35 hrs a week at about 23 cents an hour which amounts to $32 a month and they say we get all bad days off which is all right. But it seems to us that we have to work any way or walk out in it 4 or 5 Miles as some of us do no matter how the weather may be and expect us to stand out in to it until 12 Oclock.

What we men want is work. And we all need it but we want W.P.A. wages. And Paid by the wk not Month. And we want 45 Cents and hour. for 30 hrs the same as they are paying all W.P.A. workers—We are willing to work on this job that way. By the hour and Not by the Month. We are willing to work at those wages and loose the bad days. We are not asking for any thing but what we are intitled too. Will you please see that this matter is looked into as soon as Possible.

President Roosevelt we are Poor People but we are human. We wish to be treated that way. The Majority of us men gave you our votes and we are intending to again at this election And we are thanking you for the good you have done us. And thats why we are writing you we feel you'll give us justice and again we thank you.

Respectfully.

W. P. A. workers.

P.S. we absolutely can't live on this small am't as some families have 10 children. Can't buy clothes or pay doctor bills and then eat. Now won't you kindly Please see this is looked into at once.

Thanking you.

---

96. We go home to nothing to eat and no fire to keep us warm

[Union City, New Jersey]
Jan. 4, 1936

Harry L. Hopkins
Washington D. C.
Dear Mr. Hopkins

I am writing to you because I am sick and tired of starving after I have done my share and worked in all kinds of weather for the money to feed and take care of my family. What I do earn is barely enough to keep us in food until the next check. Every check I get is so late that I am in debt up to my neck when it gets here and by the time I get through squareing up for what I owe for food and coal and medicine there isn't enough left for one decent meal. My check is so small that I can't afford to even buy myself a pair of underwear to wear while I work out in the open and so half the time I am sick with the gryppe. There are six in my family and their whole expense is on my check. My last check is overdue since Dec. 31st, 1935. We go out in all kinds of weather and they say "you get your check today sure when we start but when our day is done they tell us Tomorrow or next day and we go home to nothing to eat and no fire to keep us warm. The relief station won't give us any help at all. Every day is the same old story. Today is Saturday and they told us sure we would get our check today and now after starving all week and I really mean starving because we are, They told us we would maybe get it Tuesday. and so we can go without fire or food till then and then it will be the old story again. Can't you please do something about this?

A Union City, New Jersey
P. W. A. Worker. Thank you

97. This is a great injust

[New York, N.Y.
July 22, 1936]

[Dear Mr. Hopkins:]

This letter concerns the recent allotment of twenty six days pay with vacation allowed to the so called white collar workers better known as the supervisory department of the works progress administration projects. Its a low down [illegible] shame to forget the laboring man who is most responsible for the major part of construction. In comparison with the laboring man your supervision is paid a much higher salary. This is a great injust especially when the greater majority of them whether on project [illegible] or in office they do not deserve it. No doubt you are aware of thos gross incompetency that exist among your select class. its a rank foul shame to descriminate so to forget the laboring man. its a shame: the man who had to depend on relief for existence along comes this supervisory element of which the greater number of them have never known what the depression is.

They have grown fat on the job doing almost nothing and now comes along another fat plum.

. . . after all the laboring man is in this respect much worthier. and how.

An American

98. Give work to the needy ones, and not to the ones that have everything

North Chicago Ill.
June 22, 1936

Hono. Harry Hopkins,

May I have the honor to inform you of how things are running in North Chicago and Waukegan.

Mr. E. T. Gurney the chief administer of the W. P. A. He sure is an honest man, you may ask me why, but here is the reason, a needy person who needs employment, very bad cannot get employment, but a person who has wealthy realitaves, with 3 cars, a farm stockholders at the foundry at North Chicago, and they own homes, and have everything under the sun, and still Mr. Gurney has given this party a position in which he is earning $1.00 per hour, awhile hundreds of poor people cannot earn one cent, why because Mr. Gurney is their best friend, but such work will not do. I am a friend of the poorer class, and I see that such work does not go either with you if you only if you knew the truth, and here it is. Mr. Gurney thinks that he will do such work long, but I hope it will stop as soon as you get this letter, as I believe you should do a little investagating here in Waukegan, and North Chicago, and try to straighten things out a little, and give work to the ones that need it, and give these people their piece of bread that deserve it. These people are worth I mean the whole family around $100,000 and I see no reason why they should get the relief work on W P A project. Now Dear Mr. Hopkins I hope to see a change and if not I write to Our Dear Mr. Franklin D. Roosevelt who saved this country from ruin, and who gave many a hungry mouths a piece of bread, and I for President Roosevelt at all times, if you do not look into this The President will, as I shall write to him, and tell him the truth, on what is going on. It makes me sick, to see such things as I my self have been on relief before, and the same thing was done to me. My husband was cheated out of 4 weeks salary in which Mr. Gurney did not forward to him, and he shall not do it this time, as at first I did not know how those things were going, but now I see a little more, and I thought that you should know about this.

I wish you would do something about this, as it means saving many hungry hearts, give work to the needy ones, and not to the ones that have everything. Hope to see a great change in Waukegan and North Chicago, and may God Bless you.

Just a Friend of The People Of
Waukegan and North Chicago Ill.

---

99. All of them in the office here have fine cars

[Eastman, Georgia
April 13, 1935]

[Dear Mr. Hopkins:]

Mrs. Maude Huckings here in charge of the F.E.R. is not doing right by the peoples here in Dodge County   the Mill hands Speailiy sece the Mill has been Colose down she says they have not had the Money   We all need clothes and food to   We just get a little Work now and then hardly enought to live on   all of them in the office here have fine cars to ride in   they did not have them a few Months ago   We dont know How much you have given for Dodge County   We think there is some thing wrong here some Where We hope you will look in to the Matter right away.

[Anonymous]

100. It looks like the relieff is just helping the big folks

[Tompkinsville, Kentucky
April 1935]

[Dear President Roosevelt,]

i thought i would rite you a few lines   we Heared in the news that you were going to give the old age and criple a Pension we think that would be the Best thing that had ever happened to this country for they is a few that sure does need it. When you first started up the R.F.C.* it sure did help the people and we realy Believe that was what you were aiming to do But it looks like the Relieff is just helping the Big Folks. so we wish you would make a change some way. to help the Poor. for they are sure who helps you. i dont want your help as long as i can do and live. But i do wish you would help the ones that is sure in need. . . .

[Anonymous]

101. Do you wonder that there is a feling of injustest

July 22   35

Dear Mr Hopkins   Relief Administ

Sr can you Pleas Give us any hope when oh when the Dollor Per week ever End: is there any ExplanaTion that the real Job So we can realy have enuff to eate be Keept Just a week or So a Head of us   But we cant ever Get to it. Just To think what Horrible Suspence The thing is Just torture oh Pleas Just Say actually When if Ever we can have the thing that we Heard about that Each man Would Work and be Able to have Enuff to Eate. And the Staff I believe is what they call it here they have Five cars and drive around in thim and the People Hungry   do you wonder that there is a feling of In-justest. And the people wonder if there Realy is Any thing better for us if So How Soon

very Respectfully

A Bunch of Hungry People
in Augusta Ga

Feeling is Running High here now.

---

*The Reconstruction Finance Corporation was, of course, started during the Hoover Administration.

102. Discrimination has lowered my respect for being good

[September 1935]

Mr. Harry L. Hopkins
Public Relief Administrator
Washington D.C.
I am sending you something to think about.

1. Why should Mrs. Burns be kept on the FERA. staff when her husband draws a big salary in the highway department—? Between $200 + $300 go into that home every month

2. Why should young girls of social prestige, and apparently not financially depressed be visitors when there are women and men who are better qualified intellectually and who have lost everything thru no extravagance of their own.

3. Why should we, whose ancestors have help to win every war before the revolution, down to the present time, and whose lives have been an asset and not a liability as most of the FERA. folks are. In what way has the great majority of these folks benefited the community, the state, or this beautiful, resourceful country? Not one iota. Yet they receive help and many good citizens are turned down.

4. Why should some receive more than their quota and in advance while others who are just as much in need must wait for two weeks or even a month after their work is finished before receiving their pay?

5. Why should teachers, who have taught all the year, be given preference on summer jobs?

I dare not sign my name. I am helpless. I am aone of many. but I have all my life been a loyal citizen, but chiseling, political discrimination, and social discrimination has lowered my respect for being good.

[Anonymous]

103. The money was taken from the laborers and given the bosses more than they ever got

Central city Pa.

4—8—36.

Mr. Harry L. Hopkins, W.P.A. Ad. Washington, DC.

Dear Sir: I am a Democrat and was for the New Deal and would be yet if it were not for the way we laborers are treated here in Central City where we have jobs on W.PA. The bosses and timekeepers get thier pay regular and $125.00 a month at that more than any foreman as ever got here. and the laborers are getting less than ever, in other words the money was taken from the laborers and given the bosses more than they ever got, well we get this "Widows Mite" whenever the autocrats in Johnstown feel like sending it, while the bosses and all thier "Assistants" (thier is two or three big salaried ones on every job where there was just an foreman before) go arround getting drunk and getting votes, but do you think they are getting them? they are practically ruining the Democrat party, strong New Dealers are turning to the Republican party. Then their is the "Pull type" who has to say who gets a job and who dont. I tell sir the Democrats are ruining them selves by thier cheap way of managing things we Democrats ourselves can see it Mr Roosevelt and I believe yourself has said politics was not to be in W.P.A. well let me tell you your word surely don't mean anything in Somerset Co then. We worked in Johnstown knee deep in mud and received no pay yet, and before we got the last pay we waited on it one month and then was short and have a promise of being short this time after waiting for a centuary to get it, the foremans have had two pays since we got one, is that our new deal? Whats the delay? There now is twenty job Holders for a job than one man did before, and still every thing is delayed more than ever. we were better off when we got relief we starve now before we get pays and have it spent before we get it and us the red a good some space will not permits us to sign our names but we are labors on W.PA. Projects in Central City

[Anonymous]

Chapter 8. The Conservative

Are there no prisons?
And the Union workhouses?
Are they still in operation?

Scrooge

he small selection of letters reproduced in this chapter provides a good sampling of the array of conservative and right-wing beliefs expressed during the Depression.

Most of the more affluent conservatives sounded similar themes. Unlike the writers of many of the letters that appear in other chapters, they were absolutely opposed to any ideas of redistribution. Some complained that laborers and "reliefers" were getting too much already.

Constantly reiterated in these letters is the belief that the down and out are in that condition because they deserve to be. The poor are said to be shiftless, lacking in frugality, prone to drunkenness, never satisfied, overly reproductive, ignorant, and often foreign, Jewish, and Communist. If only these lazy "human parasites" possessed the virtues of industriousness and thrift during good times, they would not be facing hardships now, said the recurring right-wing theme. If such people still would not work, the taxpayers should not be burdened with caring for the "pampered poverty rats." As the writer of the remarkable first letter below put it, "let each one paddle their own canoe, or sink." "As for the old people on beggars' allowances," this twentieth-century Scrooge went on, "the taxpayers have provided homes for all the old people who never liked to work."

The last two letters in the chapter are from less affluent people who do not express the full gamut of conservative views, but who make enough right-wing statements to provide a taste of the sort of Depression victim who blamed his fellow sufferers for his plight.

---

104. Let each one paddle their own canoe, or sink

Dec. 14—1937.
Columbus, Ind.

Mrs. F. D. Roosevelt,
Washington, D. C.

Mrs. Roosevelt: I suppose from your point of view the work relief, old age pensions, slum clearance and all the rest seems like a perfect remedy for all the ills of this country, but I would like for you to see the results, as the other half see them.

We have always had a shiftless, never-do-well class of people whose one and only aim in life is to live without work. I have been rubbing elbows with this class for nearly sixty years and have tried to help some of the most promising and have seen others try to help them, but it can't be done. We cannot help those who will not try to help themselves and if they do try a square deal is all they need, and by the way that is all this country needs or ever has needed: a square deal for all and then, let each one paddle their own canoe, or sink.

There has never been any necessity for any one who is able to work, being on relief in this locality, but there have been many eating the bread of charity and they have lived better than ever before. I have had taxpayers tell me that their children came from school and asked why they couldn't have nice lunches like the children on relief.

The women and children around here have had to work at the fields to help save the crops and several women fainted while at work and at the same time we couldn't go up or down the road without stumbling over some of the reliefers, moping around carrying dirt from one side of the road to the other and back again, or else asleep. I live alone on a farm and have not raised any crops for the last two years as there was no help to be had. I am feeding the stock and have been cutting the wood to keep my home fires burning. There are several reliefers around here now who have been kicked off relief, but they refuse to work unless they can get relief hours and wages, but they are so worthless no one can afford to hire them.

As for the clearance of the real slums, it can't be done as long as their inhabitants are allowed to reproduce their kind. I would like for you to see what a family of that class can do to a decent house in a short time. Such a family moved into an almost new, neat, four-room house near here last winter. They even cut down some of the shade trees for fuel, after they had burned everything they could pry loose. There were two big idle boys in the family and they could get all the fuel they wanted, just for the cutting, but the shade trees were closer and it was taking a great amount of fuel, for they had broken out several windows and they had but very little bedding. There were two women there all the time and three part of the time and there was enough good clothing tramped in the mud around the yard to have made all the bedclothes they needed. It was clothing that had been given them and they had worn it until it was too filthy to wear any longer without washing, so they threw it out and begged more. I will not try to describe their filth for you would not believe me. They paid no rent while there and left between two suns owing everyone from whom they could get a nickels worth of anything. They are just a fair sample of the class of people on whom so much of our hard earned tax-money is being squandered and on whom so much sympathy is being wasted.

As for the old people on beggars' allowances: the taxpayers have provided homes for all the old people who never liked to work, where they will be neither cold nor hungry: much better homes than most of them have ever tried to provide for themselves. They have lived many years through the most prosperous times of our country and had an opportunity to prepare for old age, but they spent their lives in idleness or worse and now they expect those who have worked like slaves, to provide a living for them and all their worthless descendants. Some of them are asking for from thirty to sixty dollars a month when I have known them to live on a dollar a week rather than go to work. There is many a little child doing without butter on its bread, so that some old sot can have his booze and tobacco: some old sot who spent his working years loafing around pool rooms and saloons, boasting that the world owed him a living.

Even the child welfare has become a racket. The parents of large families are getting divorces, so that the mothers and children can qualify for aid. The children to join the ranks of the "unemployed" as they grow up, for no child that has been raised on charity in this community has ever amounted to anything.

You people who have plenty of this worlds goods and whose money comes easy, have no idea of the heart-breaking toil and self-denial which is the lot of the working people who are trying to make an honest living, and then to have to shoulder all these unjust burdens seems like the last straw. During the worst of the depression many of the farmers had to deny their families butter, eggs, meat etc. and sell it to pay their taxes and then had to stand by and see the dead-beats carry it home to their families by the arm load, and they knew their tax money was helping pay for it. One woman saw a man carry out eight pounds of butter at one time. The crookedness, shelfishness, greed and graft of the crooked politicians is making one gigantic racket out of the new deal and it is making this a nation of dead-beats and beggars and if it continues the people who will work will soon be nothing but slaves for the pampered poverty rats and I am afraid these human parasites are going to become a menace to the country unless they are disfranchised. No one should have the right to vote theirself a living at the expense of the tax payers. They learned their strength at the last election and also learned that they can get just about what they want by "voting right." They have had a taste of their coveted life of idleness, and at the rate they are increasing, they will soon control the country. The twentieth child arrived in the home of one chronic reliefer near here some time ago.

Is it any wonder the taxpayers are discouraged by all this penalizing of thrift and industry to reward shiftlessness, or that the whole country is on the brink of chaos?

M. A. H. [female]
Columbus, Ind.

105. The more you give the lower classes the more they want

[Fayetteville, W. Va.
Nov. 4, 1936]

[Dear Mrs. Roosevelt,]

. . . Personally I have found that the more you give the lower classes the more they want. Never satisfied. In my charitable work I become discouraged and it makes me know what your husband is up against. The people (some) are so simple-minded. They think the President is going to keep on giving. My gardener (White) and my maid (col.) voted democratic this election, not from coercion on my part but because "Roosevelt will take care of us."

Some of us (conservative democrats) regret the prevalence of certain graft in minor county officials, Relief offices, Welfare, etc. but I know it's all too far away for you to control.

. . . You may be assured I am not looking for a position, and I have no axe to grind. I merely wish to help in what I know to be a most crucial situation, and most difficult to solve. My only solution is the hope of work for everyone. If ONLY the wheels of industry can keep humming we may see our way out. Otherwise it may be serious.

With congratulations and my very best wishes for you and President Roosevelt during the coming four years.*

I am very sincerely yours,
Mrs. N. J. S.

. . . I feel that you and your husband are earnestly trying to solve today's problems.

106. The so called social security act . . . is nothing but downright stealing

[no address]
Jan. 18, 1937

[Dear Mrs. Roosevelt]

I . . . was simply astounded to think that anyone could be nitwit enough to wish to be included in the so called social security act if they could pos-

---

*The letter was written the day after Roosevelt's huge victory in the 1936 election.

sibly avoid it. Call it by any name you wish it, in my opinion, (and that of many people I know) is nothing but downright stealing. . . .

Personally, I had my savings so invested that I would have had a satisfactory provision for old age. Now thanks to his [FDR's] desire to "get" the utilities I cannot be sure of anything, being a stockholder, as after business has survived his merciless attacks (if it does) insurance will probably be no good either.

. . . [She goes on to complain about the lack of profits.]

Then the president tells them they should hire more men and work shorter hours so that the laborers, who are getting everything now raises etc. can have a "more abundant life." That simply means taking it from the rest of us in the form of taxes or otherwise. . . .

Believe me, the only thing we want from the president, unless or if you except Communists and the newly trained chiselers, is for him to balance the budget and reduce taxes. That, by the way, is a "mandate from the people" that isn't getting much attention.

I am not an "economic royalist," just an ordinary white collar worker at $1600 per. Please show this to the president and ask him to remember the wishes of the forgotten man, that is, the one who dared to vote against him. We expect to be tramped on but we do wish the stepping would be a little less hard.

Security at the price of freedom is never desired by intelligent people.

M. A. [female]

---

107. I have spoken to one Italian whom I met

[New York, N. Y.
October 1933]

[Mr. Harry Hopkins
Washington, D.C.]
[Dear Mr. Hopkins:]

Will you please investigate the various relief agencies in many cities of the United States. The cities where there are a large foreign and jewish population. No wonder the cities are now on the verge of bankruptcy because we are feeding a lot of ignorant foreigners by giving them relief. And, they are turning against us every day. I would suggest to deport all foreigners and jews who are not citizens over the United States back to any land where they choose to go and who will admit them. As America is now over crowded with too much immigration and it can not feed even its own citizens without feeding the citizens of other foreign nations. I have found out after careful investigation that we are feeding many foreigners who send out their wives to work and who have money in the bank. While the men drink wine and play cards in saloons and cafes. I have spoken to one Italian whom I met. And I ask him what he was doing for a living. He said me drinka da dago red wine and play cards and send the wife out to work. Isn't a very good thing for us to support them. No wonder the taxpayers are grumbling about taxes. Most of them are a race of black hands murders boot leggers bomb throwers. While most of the sheeney jews as they are called are a race of dishonest people who get rich by swindling, faking and cheating the poor people. Besides the jews are responsible by ruining others in business by the great amount of chisling done. And selling even below the cost prices, in order to get all the others buisiness. The foreigners and jews spend as little as they can to help this country. And, they live as cheap as they can. And, work as cheap as they can, and save all the money they can. And when they have enough they go back to their country. Why don't we deport them under the section of the United States Immigration Laws which relates to paupers and those who become a public charge. The Communist Party is composed mostly by foreigners and jews. The jews are the leaders of the movement and urge the downfall of this government. . . .

A Taxpayer

---

108. The administration at Washington is accelerating it's pace toward socialism and communism

Hornell, New York
March 7, 1934

My Dear Senator:

It seems very apparent to me that the Administration at Washington is accelerating it's pace towards socialism and communism. Nearly every public statement from Washington is against stimulation of business which would in the end create employment.

Everyone is sympathetic to the cause of creating more jobs and better wages for labor; but, a program continually promoting labor troubles, higher wages, shorter hours, and less profits for business, would seem to me to be leading us fast to a condition where the Government must more and more expand it's relief activities, and will lead in the end to disaster to all classes.

I believe that every citizen is entitled to know the policy of the Government, and I am so confused that I wish you would write me and advise me whether it is the policy of this Administration, of which you are a very important part, to further discourage business enterprise, and eventually set up a program which eliminates private industry and effort, and replaces it with Government control of industry and labor,—call it what you will: socialism, facism, or communism, or by any other name.

I am not addicted to annoying public office holders with correspondence, but if there are any private rights left in this country, then I would appreciate an early reply to this letter, so that I may take such action as is still possible, to protect myself and family.

With kindest personal regards,

Yours truly,

W. L. C. [male]

WLC:JFE
U.S. Senator Robert F. Wagner
Senate Building,
Washington, D. C.

---

109. If its colored + foreign your so interested in place them to themselves + not amongst "humane" people

[New York, N. Y.
May 1936]

Mr Hopkins
Dear Sir: When you opened that "Sewing Project" at 18 St N.Y.C. did you forget that there are still a few "white Americans left. Its the worst thing as far as placing is concerned. Nothing but colored, Spanish, West Indies, Italians + a hand ful of white   Every colored that comes in is placed as "clerk, head or boss over tables + Knocking other people around. Well, if you dont see a race riot there its a surprise. If its colored + foreign your so interested in place them to themselves + not amongst "Humane" people— You just making the whites take a back seat. Its a very good useful project + hospitals + poor need the things that are made   But the system is rotten Just like a lot of cattle Being driven around when its time to go home they all rush no matter who they bump into. Too many bosses + no one seems to Know whats to be done—Maybe a few of us whites would like to be placed in something else but a "Sweat shop" work 6 days a week its a wonder they let you have Sunday off. If you dont give American people more of a Show we will take up with President Roosevelt who did this good act so Americans dont starve.

A disgusted
American

110. They should kick them all back to Europe as the majority of them are absolutely nogood

August, 12, 1935.
Chicago, ILL.

Mr. Harry L. Hopkins
Works Progress Administrator,
Washington, D. C.
Dear Sir:

I have been following the editorials, in regards to this—Works program, and note the difficulties that are arising practically all over. Well our government doesnt think that the, Communistic element is worth bothering about, however I have worked for the government for the past ten years, and I am still working for them temporairly. The—whole trouble is that the majority of those involved in these strikes, and other troubles, are nothing more than the worse kind of radicals. They not only try to disrupt business, but they are paid by Russia to get in every military organizeation, and create discontent and do damage where ever they possibly can. They are in every large or small factory in the Country. Do you think all those so called accidents that happen to are ships and aircraft just happen, not much, they are the work of very clever radicals in practically every instance. It is high time that this country "woke up" befor it's to late.

I was formerly employed as a laborer, then was promoted to Timekeeper, well I know that the C. W. A. was drawn up in a hurry, and that they had quite a time in eliminateing the graft, in a City like Chicago, but now that they have taken more time with this new program, they will be able to cope with the situation. I also realise that the wages they are paying the men, on these diffrent projects are lower than on the—other job. However if they wanted to work, bad enough that wouldnt stop—them, its only these racketeering Unions, and a lot of city politicians, that think they can get their hands on some graft. Well its a wise move to stand pat, and show them that they will get nowhere with there strikes.

Although their must be some way to overcome these "racket Unions", I—wonder if the men were made Temporairy Fedral Government Employees, Then the racketeers wouldnt have the nerve to monkey with them, as—they would never try to fool with the Fedral Government. One more point that I would like to suggest, Their were hundreds of Timkeepers whose work was perfect and far above reproach, well as the majority of those fellows like myself have good discharges from the different branches of the service. So far all these jobs only benifit the majority of foreigners on relief. I think all former C. W. A. employees in good standing should be given jobs corresponding to the ones they held on the C. W. A. After all those men have had the experience, and if their work was done right, they deserve a job, a lot more than the majority of those foreigners, Do you realise that there are Thousands of young men like myself that have done something for our country, and have tried to stay off the relief rolls the past two years. Well if anyone should get a decent job those men should. The majority of Foreigners think its smart to get on relief, drive a car, have two, or three others in the family working and live off of a big-hearted Uncle Sam. They should kick them all back to Europe as the majority of them are absolutely nogood.

I have worked around some of the largest Navy Yards in the U. S. and these racketeering Unions never tried to monkey with the work men, because they were Government employees, well the same thing could be done in this case. On our C. W. A. project their was no graft, and the job went along with little or no trouble. However even then those Comunistic reds tried to disrupt the workers, they would usually have girls distributing booklets or papers, but the investagators could never seem to get the ones at the head of their organization, we had the same trouble in the service. It is time something should be done, after all it is an offense against the government, in a lot of cases. They send stuff through the mails, that any other country, would throw them in jail for, they have tried to wreck Army equipment and in some cases have succeeded in causeing serious accidents, if they are allowed to continue they will eventually try to cause a revolution in this country.

And you can take it from me, that if their policies were any good they would be useing them over in their own country. I've seen the other Countries and their are none that could even compare with it, well the only way to keep it that way is to be prepared to defend it against any and all enamies. The foreign element in this country are allowed entirely to much leeway in practically every respect, even befor they are Americanized. Take the Chinamen they get here open a business, make a fortune and it goes directly back to China, well the other Foreigners do the same thing, yet if we tried to do that in their country you wouldnt last a month. Those japs never should have been allowed to buy land here, as they under work the american farmers, The most of those foreigners live good on a tenth of what a white man could exist on. Well heres hopeing something will be done SOON to relieve the present employment situation in Chicago, For those not on relief.

The Civilian Conservation Corp, is one of the best places for the boys of this country. It should be open to all boys from 17 to 30 and it should be for a year instead of six months. Their conditions could also be improved.

Respectfully
An Ex-Leatherneck

Chapter 9. The Desperate

*No work, no hope; just live from one
day to the next. Maybe better times
are coming. Personally, I doubt it.*

A small-town housewife, 1933

Desperation was a common reaction to the Depression. The writers of many of the letters in other chapters were plainly desperate. The letters reproduced on the following pages, though, seem particularly illustrative of various forms of desperation.

Some people who were pushed to desperation simply lost all hope. Few such fatalistic people wrote letters. The very act of writing for help showed that a person was not completely without hope, no matter how desperate his letter might be.

Desperation was breaking into an empty building to find a place to sleep; it was fathers and older children staying out of the house while youngsters were fed, so that the demands of empty stomachs would not lead to the literal taking of food from the mouths of babies. Desperation was staying in bed in order to keep warm and inactive and thus conserve both fuel and calories; it was children taking turns, from day to day, at eating. Desperation was searching the docks where garbage scows were loaded, hoping to find spoiled vegetables that could be eaten; it was finding something edible and gathering the family (and perhaps some neighbors) for a primitive gorging. Desperation was living for the moment, with little thought of the past or future. Both were too disturbing to contemplate. Desperation was lessening pleasure, deemphasizing sexual relations, and eating for survival, not enjoyment. Desperation was, in short, living as if you were largely dead.[1]

The development of apathy was perhaps the final step in the sequence of desperation. Signs of such hopelessness were found by the Lynds in Muncie, Indiana, in the early thirties. For many, particularly in the working class, pessimism was replacing the traditional American optimism. The American dream had not vanished entirely, but it was thought to be much less possible to attain than it had been in the twenties.[2] Pessimism could lead to hopelessness and apathy, or it could lead to discontent directed toward social change. The direction that desperation and pessimism took would depend, at least in part, upon the actions of the government. The New Deal's activism renewed hope for many, but for those who remained unaided by its programs, desperation grew worse as the promises of the Roosevelt Administration were, on a personal level, not fulfilled.

The writers of most of the letters in this chapter did not blame themselves for the conditions in which they were forced to exist. Many of them swallowed their pride with great difficulty, seeking help only when their situations became genuinely desperate. Their plight in the 1930s was without precedent in their own lives, and they simply did not know where to turn. As the letters show unmistakably, one direction in which desperate people were likely finally to turn was toward the Roosevelts.

Some among the desperate letter writers expressed resentment at the way things were. Rather than moving toward helplessness, they seem to have been moving toward discontent. Yet there is little to suggest that such resentment or discontent was aimed at the New Deal.

---

111. All else has failed

Cambridge
May 16, 1934

[Dear President Roosevelt:]

. . . I am now at the point of despration. But as I have 19 grandchildren all under 14 years of age 9 of whom are boys, to do anything desperette now they would never live down the disgrace. I was always a hard worker saved money invested in the auto business and lost. Am 55 years old. . . . I would not wish at the cost of my life that any one should know I wrote you this letter [seeking a loan]. All shall be returned in do   All I want is a chance. . . . It is my last hope and effort   All else has failed.

[Initials omitted because of writer's request]

---

112. Please help me please

High Point N C
Dec 15. 1935

Mr Roosevelte   I am In nead Bad Please help me I have 7 children and is Sick all the time one of my children is Sick and has Ben for a lone time and I have No under clothes for none of the famiely we cant harly hide I Self with top cloths   I ned Milk and my Boy need milk   Please give my childrens and my Self Some under cloths or we will freze to Deth this cold wethr we can not Make it pay Rent get Something to Eat and get wood and coal no one work But my husBan he make $6.75 per week no way way I can get any under cloths for the famely please help me I have not a teeth in My head wen I Eat I nely Dieys   no way to get any please help me please.

[Anonymous]

113. Which would be the most human way to dispose of my self and family

Latrobe, Pa.
April 4, 1934

Mr. Bruce McClure*

Dear Sir:

In regards to relief and NRA, I wish to call attention to my case, I was forced onto relief by the Latrobe Borough Council. I had been employed as Patrolman of the Borough until Jan. 8-34, then without any just cause whatsoever, I was let go. Just to satisfy Mr. William McCafferty and Mr. V. B. Stader, two of the Honorable Council of said Boro, they replaced me with a man who was working 5 days a week at Latrobe Electric Steel Co. and sent me out on the mercy of the relief with 6 children and a wife to support. Now I am forced with proposition of being set out of my home because I cannot pay my rent. I have 10 day to get another house, no job, no means of paying rent. Can you be so kind as to advise me as to which would be the most human way to dispose of my self and family, as this is about the only thing that I see left to do. No home, no work, no money. We cannot go along this way. They have shut the water supply from us. No means of sanitation. We cannot keep the children clean and tidy as they should be. They are all 6 in school but will soon haft to take them out if something is not done. I want work and money enough to support this family. I am getting relief to partly feed them but where is the shelter and water coming from and clothes. I lost my work through no fault of mine and for no just reason whatsoever and I feel I am entitle to some consideration. Thanking you in advance for any help, I remain

Yours truly,
J. S. H. [male],
Latrobe, Pa.

*Secretary, Civil Works Administration.

114. If I wasnt so poor I wouldnt ask you for a favor

Nov. 22 [1935]   Friday   Granby Mo

Mrs Franklin D. Roosevelt.

Dear Friend as I understand you are a good ladie friend I will ask you to do me a favor   I halve a little Boy of school age 13 years old only in the 7 grade cince he had to stop school as he has Bad eyes he cant see to get his lessons   I ask you if you will be kind to send him the money to get him a pair of glasses   I taken him to our Dr which is Dr Rollens and he said the Boy needed glasses and I halvent no money to get them as we are on the Relieff and you know we dont halve no money so am asking you to be so kind to my Boy so please send him $5 or $6. dollars to get some eye glasses if I wasnt so poor I wouldnt ask you for a favor he wants to go on to school so bad. so please be kind to the Boy. he was operated on about a year agoe and that put him back in school then now. tis his eyes so please send him the money dirrect to [D. C.] Granby Mo

to Mrs Roosevelt

Ans in return mail sose he can get back in school

115. Give me sume thing to eat my chrildren are hongre my wife are ded

Mobile Ala   May 11—1936

Mr Roose Velt Sor i was working on the P W A. and the took me off to Put me on the old Age Pension   i have bine off From worke Every Sence the 20 of April and the haven Put me on The old Age Pension yet   All So i was Geten 19¢ Per Hour for 8. Hours worke   Mr. Roose Velt Sor Please Sor tell Miss Davis Please mam Give me Sume thing to Eat my Chrildren are hongre my Wife are Ded   She Died may the 5/1936

Miss Davis is Working Wel Far 750 St Michael St.

I have Give them my age and them wont Rite me up   i was Born 1870 oct.

[Anonymous]

116. They laughs and make fun about me asking for something to eat

Augusta Ga
Oct 22, 1935

Dear Sir Mr. Franklin D
Rosevelt, the president of the United state of american, I am wrighting you a few lines to let you know how I am getting alone. I had to whight you, to tell you, a few things about my condition. I am out of work I aint got nothing to do, and been beggin feelworkers of the relief for work and they wont give me anything to do, and they tells me that we cant give you any work and cant give you anything to get food with, they laughs and make fun about me asking for something to eat dear Sir, Mr president I haven,t even got a bed no beding of no kind of my own and old lady iS funishing me Some old beding to use until the relief give me something and they wont do nothing for me but 12 lb of flour and four cans of beef and 4 lbs of prunes, and nothing to cook it with, and can you please Sir give me something to do. its is people that haves their own homes, and plenty around them gets it and I can,t get work and nothing and please Sir, do Some thing for me and my three children and my old 70 years old mother, we ain,t got nothing to eat nor cloth, I went and redish for work and I went back and beg for help I owes about $ 3 for grocery and I owes a $1.50 for rent and nothing to do to get it, and the folks I owe is calling on me for it. I have taken the feelworkers in the home where I was living and let her investergated the house through and through to show her that I did need it and they wont do any thing for me I am taking my child up to the office, with me to show them her size, and Just because the didn me clothing to go to School with they give me Some dresses to Small and to Short its the way the order was wrote, she wears about A 14. and they give me a 12 for her and then wouldn do any thing about it but laugh and wink their eyes from one to another, I carried them back to them amergency relief office it was four dresses which was Size 12 now dear Sir mr president will you tell them something to do for me please sir tell me what to do, I am eating flour bread and drinking water, and no grease and nothing in the bread, one of the field workers which was mrs Sicilches told me to go and with a white on her place and work for her me or my old mother one and I aint even got beding to sleep on and you know mr president that white lady aint going to give me bed cloth and wearing cloths and my children clothes and shoes and feed them and pay me to work for her when they

wont pay me to do their work So please sir do some thing for me and my children have wrote for them to give her so cloths and she had to stop School cause she had cloths and shoes

[Anonymous]

---

117. I very often thought of suicide as the best way out

[New York, N.Y.
March 1936]

Dear President,

why is it that it is the work-man that is always kicked when things go wrong with the officials   my Husband has worke on W.P.A. for some time a carpenter @ 85 dols per month + this morning he was reduced to timber-man @ 60 per month   I know there was a mistake as he is a good carpenter. I am sorry to trouble you but please Dear President I need that 25 dols he is cut   Do you know what it is to have money then find yourself broke, next children, + finally live in a cold water Dump get up to two children at night and find them nearly frozen from lack of clothing well I do, + struggled along although I very often thought of suicide as the best way out. I am not a coward but good Lord it is awful to stand helpless when you need things.

When that letter came from Project Labor officer Frank C. Hunt W.P.A. N.Y.C. this morning informing him that he was reduced to 60 per month. well I hate to think of what will happen. Please, get him replaced as carpenter again his tag number is "123986" + he works at 125 St. N.Y.C. I am sorry I cannot give you my name as I do not want publicity though I see no way of avoiding it if things do not pick up. Thanking you for favours + forgive scribbling as am all nerves.

[Anonymous]

118. My last chance now is to beg

Rossville Ga
Gen. Delvry
[1936]

Mr. Franklin D RooSevelt.
Executive ManSion
Washington D. C.
Dear Mr RooSevelt

I have tryed every Effort to get work thought mabe I would have a few days of SuCCeSS. I am not eligiable for help from the W.P.A. and Can not oBtain help from the City   well my LaSt Chance now is to beg. I am going to go to the one I know can help me   my husband is dead Leaveing me with one daughter   my daughter and I are about half Starved to death and almost with out Clothing   I havent any one to help me make my way   I havent either Mother Father Brother nor SiSter JuSt my daughter and I we have no place we can Call home. I am almost a cripple at times I have bad Spells with rhumatism   I would work regardless of my Spells if I Could get work I want to make my Liveing honest and by working. as I Cant get work hope you can See a way out for me   I have no Education So I gueSS I am out of Luck. well this is our preSidentS year who Ever he may Be   I CaSt a vote for you in 1932 and were Sore afraid you were not going to be PreSident and prayed both night and day   my prayers were SuCCeSSful altho it has not proven SuCCeSfull to me   I do not know what to do this election   I havent got money to pay my tax   Mr PreSident I know there will never be a day I can ever help you only to CaSt a vote I Cant take my Child to Church on aC-Count of haveing no ClothS. Well Mr. President if you Lend me a helping hand I will be over Joyed and if there Can be Some things I Can do to get Votes for you I will do that well if you think my Child and I are deServeing and help me out of this rut I am in I will never forget   I know the Lord will repay you for any thing you Can do will Cause me to gain me a home it is So EmbarreSing to Sign my full name I will Just give my initials   I never have been in Such CirCumStance in my Life. I know God will Spare me Some way out So if you Can See a way out for me.
please do ans. on return mail as I am So worried Sick will Highly appricate any thing you can do.

Mrs. N. K. G.
Rossville Ga
Gen. Del.

119. Winter is coming and we have no coal

September 15, 1935

Dear President

I have written to you before, It is worse than it was before   I can not get a job and my mothers shop is not doing well   pretty soon she will be laid off

Dear President we had to borrow money of my mother's policy the amount was $75 off of Handcock our insurance to pay taxes

Dear President Winter is coming and we have no coal I haven't got a suit of clothes, to where to church I hope you will give me a good answer and may God Bless you and Family You see I am the only boy and I am worried bot my mother   I don't want to lose her   I hope you won't forget me.

Good Bye

My address is Jefferson Street, Troy, N.Y.

120. I have waited and waited for work until every thing I had is about finished

Philadelphia Pa.
Feb'y 19, 1935.

Dear Mrs. Roosevelt:

After Seeing So many of your pictures in the Magazines and papers, and seeing that you always look so well dressed, a thought came to me. that you may have a few old discarded dresses among the ones that you have tired of that you would like to get rid of, and do some one good at the same time. I have waited and waited for work until every thing I had is about finished. I can sew and would only be too glad to take two old things and put them to gether and make a new one. I don't care what it is, any thing from an old bunch of stockings to an old Sport Suit or an old afternoon dress, in fact. Any-thing a lady 40 years of age can wear. I will await an early reply.

Thanking you in advance.

Mrs. E. T.
Phila. Pa.

121. The big fish just eat up the little fish down hear

Savannah, Ga.
April 16, 1936

Dear Mr Roosvelt,

The number of women Cut of got no husbun and no way to get any money and got a house Full of children. Some wich got husbun sick down in bed and got no why to get bread or money to Feed their husbun and Children and when the Women get pay we have to wate three week before we get it. and they dont pay But $13.50 and they dont give any wich the cloth. and they Cut all the Woman who got Children to Look after. and let the young women work who got no expense to Look at. and if you could only no the number of women who got Cut off and got nore where to to get bread and no money and the big fish Just eat up the little Fish down hear and we all know you was given us bread since you was a president. And no way to get Bread to feed our Children and S. Georgia is Just on a noning for all the Color People who was Cut off. the one who need do not get no help but the one who got get help. if you Come a [illegible] Later duck a [illegible]
number Cut off 250   Pleas help

The People who was Cut
off   Thank you

122. We don't have no plesure of any kind

[Fair Haven, Vermont
June 1934]

[Dear President Roosevelt:]

. . . We have certainly seen some hard days. we have been to bed good many night with out nothing to eat. + some days all we would have was black Berries. I would go + pick Black Berries last summer + we would eat them for dinner then my oldest boy 9 years old would take care of the smallest children while I + the next one to hime eight years old would go + pitch on hay for mr. Ferguson. When my baby girl was born last Dec. I didn't have a thing to put on her   I wropt her up in one of my dresses until the Doctor got a few things for her. that is the way we are getting use. We didn't get only two quilts + one Blanket that you sent out for the poor. + there is one person not far from here has got so many Blankets she has got them stored away. . . . I am not complainin for it don't do any good. but it makes me feel bad. when some gets all they want + others can't. I know a party that has got a radio + spends some of his money for beer. We don't have no plesure of any kind. . . . + also tell us what we will do about the house   I hate to lose it when I have seven little children + no place to go. . . .

Mrs. A. J. F.

---

123. They are people dont need it and they get every thing

> New Orleans La.
> City
> Sunday October 27th 1935

Dear President Roosevelt i take the Pleasure of writting to you these few lines asking you could you help me Please   i have 10 Children and i have 4 has to go to School and i cant get them No Clothe   my husband is working for the City But he dont work every Day   Some Pays he makes 3 Days and Some Days he makes 4 Days and how could i Pay Rent and Buy Cloths for my Children   other People get more than i do i use to get 5 Dollars a week from the fera and they cut me down to $405¢ cents and they are People Dont Need it and they get every thing i even told them i Need 3 quilts and they only gave me anorder to get only one   theres a Woman only got 5 in her famliey and i got 12 in my famliey   answer my Letter Soon as you can and She has her husband working and She get 2500 dollars every Month and i dont get that much   Please answer my letter Soon   i wouldn't mind if they Would give my Big Boy a job But they wont do it. if my Boy was working that would help a hole lot   Please Do Somthing for me and my 10 Children half the time my Children has Nothing to eat at home. Please write to me Soon   here is My address

> [Anonymous]
> New Orleans La.
> City
> Please write to me Soon.

124. If I wont get any help from you dear Mr. President than I will take my life away

Detroit, Mich
Oct 2—1935

Mr. Franklin D. Roosevelt.

Dear Mr. President.

In this letter I'm asking you if you are kind enough to help me out. I'm a girl of 18 years old. And I need a coat. I have no money to buy a coat   I need about $25.00   Dear President are you kind to help me and send me the money so I can buy my self the coat.

My father isnt working for 5 yrs. He has a sore leg they wont take him to work any place because of that sore leg. He cant buy me a coat. Were on welfare

Dear Mr. President my father voted for you   he also told lot of his friends to vote for you. He help you so please help us now.

I know that you have a kind heart and wont refuse a girl that needs help Others are dressed but me with out a coat   If I wont get any help from you Dear Mr. President than I will take my life away. I can't stand it no longer. We were thrown out on the street few times   I hate to live the way I'm living now.

Again please be kind and help me. I'll be waiting for your answer.

Yours Truly

M. L. [female]

Detroit, Mich.

My father reads the Bible and he has a picture of you in the bible.

125. I am just in hard luck and do not know which way to turn

Girard, Alabama,
September 4, 1934

President Franklin D. Roosevelt,

Washington, D. C.

Dear Sir:

I hope you will take time to read this letter from me. I am an employer of the Eagle and Phenix Mills. They have been on a strike for about three weeks.

It had not been but about seven weeks befor the first strike.* Dear President, I am a widow with one small son, an aged mother and a sister to care for. Mother and I both are under treatment of the doctor and have been for about three years. Before the NRA, I made 17-1/2 cents per hour, after the NRA, I made twelve dollars for 40 hours. I guess you see it has been a scant living for our family. School will soon start and I have no money to send my son to school. Winter is coming and we have no coal to burn. I am trying to give him schooling, so if it is the Lord's will he won't have to go through the hardships that I have gone through. Dear President, before I ask the favor, I want you to know I am not begging I only want you to please let me have some money and when I go back to work I will pay you back. If I have to pay you only one dollar per week until I get it paid back to you. All I have got to give you is my word. But I try to let my word be my bond. I have always been honest and square with the world. I am just in hard luck and do not know which way to turn, Since the strike and I have been out of work. I have not sit down I have tried everywhere to get work but can't. I hope you will grant me this great favor as it will be a great one to me.

Dear President, I hope you will not feel the least hard at me. I just did not know any other way to turn. I hope you will see this the way I do for my loved ones sake.

I will close
I am yours,
Respectfully,
Mrs. P. C.
Girard, Alabama.

P. S.

Dear President:

I was borned and reared in this little town. It is just across the Chattachie river, the river divides Girard from Columbus.

---

*A huge strike of cotton mills from Maine through Alabama was undertaken by the United Textile Workers of America in September 1934. Some 376,000 workers joined the strike. It failed completely.

126. Cant get eny more groceries until we pay up

[St. Louis, Mo.
October 25, 1935]

Mr. Franklin D. Roosevelt
Dear Sir
Is there eny thing you can do about people not getting their pay from Mo State Emp. office   no one has had eny pay for 3 Months and our family as with dozens of others are in Verry bad Circumstances   People are in Much worse Shape than the ones on Relief   gas + Lights have been Cut off and Credit stopped and furniture houses are taking the furniture away when some have these things about paid for—one family has 4 children that was not able to start to school by their dad not getting his pay. We all need help badly   I wish I could sign my name but if I did my Husband would be let out So please do something if you can   we had to buy a few Bushels of coal on credit but cant get eny more Groceries until we pay up and they are all in the same fix. So thanking you in advance

I Remain
yours Truly.
[Anonymous]

127. The doctor came said that they was not getting enough to eat

Middletown, N.Y.
April 10, 1934.

Mr. F. D. Roosevelt,
President of the U.S.A.
Mr. President:
I am badly in need of your help. I have a home but I have a mortgage and they have hand me notice that they are going to close said mortgage because I am not able to pay interest and I cannot pay taxes for 3 years and they are going to close my water which I am not able to pay. I have asked for the home loan but I have not heard from them. Mr. President, I have 5 children, the oldest is 10 years of age. I have been working on the relief 3 days a week and making $12.00 week is not sufficient to feed a family of 7. I have asked

different times for little help from the town but they said that I was working and they would not help me. This winter they gave me 2 orders, one for $5.00 and one for $4.00. Now I have one of my child sick. I asked for a doctor and I had to fight to have one sent to me and they sent it 2 days later and the doctor came said that they was not getting enough to eat. Now, Mr. President, we are in a land of plenty but I see that good many of us are starving. I am a world war veteran. Mr. President try to Help me in this thing if you can. I do not ask this for me but for my children.

Thank you.

Yours truly,
F. D. [male]
Middletown, N.Y.

---

128. No one know how it is until you experience it

Beaverdam, Va.
Oct. 23rd, 1935.

Mr. Franklin D. Roosevelt
President of United States
Dear Sir—

I wish to express my thoughts of our poor and needed country. first we are looking for work, but never can't find any to do. Need clothes, food, and in debt so bad. You know merchants don't want to credit people now. Every body after money now days. We have tried to get on the relief work but they claim they takes care of no one but those with heart trouble, sickly, and widows with no one to help take care of their children. But they don't do that.

But that's not right if we poor ones with husbands and little one to raise and send to school, can't get any work what more is it for them on the relief to starve than it is for us?

A friend of mine said she thought it was a fine thing for sick folks but I told her it was no more for the sick to not have help than it was for healthy men and couldn't get work.

The State highway dept. has men working regular for years, making good money, Why don't they take them off so they can feel our heart ache and needs and let us who don't get work, work in their places. It nothing fair.

We right now, have no work, no winter bed clothes but ragged quits no winter clothes, Wife don't even have a winter coat. What are we going to do through these cold times coming on? Just looks like we will have to freeze and starve together.

Mrs. Folkes, a head one of the relief Adm. Says poor folks must take what they can get, says musn't but one at a house work at the time. But she and her husband are both working. Don't need it as bad as I do.

That's what the matter why we can't get work because the head bosses get all the easiest work and most money. My little boy was speaking of Santa Claus "He says Why is it most children gets pretty toys and so many seems like they are rich and we so poor   This made tears come in my eyes. Then I told him if we are ever lucky enough to get work we will try to get him something pretty. I have to tell him of some happy day which may come.

Once I was sick, went to Dr. he waited on me, for his money and I still owe him to-day. Then I went to the Druggist   no we credit no one here, So I had no money and no way of making any   Wasn't I in a bad shape?

No one know how it is until you experience it.

Right now, we have to find a place to go, no money on hand to move or pay rent. If it's anything you can do to help please be kind enough to help us. Just give us work to do and we will be only too glad to do it. We never can go to church for we never have money enough to pay for a trip seem so dishearten in life to live like this when it use to be plenty of work for every body.

Hoping we have have more work to help feed our loved one. For I know it's One above who cares for all.

Yours Truly,
[Anonymous]
Beaverdam Virginia

Chapter 10. The Cynical

. . . an' ever' time since then when I hear a business man talkin' about service, I wonder who's gettin' screwed. Fella in business got to lie an' cheat, but he calls it somepin else. That's what's important. You go steal that tire an' you're a thief, but he tried to steal your four dollars for a busted tire. They call that sound business

John Steinbeck, *Grapes of Wrath*

hose who did not blame themselves for their Depression-related problems often blamed others. Many such people became cynical. If not always quite resigned to their fates, they at least saw little likelihood that most people were concerned about anyone but themselves.

Scorn for the motivations of politicians was widespread during the Great Depression (as it has been throughout most of our history). Oddly, though, many who were cynical about politicians in general seemed to trust the master politician of the age, Franklin D. Roosevelt. A number of the letters that follow bitterly mock the putative motives of local and state politicians (along with those of most other people), yet ask the president to do something to help the poor. For some, of course, cynicism carried over to the New Deal and to FDR himself. The New Dealers had never suffered, some poor Americans wrote, and they did not understand or really care about the problems of poverty. Such Roosevelt critics were less common among the letter writers, however, than were those who sneered at almost everyone *except* the president.

Politicians were not alone in being viewed with cynicism in the thirties. Letter writers commented cynically on bureaucrats in relief and other government agencies. Relief was said to be just a political game. People said that agencies were filled with grafters seeking to help themselves rather than the poor. The red tape and excuses commonly encountered in administrative hierarchies were viewed as part of a system of self-serving bureaucrats, sometimes characterized as "parasites."

Another favorite target of Depression era cynics was the rich. Here cynicism begins to shade into rebelliousness. Forgotten men and women mocked the pious platitudes uttered by the rich. They jeered at businessmen's calls for frugality on the part of the poor. They ridiculed millionaires' hollow defenses of democracy. Some even scorned "the system" itself. It is here that cynicism ends and rebelliousness begins. The latter reaction must await the next chapter.

---

129. Just stay at home and watch others have all the fun

Louisville, Ky.
May 8th 1936.

Dear President Roosevelt.

I am enclosing a article from our paper here in Louisville. Happy Chandler our Governor got in the office by making speeches against all sales tax.

Now please read what he is doing to us poor people who really can't afford all the extra cost.

What about the children who's parents can't give their children the little things in life such as a cone of cream or a 1^cts piece of candy or a soft drink once a week. Who will get the blame for this neglect   The father of course. It would be perfectly all right if the bread earner made $40^{00} or $50^{00} a week. But what about some labores who only have the pitiance of $7.^{00} and $8.^{00} a wk. with 5 and 6 children to support. Tell us Kentuckians how we are going to live and what to eat after we pay rent and other expences. Really Mr Roosevelt such happenings as this is making against you who is really trying to help the ones who can't help themselves. Please can't you have some one to look into this. For I have heard people all over town saying if the Democrats keep on putting taxes on everything just as well to quit and leave them support you for at the end of the week you haven't any money left as it is. Do you think it is right that we poor never have the pleasure of a show or a trip back home. Just stay at home and watch others have all the fun good eats fine autmobiles town houses, country homes fine smokes off the taxes they collect and all they do is talk about 2 Hours aday and they are through with their work. and they make up in thousands of dollars a year they can afford the extra pennies But there are more who can't. So if you will take the time to read this you will have the thoughts of more than one Kentuckian on paper and Maybe you will find a way out for us. With a prayer for your support

I'm sincerly yours
A Democrat Voter.

---

130. We dont want the millionairs to buy the next president into the White House

I HOPE THE PRESIDENT HAS A CHANCE TO READ THIS FOR HIMSELF

MARCH 22 i9 36

san francisco cal

DEAR PRESIDENT ROSEFELT

TO NIGHT BEING SUNDAY NIGHT I SAT IN MY CHAIR THINKING OF THE TERRIBLE THINGS PEOPLE DO WITH THE MONEY YOU YOU INTRUST TO THEM. HERE IN SAN FRANCISCO WEATHER YOU KNOW OR DONT KNOW I JUST COULDNT HELP BUT WRITE YOU THESE FEW LINES   IT SEEMS EVERY TIME YOU ALLOW SAN

FRANCISCO MONEY FOR ITS POOR PEOPLE IN WORKING PROJ-
ECTS THESE HIGHER UPS ARE EITHER GRAFTING A PART OR
HALF FOR THEM SELFS   THESE PEOPLE U INTRUST THE MONEY
TO THEY HIRE THE POOR CLASS FOR A LENTH OF TIME WHERE
THEY COULD KEEP US A GOING TILL THE MONEY RUNS OUT
INSTEAD THEY EMPLOY US A PART OF THE TIME AND USE HALF
OUT OF EACH ALOTMENT TO HIGHER THESE RICH CONTRAC-
TORS PAYING THEM HUNDREDS OF DOLLORS A DAY   USEING
THESE CRANES AND CATTER PILLER TRCATORS ITS A SHAME
YOU PUT UP THIS MONEY FOR US FOR HAND LABOR AND THESE
BIG SHOTES AS YOU CALL THEM USE THIS MONEY FOR GRAFT
AND CONTRACTORS   I SUPPOSE ITS NOT ONLY IN SAN FRAN-
CISCO BUT ALL OVER THE UNITED STATES   WHAT WE NEED
PRESIDENT ROSEFELT WE WISH YOU WERE DICTATOR FOR
AWHILE AND WE HOPE AND PRAY THAT YOU WILL BE OUR NEXT
PRESIDENT   FOR WE DONT WANT THE MILLIONAIRS TO BUY
THE NEXT PRESIDENT INTO THE WHITE HOUSE ONLY BY A TRUE
VOTE   WE DONT WANT A BOUGHT IN PRESIDENT LIKE THE
GOVERNER OF CALIFORNIA WAS BOUGHT IN BY THE MILLIAN-
IARS* PRESIDENT ROSE FELT I AM NOT A CRANK ONLY A POOR
MAN THATS ALL JUST TARE THIS LETTER UP WHEN YOU GET
THRU READING IT   MAY GOD BLESS YOU
[Anonymous]

---

131. You are multi millionaries, what do you care
for the masses of people

Los Angeles, Calif. Sept. 9, 1936.

Mrs. Roosevelt
Washington D.C.
Dear Madam:

I was just reading how rich Pres. mother is, read this article.

You are multi millionaries, what do you care for the masses of people,
burned the corn, cotton, destroyed the cattle, now the Lord is doing it for
us, to punish this nation, by drought. Condemning big concerns, when you

---

*This is a reference to Republican Frank M. Merriam's victory in the 1934 California guber-
natorial election over leftist Democrat Upton Sinclair. The campaign against Sinclair is generally
acknowledged to have been one of the dirtier ones in American political history.

people are heavy investors. You husband said Constitution is a Horse and Buggy affair.* Yes, but he strives to be President after condemning our Lovely "America."

I am an American through and through. I stand for America.

Mrs. H.

Los Angeles, Calif.

---

132. By starving the people they think they can make them vote the way they want them to vote

[Port Henry, N.Y.]

March 18, 1935

[Dear Mrs. Roosevelt:]

I have been reading the papers about what is going on at Washington. It is a pity those Senators do not seem to understand how serious the condition of this Country is and why does President Roosevelt want all this Money to give to people who have penty by not giving the working people a living wage. You know the depression has lasted to long. And the people in charge of the Relief want it to last at least for two years more. This Relief is the worst scandal in the history of this country. I can not see why President Roosevelt can not see it is only food for the 1936 campaign for all in charge of the Relief are Republicans and they will not do what is right, by starving the people they think they can make them vote the way they want them to vote. The poor people are not getting this money. . . .

Mrs. C. C.

Port Henry, N.Y.

---

133. The luxury of an open fire

Columbus, Ind.

[January 1936]

Dear Mrs Roosevelt.

I would give ten years of my life to be able to have the luxury of an open

---

*After the Supreme Court invalidated the NRA in May 1935, Roosevelt told a press conference that the decision was based on a "horse-and-buggy definition of interstate commerce."

fire just one evening, as you write about in the Indianapolis Times.*

N. T. [female]

---

134. Try living on that Mr Hopkins but you won't as long as you are in politics

[Los Angeles, Calif.]
January 9-1936

Mr Harry Hopkins
Washington, D. C.

Are you in favor of the Townsand Plan? You are certainly playing right into their hands by this continued unemployment in Los Angeles County and this continual cut of relief checks, one last week and another this week and the promise of others until we single women will be trying to exist on $17.50 per month. try living on that Mr Hopkins but you won't as long as you are in politics. How come that when the treasury is low for are relief money, the higher ups never take a cut in salary but hold meetings at the Biltmore Hotel and fill their bellies to deside to reduce our budgets to empty our bellies, some system and it is the worst thing can happen for the New Deal and Pres. Roosevelt also for you fellows dealing it out to the President's forgotten men and women for without this part of the administration you fellows would have no jobs and wouldn't be pulling out the plumbs from the pie. Also, why don't you get yourself informed as to how these local relief adminestrators are handling the funds and the the work program. <u>Why</u> are the Mexicans and niggers being given white colar jobs and white Americans still are on the lousy dole or doing work entirely foreign to their calling. If our local distributors have no sense of justice, as the head of the whole lousy concern you should do your part to reajust this condition. Los Angeles County has more dishonest and paracitic officials than exists elsewhere in the whole world and I guess you all at Washington have found that out. If I have to continue much longer being unemployed and trying to exist on this low down dole which gets lower down each check, then I am off of the New

---

*Mrs. Roosevelt wrote in her "My Day" newspaper column on 30 December 1935: "I wonder if anyone else glories in cold and snow without, an open fire within, and the luxury of a tray of food all by one's self in one's own room? I realize that it sounds extremely selfish and a little odd to look upon such an occasion as festive. Nevertheless, last night was a festive occasion for I spent it that way."

Deal and will not vote for Roosevelt   I hope your undersecretary permits you to read this as you should know these facts.

Yours truly—

A Los Angeles County Victim

---

135. You are getting yours, and never have suffered like our people have, therefore you do not care

Sept. 21, 1935.

Mr. Hopkins,
Relief Administrator,
Washington, D. C.
Dear Sir:—

Why are the Relief Projects being help up in St. Louis? The Projects that have already been started and are being help up for no one knows why, but you and I do not think you know. They could be continued and at least put some of our men to work right away and not wait until all the rest are ready, for if that is done and you fool around and pass the buck like you have none will be started at all.

We are not getting the allowances we did and our children are suffering for lack of food. And some have no clothes where with to attend school. Now is that right? And we will soon need coal and will not receive the funds for it, then what about that?

Of course, you are getting yours, and never have suffered like our people have, therefore you do not care. You have never been hungry and without all the luxuries of life, let alone the bare necessitities. It is not the fault of our people that this condition exzists here, for they have tried and worked at anything at all to make a few pennies, but there is not the work to be had here.

Now there is work waiting here for some of our men and you are responsible for them not getting it. How can you answer to these people for that. They demand some consideration. And I am afraid they will soon tire of this delay and take some action themselves. They have been held down long enough through your petty Political Playing. That is all it is. The red tape could have been cut long ago. But that is your excuse. We know it is not true. Petty Politics is the answer. You will never get yours later by such actions.

Your plate at the table is full. Your family can enjoy life from the peoples money, and not have a care where this and that is coming from.

You were put in that position to do a real job and now you find you cannot fulfill it, and are playing around to the interests of the most moneyed men and starve the real working people of the country. God rights everything. And I hope to live to see the day that you and yours will have a little taste of what you are giving us daily for your food. NOTHING.

The Press all over the Country is razzing you and you think you are doing a swell job. Well people are something like elephants, they never forget. And the year 1936 is not far off.

You may not take this seriously but I have heard so many comments from people who have waited and waited for you to do something and the time is not far off when they will take action themselves. No one will be to blame but you. And now you want to pass the Buck to the State Administrators and in the next word you say they cannot pass finally on these unless they are O.K'd by Washington, which is BIG YOU. Well get busy and learn how to do something for some one besides your self.

Roosevelt is a coward like you are, he was afraid to come to St. Louis to the Legion Convention and you would be afraid to come too at an invitation. You are so yellow, but it is your type that holds such positions and should but put out. If you are afraid to fulfil your duties, why resign. there are many better and nobler men who are not afraid to do the right thing by the working people.

The women are the real ones that have to suffer when they see their children underfeed. And then they advocate to eat more food. Yes we would gladly eat more feed and give more to our children if we had work where we could earn them money to purchase more food.

Please take this situation seriously and grant these men work right away. Start them on the work that is laying waiting for them to take up. The Winter is going to be hard enough, when we are all needing so much and nothing to get it with and we are being cut here and there on our allowances. The children have to suffer.

Put a small amount of men to work and by doing that it will take that much burden off of the Relief Rolls and give more for those that have to remain on.

In the name of GOD, Start our men to work NOW. There is plenty for them to do.

A distracted Mother.

I have tried to get work and there is nothing for a woman of my age to do. There are too many young married women allowed to keep their positions after they marry and in that way throw men out of work and our young single girls who have just finished college and should be allowed to hold a position are prevented from getting one on this account. That is something else that should be taken up all over the country. Preventing young married women from continuing in their positions after marrying in order to lay up a large sum of money and there-fore keeping men out of work. When you have nothing more to do than you are doing now you might try a hand at trying to remedy this situation.

Chapter 11. The Rebellious

Rush, says the boss,
Work like a hoss;
I'll take the profits and you take the loss,
I've got the brains, I've got the dough,
The Lord Himself decreed it so.

"Mammy's Little Baby Loves a Union Shop"
(CIO Strike Song)

The letters that follow fall into three categories of rebellious Americans. The first includes poor, angry people who complain bitterly and generally seek a greater degree of justice and equality. These people, despite their egalitarian attitudes, show scant signs of adherence to a formal socialist ideology. Most such writers appear to have been poorly educated.

Letters in the second group do express ideological commitment. Such leftist terms as "industrial slaves," "oppressors," and "financiers and capitalists" dot these communications. It is apparent, too, that the authors of these more ideological letters were better educated than most of those of the first selection of letters. It is interesting to note that the writers of some of the ideological letters identify, in spite of their obvious education, with poor, working-class people.

Although the fact is often ignored, it should be noted that discontent and rebelliousness were no monopoly of the left. Indeed, these basic feelings are without ideological content. The existence of rebellious Americans of the racist and protofascist, rather than the egalitarian, stripe should not be overlooked. The career of Father Coughlin makes the point well. At the height of his popularity, the radio priest's criticisms seemed to be of a leftist nature. Later in the decade, however, it became clear that Coughlin was an anti-Semitic supporter of fascism and Hitler. As his views became more plain, Coughlin lost most of his followers. While this is comforting to those of us who would prefer not to find much potential for fascism in the United States, some consideration ought to be given to those rebellious Americans who actually were protofascists.[1] The last letters of the chapter are examples of this third category of discontent.

---

136. You have every comfort that the common people of our great nation is toiling to provide you

Livingston, Calif.
January 25, 1935

[Dear Mrs. Roosevelt:]

. . . you have been writing in the various magazines about the way you think the common people of our nation should live on 7¢ per meal. Are you and President Roosevelt Roosevelt <u>really</u> living on 7¢ per meal. absolutely no. Impossible. And I as one member of our great nation want to give you and President Roosevelt to understand that this 7¢ per cent meal is out of the question for any man or woman to live on. who is working fifteen hours a day to keep you and President Roosevelt in our Nation white House. in all the good food. that the Nation can produce. Cars and airplane to travel and take vacations. you have every comfort that the common people of our great nation is toiling to provide you you. and you are doing nothin in return for us. only to tell us that we should provide ourselves with 7¢ meals. each day of the year.

Is this right? Why just think of all the terible tax the people are paying. . . . This really is the Condition of the Country I really know. I am a music teacher and am working 10 hours per day. to make my living and I know what people are doing. . . . Now Mrs Roosevelt, this is what I am doing, a woman who you might call the common trash. But this is what I am doing— and are you doing any better for Our Nation. and the nation. White House you are now in. and being suported by common People as the capitist who are not doing their duty but are being upheld By the rulers of the white House. of our great Nation.

very Sincerely
L. C. [female]

---

137. The poor class of people down here is treated like dogs

Miami Okla.
Nov 15 -35

Mrs. F. D. Roosevelt

Dear Friend

and Lady of the white house. I am asking you a few questions in regard to the way they are doing down here about the reliff ward. we have a family of 8 children and have get nothing to live one, and cant get any kind from. the government. we go over to miami and talk to them they just make fun of us. and laugh. and Say we will See that you. are taken care of but thy never do any thing we have always tried to get by without help, the drough. last year. and this year. has put us where we cant feed our Family and Clothe them they told us. to live off 25 hens & 3 Cows. with no feed to feed them   we are all barefooted. And no clothes to wear. and Can not Send our children to School. Thy put us off the relief in July and. my Husband. Cant get back on. but there is men on that has got Enough. to make a living with out it. we have got nothing to Sell. it is hard to try and feed 8 children on bread & milk and. part of the time no bread. there is Several families in this community in the Same. shape we are in the only ones they will help is the ones that can ride in fine cars. the poor class of people down here is treated like dogs, there is about 50 in office at miami, thy are the ones that are living fat. there is one girl in office from our. community her father is a big farmer. and holds. 2. Jobs. one Job is boss on the relief and one County road Job. my girls asked for an office Job and they told them thy couldnt make their board, and thy cint do the Same work She is doing. I would like to know how us poor people can get any help, if there is any Share for us in government help.

Visit miami. dressed. like us poor people. and ask for help and See how. you are talked to for your Self. . . .

yours truely
Mrs F. O. S.
miami Okla.

---

138. The man that works with the shovellis wirth more than you fellows are becaus yous perduce nothing

Manistique Mich. Mar. 12 th. 1936

Mr. Harry L. Hopkins.
W. P. A. Director.
Washington D. C.
Dear Sir.

I seen in the press some time ago a notices inserted, notifing W. P. A. workers would be discarged if caught lofeing while on the job. I wish to iquire if you ment to enclued the W. P. A. offices staff. I viseted about all the office staffs in uper Michigan and found that was about all they was dewing. Seting around telling stores smoking cigretts with thair feet stuck up on the desk haveing a good time.

Do you think that a man of the age of 60 or 70 years old can do the work that a man can do at the age of 25 he can not he would collapes. When old age creaps upon you. you come incontact with all kinds alments akes pains nerviness sleepless and sightless. There is know 60 per cent of the W. P. A. workers over 60 years old. The younger class seems to forget the forfathers. And denie the old age the $ 200. a month old age pention something that would give the old age a little pleasure for the last few years they have to live. Such pention plan is the only thing that will brin back this cuntry to normal and prospairty a decint liven and liveing wages.

The forfathers of this nation built schools and collages to educate the younger class that is know in power. And know by that class are refused a decint liven thay forget old age mother and father and gray hair. Why shuld we be ineed in the mist of plenty. Our public servints is the caus of that no one elce. Rembter that old age gray hair and deth will catch up with you and nothing leaves this eirth.

The $ 200. old age pention plan of Townsend and Rev. Coughlin social justice plan is the only plan that will restore this nation to prospairty and hew disputs it is not telling the trough.

If the W.P.A. would of set preavailnig wages for 8 hours no they cut wages for the industry why becaus the industre man said if you dont want to work for $ 42. a month go back on the W.P.A. Dew you call that prospairty labor is the foundation of the world you can not egist without it the man that works with the shovellis wirth more than you fellows are becaus yous perduce nothing.

Here is a example of five in familey the head of the familey gets $ 42. on the W.P.A.

Will you allow them 25¢ each a day to live on a total of $ 1.25 per day for

one month 31 days a total of	$ 38.75
will you allow for rent	6.00
will you allow for light	1.00
will you allow for wood	3.00
will you allow for water	.75
will you allow for wareable afects	3.00

. . . . . . 3xpence $ 52.50

A total of $ 52.50 Credit   42.00

. . . . . .

$ 10.50 In debeth

A tak payer.

---

139. Poor people are human and it sure isnt his fault he is poor just because some have hoged it

Kalamazoo Mich.
Nov. 21 1935

Harry Hopkins:-
Washington D.C.

Dear Sir:—I am writing to you concerning the W.P.A. . . . We are completely out of coal and how can he [her husband] work without no food her clothes. I dont see how times are going to get better if men have to work for so low wages and food stuffs so high. and rent has raised. The government put out clothing and sheets and pillow cases blankets & etc but how many got them and those that did had to fight to get them and they never gave us any clothes at all and now that we are asking for a little help till he gets started they wont help us.

It was simply a graft the things were put places they weren't supposed to be and the poor people went half starved as there were three grown up's in our family and they gave us $3.50 a week to live on my son had to go through a physical exam and Dr told him he hadn't the proper food   But still President Roosevelt says he doesnt want any one to starve why keep them going on existing   I think Mr Roosevelt means all right but it is others that put out these cheap projects it just keeps him down   everybody should work with him instead against him   I am going to register and believe me my vote will be placed right as I think he means for this money to be put to a better advantage. Instead of a man trying to keep up a home on $13.00 a week and go out and grub stumps without the necessary food.

There sure must be a way figured out that a poor man can live instead of being half starved when there is so much money in this country and a poor man is the one that does the work and gets nothing in return.

Well anyway I would like for President Roosevelt to know what is being done to the people he is putting this money out for.

. . . This W.P.A. allready has lead a mean with a family to crime he cant live on $13.00 or no one else can he got busy the other evening and brought home some extra money. poor people are human and it sure isnt his fault he is poor just because some have hoged it.

This is just a letter to let you know what is going on in Kalamazoo what people must endure for a very little food.

Yours Truly
W.P.A. Workers
Wife.

---

140. How can these rich eat and sleep and be so happy when they know there are millions starving

Oklahoma City, Okla.

June 10, 1934

Dear Mrs. Roosevelt, I am asking you to talk with the President for us thousands of the unemployed—for the aged and the sick—there will have to be something done. So why starve the people any longer. Its only a few of the younger people and those with a pull who are getting anything. There has got to be an old age pension—so why not now. Why make these people who have given the best years of their lives to the work of their country—why make them suffer and starve longer. Congress voted thousands of dollars to themselves they are all rich men. Thousands to the veterans—thousands of them already rich men. There is no use talking about us of past 50 years getting a job even the man past 40 is the same as out. Now another thing the unemployed have been so long with out food—clothes—shoes—medical care—dental care etc—we look pretty bad—so when we ask for a job—we dont get it. And we look and feel a little worse each day—when we ask for food they call us old bums—it isent our fault. I had enough money in the bank to take care of myself but the bankers got it—hundreds were the same —we have lost our homes—but it wasent our fault—no we are not bums— and we past 50 years have done our share of the work and we are entitled to some of the profits—the same as the rich—the young men are beginning to think and talk about what will happen to them at 40 years or so—they dont like it. So when we unemployed ask for bread—they dont even say give us cake—but they give us gas—the club—the gun, and turn water on us. It was a disgrace the way they gassed and nearly drowned the women and little children here—because they wanted food—they are still holding the mother of two little children because she stood her ground and ask for food. They never report to you the truth of it to you. They just yell <u>Red</u> and make out they have done a wonderful thing. These poor people havent enough food to give them the life to be even pink. Now all the rich ought to begin to see that they cant hold every thing all the time. Both Mr. Hoover and Mr. Roosevelt said the wealth of the country should not be held in the hands of the few—but scattered all over the country among the people—but they have done nothing about it—about the Morgans etc. Wall Streeters, etc.— let him. If it comes on another winter of suffering—the people may save him the trouble. I'm just writing you what I hear every day. All this news paper talk and N.R.A. etc reports is bunk. The people see and know just how much good they are getting—Now these rich who have more land than they should have more houses than they can live in—more clothes than they can wear—more food more money than they can spend—tell me why shouldent they be taxed so the men and women who have starved to make that wealth should have a share of it in their old age. Not only a pension but medical care dental care—and at the end—all funeral expenses should be paid—Why give our veterans so much and the people who give and give till it hurt and payed the bills and still paying get nothing. Last year we saw an old woman buried in the potters field One of the first women to come to this state and slave to make it safe for the millionaires. No wonder these young fellows laugh when they say love our country and our Government. Do you know the debts of this country can never be paid—if we had 45 times the money of the U.S. it would take it all—and we all would have to start again with out a cent. So why bleed the people for more interest to put into the banks for the money to go. Why go on borrowing more money to take more interest out of the people—to make more debts that can never be paid. Please read "The Book" by W. H. (Coin) Harvey Monte Ne, Ark. price 25¢ You may be surprised to learn the U.S. Government never intended we should borrow money from the banks & pay interest. The Gov. should make its own money the people are finding out how much bunk has been put over on them—Now anyone with half an eye can see that what brought on this problem of hard times is not at all hard to solve. Its just that the over rich got all the money in their hands. When all the moany is in the hands of a dozen men and controled by even fewer nothing else can happen—and the rich dont want it solved—they want to get the masses a little lower—so to get more of the things of which they already have to much—Read the Declaration of Independence—Read what the Bible says—Read what the very few statesmen we have ever had say about the wealth of the country in the hands of the few. Call Huey Long in "whether you like him or not" ask him about spreading the wealth—maybe the Wall Street gang have killed him by this time. Anyway the more the Morgan controled newspapers say and make fun—the more the people are for him. As we see it Huey Long is the only man in Washington who is trying to do anything to help the old people. He just dont go far enough-$30 a month is alright for the old people who have a home— but for right now there are thousands who have no home—I have no home and for writing this letter I get to sleep on the bare floor along with 5 other woman tomorrow night it will be some where else. I am a victim of the money hogs—like all the rest—look at the packers strike here—those people working for 8 & 9 dollars a week to keep a family—those packers are millionaires. They want more money—and to have the honor of paying dividends on watered stock which they own most themselves. Where is the N.R.A.—its a joke anyway—But it does help the big fellows that they wont now have to bother about   I know a man 60 years old who works in a store from 9 in the morning till midnight. $7 a week 7 days a week. They say you are an old man and we cant pay you much—yet he knows more about the business than the bosses. and works all round all of them—and you N.R.A. and all the rest of the alphabet. You see why we sometimes get a laugh—We all pick up the papers as the rich glance at the stocks etc. and throw them down—so we read of all the very wonderful things our Gov. is doing for us. And we are on the ground and cant get any thing to do—so we or some of us get round a little see and hear what is going on—oh that $7 a week man has a wife to keep. Well the N.R.A. did put the price up and the chain stores have reported a big increase—More money than for a long time—the chain stores and chain everything else has got to go—no one should have more than one store or one of any kind of business no group of people should have more than one of any kind of business. that would give the little hometown man a chance to make a living and keep the profits in his home town not all the profits go back to Wall Street. A bunch of Jews own all the theaters, the Hotels are chain—the restaurants everything is chain. They all employ all young people and pay very little. Its all under a book of prints so one dont have to know much. Show this to your husband, talk to him these old people must be taken care of. Congress can vote the pension right now—it must be enough to take care of the people $30 a month is not enough and there must be medical & dental care go with it. for old people who have a home $30 a month might do—the army, navy, and veterans have medical care. It wouldent take enough from the rich to hurt them—only their greed—they would still have more than they can use—How can these rich eat and sleep and be so happy when they know there are millions starving. Read what the Bible says about it—the papers make a big talk—but they do not fool the people who are there see and hear it all—Do not make the poor the old & sick suffer any longer—this relief and old age pensions has to come why not now it will put money out all over the country in a way it would do real good even if it all went into the chain stores and back to Wall Street—then they wouldent feel so bad that they had to part with some of the maoney they couldent use. Dont you see if all these older people were taken care of with a pension—every dollar would have to be spent every month—It would all come right back and just about the first month is all that would be payed out it would be used over and over. It would give work to thousands of the younger. cut the hours of work—make the stores and all works put on more help employ the people even if they never make a profit or pay a dividend. cut these big salaries—spread the money   Its got to be done some time— Huey Long has a good idea of it—So has Coin Harvey. Huey Long don cut the rich man enough or give enough to the poor ask him for a manual of share our Wealth—Do not give the maoney to some rich man to get richer on but pay it from Washington. And give these people you pay a pension to the same right the veteran has of going from one state to another—they are the same as a veteran who has done his share of the Gov. work—he is now old and should have his freedom which he has never had before—he has always been a slave in supposed to be the land of the free—Free for who— Do not let Congress go home with out doing something for the suffering people. Thank you. I have no address

Mrs. S.

141. This nation is hanging over a giant powder keg just waiting for someone to light a match

Nashville,
Tenn.
8/15/36.

Mrs. Franklin D. Roosevelt,
Dear Lady

Will you please warn the people of whats going to happen in America if these property owners dont quit making industrial slaves out of their laborers and working them on starvation wages, paying them a wage whereby they cannot obtain the desires of life, or else installing machinery and laying the common laborer off of his job to starve to death.

We dont want a revolution in this country where innocent men, women, and children will be shot down without mercy like they are doing in spain and also like they did in Russia. We want peace on earth good will toward men. You know mrs. Roosevelt with the majority of us poor people we desire good things as well as the higher classes of society. For instance we desire a nice home to live in with sanitary surroundings. we desire a nice refrigadaire, electric stove, fan, nice furniture, radio, a nice car with money to take a vacation, but one cannot have these desires of life at a wage of 8.00 10.00 or $12.00 per week, and if we could, we could not accumalate no money and would have to go on being industrial slaves and our children would fall under the same yoke of bondage that we and our fore parents were under. And never be considered no more than an ordinary slaves.

After all it is natural with any human being to want to obtain the desires of life with the least physical exertion possible. But the great majority of the men that wear the overalls and are forced by the task master or property holder to exert their bodies strenously every day do not get even proper and sufficient food to maintain their bodies while at work.

When man, woman, or child fail to get proper and sufficient food to maintain their bodies they are gradually starving to death, and become so weak and run down that some disease develops and they die. How many little children in america that are failing to get sufficient milk even to maintain their little bodies. I can see little children all around me looking hollow eyed, peaked face for the simple reason that they are not getting proper food.

Mrs. Roosevelt can we believe for a minute that our young men and young women that are growing up, being educated, educated from an eighth grade to a college education, educating them selves especially on the economical conditions of the world, are going to be willing to become industrial slaves on starvation wages.

This alone will bring on a revolution if it is not remedid. There would not be so many crimes committed if every man and boy were out from under bondage of hard labor and were getting the desires of life. we have plenty of young John Dillingers, pretty boy Floyds, Jessie James roaming all over our land today wanting jobs, desiring to marry and settle down and live a comfortable life and cannot get hold of enough money to buy a marriage license. and the next thing we know they strike back at the ones that are responsible for their being in that condition.

Mrs. Roosevelt this nation is hanging over a giant powder keg just waiting for someone to light a match. You see I am forced to mingle with the poorer classes and I hear what they have to say. As far as I am concerned I dont believe in taking the carnal weapon against my fellow man. Therefore all I can do is stand still and see the salvation of the lord. I am thirty four years old married and have one daughter. I have a eighth grade education. I got a job last week as labourer on the new courthouse here, although I am a painter by trade, and just because I am a little crippled on my right side the contractor would not work me, he said the insurance company would not allow him to.

And so I cannot see a very bright prospect in life. Although my wife slaves in a cotton mill but I want a job so as I can get her out of it, for I am afraid she has contracted tuburcolosis. hoping an answer   I remain

Yours,
Sincerely,
D. B. P. [male]

---

142. The rich are the laziest people in the world

Asbury Park, N. J.
August 3, 1935

[Dear Mr. Roosevelt:]

My soul shall not rest in peace until the last bit of slavery is removed from the land, and righteousness abide therein. Even now the Oppressors are digging their own graves. You have the power to replace the dirt into the graves of your entire family if you care to. These things the people realize from suffering and are teaching their children. 1—The Rich are the laziest people in the world. 2—They rear their children to be oppressors. 3—They never do anything for the uplift of suffering humanity. 4—They make the laws to suit their own pocket books. 5—They create wars and send the innocent out to fight for them. 6—They drain the world of the little money that is left in it. 7—They make life miserable for every man, woman, and child. 8—The Laws of the Land are being misused. How can you, having never faced a real gun, eat the best of foods and sleep in the finest bed, while the sons of men who risked their lives to save this country lay dying with their families for the want of food, clothing, shelter. . . .

J. J. [male]

---

143. They did not build this country so that their posterity should starve in it

Apr. 10, 1936
N.Y.C.

Harry Hopkins
W.P.A. Administrator
Wash. D.C.
Dear Sir,

I am a W.P.A. worker—I have heard of your plans to lay off the W.P.A. workers and I am very much opposed to it. I come from an old American family who pioneered this country—They did not build this country so that their posterity should starve in it. I believe that this country owes a living to every man woman and child and if it cant give us this living thru private industry it <u>must</u> provide for us thru government means—I am ready to fight for what I believe to be an inalianable right of every person living under this govt.

A. B. [female]

---

144. This U.S. could be a paradise instead the habitation of misery + want if leaders but let go of selfish interests

Ypsilante Mich Jan 24-36

Hon Pres and Mrs Roosevelt—Washington D. C.
Dear friends—A few words from one whom you represent. When Pres. Roosevelt gave his promise to drive "The Money Changers from the Temple" listeners had great hope that at last the common people of the nation would have a hearing but so far he seems zealously to be watching over

the interests of financiers and capitalists and the common people are allowed to view a mirage with wonderful promises which disappear on approach—They are however not deceived which you would fully realize if you visited their quarters in almost any large city. Pres R. security program is ridiculed and to all of us it is a great disappointment. Common people have maintained the morale of this nation + not the visitors to Reno or those sitting in cocktail hotels—Uncle Sam had millions to spend to destroy food and cotton but a paltry $50.00 @ mo for 3-1/2 million working men to maintain a home and family in decency and health. and 49-1/2 cents a day for the aged to keep up the old home but coal—food + clothing after all of these have been raised to highest prices by him. We all know streams of money have been steadily flowing into Wall St from all the corners of this nation and it is by the Federal Gov't alone which has access to all these treasuries that Old Age Pensions should be paid. It is Wall St. that has made corners and pools in stock markets. Created Holding Co.s-Sam'l Insull's and Henry L Dohertys with money for sky scrapers and Every conceivable luxury but no money to pay interest to honest people who paid their $100 per share with the promise to get this interest monthly as old age pension—There is as much wealth as ever, but where is it?—In the hands of a comparitively few and most of them in Wall St. Why cannot Pres R. understand the people know this and are demanding a re-distribution of wealth instead of a program of debt-debt-debts-for unborn generations to pay. Why is he not taxing the fountain heads of this wealth if he means business. —Not borrow $4,800,000,000. to pay to workers at starvation wages and have most of it go to political overlords. Closed banks with receivers who know nothing about banking yet get $4000 @ yr or more because they are Dem. politicians + eating up assets of depositors who are in want   The Townsend Plan while it looked like a fairy tale or the Milinium at first yet as we think of it + examine its details we believe it is workable if really tried—It does not put all the wealth in one hand to distribute as he sees fit as a Hitler or Mussilene giveing him all power (and why ask it) but it distributes it to all the corners of the nation from which it was filched by means our Gov't should have outlawed before birth. Not even a large amount to any one person at any given time—but honest people who have lost as heavily as the 60- or 65 yr olds have—can much more be depended upon to spend the $200.00 @ mo. justly than any youthful politician I know, together with whatever income the recipient already has—to be paid by local banks on a percent basis will help the banks as well as the workers of every industry and this pension should be given to every industrious citizen of U.S. for past 10 or more yrs.

Pauper pensions tend to break down self respect. We know many who have lost practically every thing thru no fault of their own would rather die than have to declare themselves penniless. Also—This plan also does not place a great debt on the nation for another generation to pay but can be paid by a general transaction tax on funds in the hands of this generation.

It is stated on good authority that one bank alone in New York City has annual clearings amounting into billions.—2% tax would not impoverish them yet do an enormous amount of good + considering the many banks of the nation beside many many other sources of such a tax. There is not a doubt but the necessary sum could readily be raised (especially if it was to be used for armament or to protect the wealthy in nation).

Of course the wealthy and insurance companies are the chief objectors. However the 8 million or more dispensers of $200.^{00} or more @ mo would put new life into all industries + help the whole nation by supplying work and its reaction would be a benefit even to the wealthy. For low wages by Gov't make large profits possible by Capitalists. + does not redistribute wealth which must be done if we ever secure prosperity.

Mass production requires mass selling. + mass selling requires mass buying + mass buying requires purchasing power in the hands of the masses and it is the failure to provide this purchasing power that has wrecked our economic machine   Townsend Plan places this power into the hands of the masses—It is useless to raise prices and then give masses no purchasing power.—It simply makes living more impossible. A man's inteligence is judged by the rapidity by which he can adjust himself to a new situation + a nations inteligence is judged by the rapidity its leaders can adjust themselves to a new order.—We are in a new era or order   Machines replacing human hands by the million-Hours of labor per day and also years of labor must be decreased but how shall the enormous profits of past yrs be distributed to those whose earning days are past + their years of industry all for naught— because of unscrupulus racketeers. This U.S. could be a paradise instead the habitation of misery + want if leaders but let go of selfish interests.

Sincerely

Mrs O. M.

145. A real white-man has very little chance for help

Elmhurst
Queens County
New York City. NY
March 4. 1936.

Hon. F. D. Roosevelt
President. U.S.A.
Dear Sir:

I think you are doing good work in taxing these huge corporations and the ultra rich, but just the same you are going to lose four votes in this family, unless you have your Postmaster Mr. Strong-Arm Farley put some of the relief and hand-out money in the hands of real Americans.

From what we see around here not much of the money goes to those who actually are patriotic and Americans and real good-living people.

Most of it is handed out to European Waps. Jews. and a certain class of Irish. Outside of these and the Niggers. a real White-man has very little chance for help.

Please look this situation over, as we are not the only ones who are wide-awake.

Yours sincerely.
An American of Fifty years.
and always will be.

146. I believe the Christians should rise up and kill Jews

[New York, N.Y.
n.d. — 1935]

My poor children
are starving

Your husband has
given all the offices
and money to Jews.

Baruch has ten
million dollars

The Jews are starving
the Christians.
Jews are all criminals

Dear Mrs. Roosevelt:

My husband says that President Roosevelt is in the hands of the Jews, and that the Jews are bringing ruin on this country the same as they did in

Germany. He says they have your husband in their clutches and that they are starving the Christians into slavery. My poor husband can get no work. The Jews control relief in New York City, and will not put my husband on relief—only Jews and Dagos get relief. I believe the Christians should rise up and kill Jews. They are all criminals my husband says. My poor children are starving and your husband is responsible, as he has given everything to the Jews.

Mrs. R. D. S.

My husband and all the Christian neighbors are going to vote the Republican ticket.

PART IV

The "Forgotten Man" Looks at Roosevelt

Now I understood how it was possible for my family to worship FDR despite all the things he had done during his administration that enraged them. They had used Southern logic to "straighten everything out just fine." It was very simple: Credit Franklin, better known as He, for all the things you like, and blame Eleanor, better known as She or "that woman," for all the things you don't like. This way, He was cleared, She was castigated, and We were happy.
Florence King, *Southern Ladies and Gentlemen*

We do not hesitate to address you as Mother, for such you are in the truest sense. Your national children have cried unto you, and you have heard and answered their cry. May God bless you!
Mrs. G. W. B. to Eleanor Roosevelt, July 1936

The issue is myself.
Franklin D. Roosevelt, 1936.

Chapter 12. The Unconvinced

New Deal? They forgot to cut the deck.
That's what we say around here.
Restaurant waiter, 1939

As undeniably the dominant personality of the Depression era, Franklin D. Roosevelt was the focal point of the feelings and attitudes of millions of Americans. There can be no serious question that a substantial majority of Roosevelt's countrymen, particularly among the working class, admired and supported him. Since this attitude was most prevalent, it seems appropriate to discuss such people in the final chapter of letters. For the moment, however, our attention will turn to those Americans who were less enamored of their leader.

Although there clearly were fluctuations in Roosevelt's popularity, the evidence of letters supports that of elections and opinion polls to indicate that the unconvinced were almost always less numerous than the convinced. This does not in any sense prove that a majority among Depression victims were satisfied with what the New Deal had done for them; it only shows that they had great confidence in Roosevelt himself.

The opinions of Roosevelt expressed in the letters selected for this chapter begin with several deeply bitter and hostile communications. Following these is a group of letters whose authors would like to believe in Roosevelt but remain unconvinced of his complete sincerity in his claims to be a friend of the common man. Some of these writers clothe their doubts by attributing them to others, saying that *they* did not believe that Roosevelt was inhumane but that many people were beginning to think he was.

The scheme of the chapter is to arrange letters in an order of increasing belief in the president. The last letter completes this trend and serves as a transition to chapter 13. The writer does not blame FDR and says that, "if our President only knew," he would help. Yet the author does not seem quite convinced of this. Certainly his conviction is much less firm than that of most of the writers of letters contained in the final chapter.

---

147. If Roosevelt would have to live on 50¢ a day he won't smile

[Brooklyn, N.Y. March 25, 1936]

[FERA
Washington, D.C.]
Dear Sir

50¢ a day is not enough as half the time I have to go hungry   Why don't you raise it to 75¢ a day as it's impossible. Do you want me to go out & steal the rest   if Roosevelt would have to live on 50¢ a day he won't smile, he smiles because he gets $75,000 & everything free.

[Anonymous]

148. If you are looking for the poor class of people to elect you we are looking for you to help us

[Rockwood, Tenn.
February 17, 1936]

[Franklin D. Roosevelt
Washington D.C.]

I don't understand why they have all this can stuff down here and dont give it out to the needy people   do you think they would have the heart to elect you a gain   they poor little children hungry and cold and I think you will want help some time that the poor Class of people is the ones that votes you through anyway . . . do you think a poor man can live with a large family [on 95¢ a day pay] it wont be long untill election day and if you are looking for the poor class of people to Elect you we are looking for you to help us

You will hear from me a gain

[Anonymous]

149. You have not been for the good of the people

Wakefield, Mass
March 9. '36.

President Roosevelt. U.S.A.

Mr. President:

I am addressing you a few lines to ask you a very important question that is I am one of the women serves on a project in this towne. where fifty or more like my self are trying to exist on your small and meagre earning of [illegible] ten dollars per week or forty six cents per hour, we had been getting 9.60 per week then 12.00 per week. then 13.00 per week and now cut us down to 21 hour week where we only get 9.00 and some small change. For the name of Commonwealth what are you trying to put over the people who put you in the office you know hold? You are not only starving us to death but you are breaking down the spirit of the good fine citizens of this U.S.A. The Politicians you have given all the money to have squandered it by their almighty graft. and we are pounced upon in this way. You have done a great damage to our people since 1932 and if Miss Perkins and Harry Hopkins and some more of your bosom friends were thrown out of office and there's no doubt in the mind of the good people who put you in, you kept the $4,800,000,000 to take care of the people in your own possission instead of turning all this money over to Hopkins that ought to be kicked out of office. You have not been for the good of the people. and it matters not much what you say. you have no word when you said The people wont starve what have you done to help! Men dying because of your disinclinations to help find work for them. couldnt earn money nor even get a job to feed their families. and here there are loosing their homes by the millions. There is a just God over you and the people you have done them such and injury in this world of plenty. Now every body is critizing your actions and you are due for political trimming for no one cares to be dictated to by a man of your tricks. I am asking of you one thing to look into immediately and it is this <u>Put us women back to our regular W.P.A. price of $52.00 a month.</u> or their will be an immense amount of trouble for you   Give us what belongs to us. Our unit here is nothing short of slave driving. and we have a Regional Supervisor by the name of Walsh a Miss Walsh she lays down the law to us. with letters from H. Hopkins. signed by him and is read to us. Now get busy and get in touch with your friends and helpers get back to our 13.00 a per so we wont starve to death. You will hear from more of us if you dont put us back to $13.00.

A Woman worker.

---

150. I am wondering if you or the president realy cared what happens

[Brainerd, Minnesota]
July-16-1937

Dear Mrs Roosevelt.
Washington D.C.

I hope you will take the time to read my letter. When I see so much suffering and crime, I am wondering if you or the President realy cared what happens. I have been reading about your son Franklin's wedding. Did you ever stop to think that there are thousands of young men that would like to get married and have a home if they could get a job, and earn enough to support a wife. Some of our best boys are in the C.C.C., Camp, where the officers get the pay and the good eats. The boys take the scrap and the little sum of $5 a month. a boy from 16 to 21 should be in school. and after should have a job and making a home for his bride. Every one is moving to town to get on the W.P.A. and the farmers can not get help to harvest what little crops they have. 75 per. cent is paid to officers in the W. PA. office.

Just where was the Presidents mind when he wanted to pension off the

Justices of the Supreme Court on over $400 a week. when every one are wealthy and he thout 15 a month pension for the old folks was plenty. What does he think the old folks live on. None has ever lived on that small sum or they wouldn't be alive at 65 now. Ever few weeks a high salaried man calls to see what you have spent the $15 for and if you can't get along on less. What do you think the old folks thinks about the President in this matter.

The answer to all, is the Townsend Plan   Why not investigate it. The old folks who have paid taxes all their lives and built this country up will live in comfort. (so many need glasses, new teeth and doctors care)   It will banish crime, give the young a chance to work, pay off the national debt which is mounting every day. So please investigate it, and you will have as many friends as our good Dr Townsend.

Yours Truly
Mrs. E. E. H.
Brainerd Minn

---

151. How we hoped and trusted that Mr Roosevelt would be another Lincoln and free us from the slavery that we are in today

[March 8, 1936]

Liberty Pa
Chairman Bethel Township
Hon Mrs. Franklin D. Roosevelt
My Dear Mrs Roosevelt

I hope you dont think I am rude in writing you this letter but I just could not help my self I just had to do this   I want you to know that I wouldent do the slightest thing in the world to hurt your feelings   I am one of your greatest admirers but things are so bad everywhere, People dont have the wherewith to procure the necessities of Life we are just slaves and how we hoped and trusted that Mr Roosevelt would be another Lincoln and free us from the slavery that we are in today but sorry to say he wants to Build huge Building Highways and a lot of Publick works Ligemet work with regular Building Material at regular cost and Pay regular Contractor the full Price which means a full Profit but because the poor laboring Man is down and out in the gutter, starving, he asks him to do a full days work for 1/2 days Pay. $50.00 per month now my dear Mrs Roosevelt how can a family live or even exist on $50 per month Rent 20 or $25 per month gas $1.50 Electric 2.50 2 People cant live on whats left and what is supposed to lift the depression how can People buy shoes clothes hats stockings Furniture rugs coal wich would make work for other idle men, take a horse thats been Idle for Years

Put him to work ask him to do a full days work on 1/2 the regular feed take a cow a chicken o whats the use any body can see how that works out I know you can but Mr Roosevelt cant seem to see it that way, Now my dear Mrs Roosevelt I know you have a kind heart I know you can see those things wont you please try and make him see this how any human being would see it paying $50 per month cant possibly even commence to budge the depression only make things worse, it makes People steal makes criminals and crooks out of people its no sin to steal under such circumstances, why cant the government make just a little bit of money to keep us from going into debt any further and be real Democrats, why in Bethel Township our People worked Their heads to drive Those crooked republicans out of office   why every body swore by Mr Roosevelt They would have gone through fire for him and surely he wont go back on us now when we are in such a predicament I hope Mrs Roosevelt you wont feel bad at anything I have said, I am just Pleading with you to see if you cant persuade The President to Change his mind about that $50.00 per month question. I am Very Cincerely Yours

C. J. M. [male]

---

152. You are just letting the wealthy . . . do as they please

[Jasper, Ala.
February 15, 1936]

[Franklin D. Roosevelt
Washington, D.C.]

. . . Some have gone hungry and hardly had fires to sit by as you can not get food + coal without the money. . . . One poor old lady came down through the snow one morning walked over 1-1/2 miles, her feet wet + nearly frozen   no shoes on fit to wear and she was docked 20¢   We get 19¢ per hour. This was such a small thing to do, such an "inhuman act," when all of the executives, foremen etc, over us are drawing good salaries, have good warm clothing fine cars to go in and any thing they want to eat all the time. . . . We do not believe that you are to blame for the way the relief work is being run for we know you do have lots of sympathy for the poor downtrodden undernourished poor of this whole U.S.A. There are numbers of people though who do think that you know how we are treated and seem to think that you are just letting the wealthy who have control of the relief work do as they please with caring for the poor. We have been treated very unfair here in Alabama. People have almost suffered for clothing + food since the relief work has been going on. We have too many in the offices also foremen etc—making large salaries when they have practically nothing to do. Entirely too many typewriting going on every where—especially people working who do not need the work drawing large salaries. . . .

Ladies of the Sewing Room

---

153. Am beginning to think I am only kidding myself, and what is the use of doing that any longer

Buffalo. 6/22 '38

Mr or Mrs Roosevelt—

Whether my letter will be considered or not, I am writing just the same, from urgent necessity.

I have always considered both you and Mr. Roosevelt very fine and humane people, and do still and have had the greatest confidence in both of you.

Have always been on the Democratic side of the question, and so have all my relatives, on both sides, but lying all politics aside I am writing on a far more important subject, and which is more vital, than all politics. It is the subject of dealing with the vital point of the Welfare in life.

Ever since I have been old enough to know what living is, I have been educated in economy. I have economized in every way, shape, and form, never having wasted anything, that I could possibly make use of, either in food or clothing, as economy has always been to me like one of my commandments in life, and always looking foreward, to having a little compensation in my future life, due to my efforts in saving. have never purchased things that I thought I could really get along without, although they were many times real necessities of life.

But now I find, it has been just an illusion. I have nothing, not even a decent home, hardly enough to eat, my people out of work, with no prospects of any for some time to come.

It cant be said that I am probably spending on running a car, for I havent any, or never expect to have one.

I would only be thankful if I had decent living conditions. I cant understand why people should be in such conditions in this wondeful Country of ours. It is just going from bad to worse, as far as I can see. I have been trying to keep my nerve and patience, and also my confidence in the administration, but now since I have experienced so much suffering and want, I am afraid I am losing it, and am beginning to think I am only kidding myself, and what is the use of doing that any longer.

Besides I am not alone in this matter. There are thousands of others in the self same condition for instance—I am enclosing a clipping from the news paper to portray just a hint of the people of this country, who are also trying to raise families of poor little children.

It is certainly appauling and unreasonable to the fullest extent. but if any trouble arose in this country of ours, these very same sufferers now, would be expected to go to the front, to defend their Country.

It is for the Almighty God to look down upon the cause of this terrible situation.

One of Many.
Mrs. N. G.

---

154. Do you really at heart want to restore the faith of this country

[Oregon
February 28, 1935]

[Dear Mrs. Roosevelt:]

I am sending you a plea for the dirty bunch, we are getting tired of being so termed. . . .

We do not dare to use even a little soap when it will pay for an extra egg a few more carrots for our children, pale and wobegone they look but dear to our hearts, dearer because of their helpless, needless, suffering.

Smoking their imported cig. that cost more for one day than growing children are allowed a month, how can these men and women that decree how much we eat, know the sacrifice of parents trying to get 21 meals out of 75¢. . . . Oh what can they know what it means for a mother to hear her hungry babe whimpering in the night and growing children tossing in their sleep because of knawing plain HUNGER.

But our faith must not falter when these children ask will Roosevelt give us work to-morrow, we must answer with conviction in our voices, I am just sure he will. We want these boys to be loyal to the standards of our ancestors and those that had the good of this country and its people at heart. We know that our President is doing his utmost for us and all this could be adjusted so easily and our country happy again like we were in just a few months

Do you really at heart want to restore the faith of this country and uphold the respect of other nations. . . .

One of the Unwashed

155. But why isn't it carried out so

[Pennsylvania
May 1936]

Dear Mrs Roosafelt

I had been interested in your talks over radio and in paper. But why isn't it carried out so.

You give so much hope of what is being done for the poor.

Yes we go and ask for it but what do we get. I have asked for help from one place too another. without results. My husband is earning 12.00 aweek I get 2.90 relief there is eight of us. For seven years I haven been going around working with a tumor to help. the family I have children that need hospital care. and cant get it. Im saving my releif check to pay for one of the children tonsils. Now where the rest of us will get care. A drunked on the street that's been hurt will be taken care of. All the talk on child welfare what child gets it.

I realize the government is giving us relief. But do we get it that need it most? As for afact I now that people will get what they dont need as much as those that need it. I have been after social service to straighted out my [illegible word] trouble for one. O well there is no use telling any more.

[Anonymous]

156. So these little faces will still look on your picture with a smile

[California
November 15, 1935]

president Rosevelt

Dear sir

I would like to ask you one question   Could you live on $13.00 Dollars a week if you had a family of 8 to support light water Gas and house rent to pay all on $55.00 dollars a month Could you do it? No you Couldent how do you expect us to do it . . . we supported you with 3. votes. and also intend to Vote for you in the Coming election you have been the best president we have ever had. but I think if you will study this situation over you will see a family cant get by on so little   I am willing to work at any thing no matter how hard if I can get a living for my family. but I cant school them on that.

They cant go to school bare footed and have only bread to eat you know that. I dont mean to be a Knocker. but I dont believe you have thought this Over. it is bound to be a mistake. you are too inteligent a man to think a man with a family can Get by on this small amount. you know undernursed underfed children cant resist the diseases that claim so many and leave them crippled for life They all hold you up as a model the Hungry child is Just as Dear as the rich child wont you think this over and see if you cant change this program a little so these little faces will still look on your picture with a smile. . . .

yours Respt

[Anonymous]

---

157. So many people get so disgusted they say well Rosevelt shurley dont care

New Phila Ohio

Dec. 31. 1934. [From FERA

markings on the letter, it appears that

the correct date was 12-31-35]

Mr. Harry L. Hopkins

Dear Sir

as we would like to know why we should work out in weather like stock and if we loose uny time we have been told we had to make it up even on sunday if nothing elce. we draw 22 dollars on the 15th and the 30eth of each month or suposed to we drawed one pay in December on the 18tenth and have not recieved another cent 1 pay in a month some peole has sick children and because they are working a Dr. wont go with out they have the money. and where 6 and 8 in family we suffer enough to get our pay ever 2 weeks with having only one pay a month. they put stuff in the papers about Rosevelt doing nothing no he can not when he has crooks making dogs out of the poor people 1,15 working in one office ever one Republicans but 2 and laughed about it. they are the ones siting in warm offices geting a big salery of Old Rosevelts money. he has put out lots of money for the needy but the big bugs is geting Rich and the poor going out on the Jobs with out uny thing to eat and the big shot has pieces printed in the paper if you dont work and put out a days work you will be sent home and give no Relief at all. take $44 dollars a month pay $8. dollars a month rent 7 and 8 dollars for cole. what is left for a family to eat and wear and then only recieve 22 dollars in a in the month. if it could be arange so the people with plenty all their life own big homes is put in all these places for Bosses and head leaders Old Montgomery is put cheese of this place here and he is cheese to. and if the men talkes how they are treated they say its your good President. it is not what is raised for the people it is the way it is wasted and spent through people dont kneed a cent of it. they have a wire house packed with stuff not been give to poor people said they was working have to buy what they got. and if they could be uny thing done for us poor out cast under the big mans thumb it ought to be done before they get all the rest swalowed up. we can not go much longer on half time eats. 22 dollars a month for large familey you know how much they suffer the land lords puts you out if you do not pay rent the cole bills hast to be paid and our table is set 1 meal a day and on short order. I realy believe if our President only knew how things was going on he would reach us a a helping han so many people get so disgusted they say well Rosevelt shurley dont care. he is geting his he dont care for our suffering but we few yet have hopes of Rescue the ones that gets full benefit of this money he put out says put a president in the white house can do not promise and not keep his promis he cant do as long as people has controle of the money and work like they have here they know how to hurt his election by doging the people and claim they do as they get orders from Washington we know no orders comes from these like they do us here in New Phila Ohio if it is the Presidents orders to make the wealthy Rich and the poor suffer on 22 dollars a month he dont kneed office So we are hoping to get some Results soone. we have Recieved one pay in December 22 dollars and this is January and they said at the big office in the Post Office today we might get it by the 3 of this month and us men cant go out to work the next 2 or 3 days because we have not a bite to eat we will get fired for not going out. we worked today it was 10 below Zero. some men nearly froze if we could have men put in these offices were suitable things would go better and less expence it taken 1 hundred and 13 to run the Relief office in this little town and the county taken it over 12 runs it better than all that saleried bunch did where is the money is it not wasted. and they brought their friends and their friends from other towns to work in the office like the men and women from town here was dum plenty of high schooled people in town on relief could been give them Jobs and not been kept on relief but they hired all well up people did not have to live on Relief to work. in the offices. now it is the 2an of January and we have not drawed for December yet only for the first half men on the Job with out a bucket and had no breakfast to day. please waiting for something done.

Singed by
P. W. A. workers.

Chapter 13. "Our Savior"

*"I hope God will forgive me for voting for Hoover.
Roosevelt is the greatest leader since Jesus Christ"*

New York businessman, in *New Republic*, 1935

Americans wrote literally millions of letters praising the Roosevelts. The small collection that follows provides some of the flavor of such communications.

The selection begins with an example of the feelings many had toward the new president in 1933. Following this letter a sampling of some of the more common views of Franklin and Eleanor Roosevelt is given. These admiring statements range from those of religiously oriented writers who compare the president to saints or to Moses through the frequent references to the Roosevelts as parents to the nation. Also included are examples of people who considered the president a personal friend and of those who complained about conditions but refused to blame FDR. As one of the letters shows, admiration for the president was even capable of moving some Americans to verse.

Occasional hints that faith in the president may not have been bottomless occur in these laudatory letters, but the vast majority of writers showed no sign of deserting their champion. The chapter closes with letters that point toward subsequent events: the third-term question and the possibility of war. The irony of the statements on the latter subject seems a suitable note on which to bring this collection to a close.

---

158. Fear has gone

March 31, 1933.

Senator Robert F. Wagner,
Washington, D. C.
Dear Sir:

It seems but fitting that we should send you a word of commendation, of sincere appreciation for the unified action of Senate and the House in getting in step, and pulling in harmony with our courageous President.

We feel proud of Congress, and rightly so—for their prompt action, losing little, or no time in pros and cons. We are proud of Congress, proud of those men, much too big to think of self interest, or to permit party or any other objective to interfere with their pulling as one to get this, our Country out of the "pit of this depression".

It makes one raise the head and square the shoulders, feeling that now indeed we can place confidence in those chosen to lead the destiny of our Country.

We now feel that in truth Washington is the throbbing heart of U.S.A. Fear has gone.

Thus, we desire to give voice to our sincere gratitude and thanks to Senate and the House for their actions, their promptness in passing the bills. We are sincerely proud of our courageous President and the splendid men in his Cabinet and Congress.

Humbly, but with grateful hearts we thank God for raising in our hour of need, a fearless leader and a courageous staff. Asking God's guidance and protection for Mr. Roosevelt, his Cabinet and Congress. We have the honor to remain

Yours very truly,
I. R. H. and friends.
Brooklyn, N.Y.

---

159. We all feel if there ever was a saint. He is one

Cedarburg, Wis.
10⁴⁵ A.M. Mar. 5, 1934

Mrs. F.D. Roosevelt
Washington D.C.
My dear Friend:

Just listened to the address given by your dear husband, our wonderful President. During the presidential campaign of 1932 we had in our home a darling little girl, three years old. My husband + I were great admirers of the Dem. candidate and so Dolores had to listen to much talk about the great man who we hoped and prayed would be our next Pres. We are Lutherans and she is a Catholic so you'll get quite a thrill out of what I'm to tell you now. That fall Judge Karel of Mil. sent me a fine picture of our beloved President, which I placed in our Public Library. When I received this fine picture my dear mother (who has since been called Home) said to Dolores "Who is this man?" and Dolores answered without any hesitation "Why who else, but Saint Roosevelt!" The old saying goes fools and children often tell the truth and indeed we all feel if there ever was a Saint. He is one. As long as Pres. Roosevelt will be our leader under Jesus Christ we feel no fear. His speech this morning showed he feels for the "least of these" I am enclosing a snap shot of the dear little girl who acclaimed our President a Saint and rightly so.

I'm sure Pres. Roosevelt had a great day on Feb. 16, the world day of prayer, when many hearts were lifted in prayer for him all over this great land of ours.

We shall continue to ask our heavenly Father to guide and guard him in his great task as leader of the great American people.

With all g od wishes for you and your fine family I am your most sincerely

Mrs. L. K. S.

---

160. Your just big and fine enough to be the wife of our beloved president

[Ridley Park, Pennsylvania]
9/1/34

Dear Mrs. Roosevelt.

I was delighted but I dont believe I was very much surprised when I received your letter. Just to look at your picture and that of our President seems to me like looking at the picture of a saint. So when you answered my letter and promised to have some one help me it only proved you are our own Mrs Roosevelt. I have told everyone what you done for me. I want them to know you are not too busy to answer our letters and give us what help and advice you can   you hold the highest place any woman can hold still you are not to proud to befriend the poorer class, well your just big and fine enough to be the wife of our beloved president   Thank you and God bless you both.

Respctfull
M. M. [female]

---

161. No greater man, ever lived

Waterbury
Conn.
[November 1936]

My Dear Mrs. Roosevelt,

I know you are the happiest woman, in the world today, after President Roosevelt's marvelous victory. I was confident of his victory. God, was good in sparing him to us for another term. No greater man, ever lived, I hope you gave him that little picture of Ste. Anne I sent him in your care. I shall begin, a nine day novena, in honor of Ste. Anne, for the cure of the President's paralysis. Have him apply the picture of Ste. Anne to his legs each day of my novena, which I shall begin, Sunday Nov. 8, 1936. If he is cured, will you both in return, bring his cane, to the Great Shrine, at Ste. Anne de Beaupre, in thanksgiving to this great Sainte, and do me the honor of your photo, and the President's. In return to this great Sainte, if she answers my prayers, I shall erect an altar, in my home, and pay her honor on the day of her great Feast, which is July 26, for ten years. This is how much happiness, I wish President Roosevelt, and his lovely wife for all they have done. I know you inspired him to great deeds, as only a wonderful woman as the President's wife could.

> With Best Wishes
> From a sincere
> and humble heart
> A. F. [female]

---

162. When he spoke it seems as though some Moses had come to alleviated us of our sufferings

> Nov 25, 1934
> Arkansas City, Kansas

Mrs. Eleanor Roosevelt
White House
Washington, D.C.
Dear Madam:

I beg to inform you that I have been reading your writings in the Wichita Beacon and I must say that the whole nation should be enthused over them. I especially was carried away with the one on Old Age Pensions. It bought my mind back to the day of the Chicago Convention, when Mr. Roosevelt was nominated for the presidency.

In our little home in Arkansas City, my family and I were sitting around the radio, to hear and we heard you when you flew over from N.Y. and entered the great hall and when he spoke it seems as though some Moses had come to alleviated us of our sufferings. Strange to say when he was speaking to see the moisten eyes and the deep feeling of emotions that gave vent to his every word and when you spoke then we knew that the white house would be filled with a real mother to the nation.

I am, or glad to say in this thought you have not failed us, you have visited the slums, the farms and homes of your people, and formed first handed ideas for their benefits. Oh what a blessing while you have always had a silver spoon in your own mouth you have not failed to try and place one in every mouth in the land and when I read in the Beacon your brilliant ideas of the Old Age Pensions. You said the only thing laking was the way to do it. So I said the first lady is seeking a way to help us and so let us help her to find it. . . .

Dear Madam, I am afraid to write more to you at this time as this is my first letter to the lady of the land as the others did not seem to be interested in the welfare of the people. Wife and I pray continually to God for your success. Every time the news boy hollers Extra our hearts are filled with fear that something has happened to the president, but as we go marching on to higher hills of prosperity through the new deal we are hoping and working to that point that all will be well. But one thing I was just about to forget I think that the home building program should be furnished means for back taxes included for repairs and etc. As many places are handicapped to get loans from government on account of being back taxes. Our heart in hand is ever with you and the Pres. to carry on.

Respectfuly Yours
P. F. A. [male]

---

163. I do think you and the president is the mother and father of this great USA

Toledo ohio
Feb 11-1936

Dear Mother

Of the Greatest country on god earth allso the father of the greatest I am one of the least and hope I am Doing Right and truely mean no Wrong By Writeing these few line   I am just a voter But I Dont mean any thing all that much But Just the same I am saying this I think the President is Doing alright But what a Pull Back he have got. so many vote for him and do Difference when it com to suporting him   I would call you som other Big Name But their is No other Name More Better than Mother and I Do think you and the President is the Mother and father of this Great USA   Well this is What I Want to say Would it hurt to Do a little investigating lot of the People is Kicking about any and every thing the father of the house hold is Done Well far as I can see the Middle class is trying to Poison the Mind of the lower class Making it as tough as they can without you noing it althou this May be so small that you may Not Pay it No Mind But little thing som time like that help a lot. . . .

[Anonymous]

164. There is a feeling of love

[St. Louis, Missouri
May 13, 1934]

[Dear President Roosevelt:]

. . . you and your family will at some time be rewarded for all the good you and Mrs. Roosevelt have already done and for all you will continue to do. We read of her good and kind deeds in our local newspapers, and the people of her country not only look up to her as the mother of our country, but there is a feeling of love. In closing this letter I wish to say that I feel very greatful to you for all the good you have already done for all of us and do hope you will be our President for many years, and then we will have good times again. . . .

J. F. F. [male]

165. This dirty work is only done to turn the men against you

Youngstown Ohio
Nov. 30—35

Dear President
Washington D.C.

I am Writing You in regards to our money on the Sanitary Water Project which I am working on   I am sending you a copy of my time and the amount of money that I have had for this month pay   Not only myself but there is about (250) on this Job   Now Mr president the bosses get there checks regulary but the labor has to take what ever they can get and be satisfied there is some men on this work that has only got ($48.) for (2) monts work. Now Mr President this dirty work is only done to turn the Men against you and our party for the Coming Election in 1936 and my card calls for ($55) Per Month but I did not get it so will you Please see that we have a set Pay day as we have to live the same as the Bosses. Mr President Why cant we get our Pay every 2 weeks. and get $27.50 say on the 15th and the last of the month but there is to Much Graft in Youngstown and in Columbus with the Mens wages. Mr President there is men working with me that is actually hungry and need there money Badly so now we are going to leave this in you care and we think you will straighten this out and evry thing will come out allright

Yours truly
Representing (250) Labors

P.S. Mr President for myself I dont like that dirty work because you have been a father to the People of this country and you Must not be forgotten in the time of Friend Ship

So Good by
Closing in F.C.B.

---

166. I've always thought of F.D.R. as my personal friend

[Columbus, Ga.
October 24, 1934]

[Dear President Roosevelt:]

I hope you can spare the time for a few words from a cotton mill family, out of work and almost out of heart and in just a short while out of a house in which to live. you know of course that the realators are putting the people out when they cannot pay the rent promptly. and how are we to pay the rent so long as the mills refuse us work, merely because we had the nerve to ask or "demand", better working conditions.*

I realize and appreciate the aid and food which the government is giving to the poor people out of work Thanks to you.

but is it even partly right for us to be thrown out of our homes, when we have no chance whatever of paying, so long as the big corporations refuse of work. I for one am very disheartened and disappointed   guess my notice to move will come next.

what are we to do. wont you try to help us wont you appeal, "for us all," to the real estate people and the factories

hoping you'll excuse this, but I've always thought of F.D.R. as my personal friend.†

C. L. F. [male]

---

*This is a reference to the unsuccessful 1934 textile workers' strike.

†This letter was not answered by the office of the man's "personal friend" but by an adviser on labor relations in the FERA. The reply was a cold letter that informed Mr. F. that nothing could be done for him.

167. You sure have been good to the Poor

Oliver Spring, Tenn.
April 25, 1936.

Franklin D. Roosevelt.
Washington D.C.
Dear President.

We are just getting ninteen Dollars $19 a month in Morgan County and if it rains us out they wont Pay us for us les we make it up and we cant make a living at that

All of the working men are for you. for you sure have been good to the Poor and help us out, and we sure do aprishate your kindness

With best wishes
J.B.

168. What wonderful man you have been

Cambridge   June 22 1936

Your honorable Mr Roosevelt

I am taking Privilage to write to you about these close the Poor should get you are so kind to send them for us   we dont get them   the fire house Cambridge at Inman St where the give out the close the have womon In charge her name Is miss Curisken she fits with the Poor if the ask her for any   the way she give them out Is no good   If you number dont come out on the wall + It never comes

It seems to bad   your so kind to the Poor   I hope god will reward In heaven   this women Is giving these close Is no good

you send the stuff to Poor but we dont get It   I am hopping you will draw there attion to   I Pray for you night + day   what wonderful man you have been   I will always vote for you   so will say good by

God Bless you
[Anonymous]

169. I know you are a wonderful man

Ansonia, Ct.
[May 1936]

To our President Roosevelt,

I wonder if you realize the damage you are doing to your re-election by cutting off the relief of the W.P.A.. Mr. Roosevelt if you knew how hard it is for us to live on $15. per week. But to get nothing at all. My God! It is awful. If you have to cut down, why not cut office force and all. It would be far cheaper to give every unemployed $15. a week. The work you are doing is beautiful but what a useless cost it is to the Govt. What the people need is food, clothing and shelter. Mr. Roosevelt, I know you are a wonderful man, you took the power in your own hands once, why not do it again. Why? there isent anything you cant do if left by yourself. You are the only President who ever gave a thought to the poor. Now you know what your Democrats are up against here. Oh. Mr. Roosevelt please see that our husbands are hired back again. When an American looks for relief he is told he does not need it. Our Mayor called us people on relief "Beggars."

But For Gods Sake, don't give the money to the States because then we will not get any relief and don't let them damned hounders (investigators) hounding us good Americans be hired again   god will surely bless you if you hire our husbands back again W.P.A.

Mr. Roosevelt, only Americans and Democrats were laid off. You are playing in to the G.O.P. hands. The G.O.P. paid $3, 5, 8 to foreigners to vote for them. They are glad you laid off W.P.A. because they will get more votes they won't have to buy. That how the G.O.P. does, turn one democrat against each other then they will get that vote.

[Anonymous]

170. But God, I think, made Franklin D.

Cleveland, Ohio
February 19, 1936.

The President of the United States,
Washington, D. C.,
Dear Sir:

"I THINK THAT WE SHALL NEVER SEE
A PRESIDENT LIKE UNTO THEE.

A MAN WHO HUNGRY MOUTHS HATH BLESSED,
UPON THIS EARTH'S SWEET FLOWING BREAST.

A MAN WHO LOOKS TO GOD EACH DAY,
AND LIFTS HIS TIRED ARMS TO PRAY.

IN WINTER AND IN SUMMER WEARS
A SMILE, THOUGH NUMEROUS HIS CARES.

UPON WHOSE BOSOM SORROW'S LAIN,
WHO INTIMATELY LIVES WITH PAIN.

POEMS ARE MADE BY FOOLS LIKE ME,
BUT GOD, I THINK, MADE FRANKLIN D."

Most sincerely yours,
W. P. A. worker 81058,
Cleveland, Ohio.

P. S.

Lest friends should say, "He seeketh fame."
I'll send this off without my name.

171. I do hope you will ask our dear president to divide up the wealth as soon as possible

New York, Dec. 3. 1936

Dear Mrs. Roosevelt:

I do hope our dear President will come home very soon, and start to divide among the people of this country the billions of dollars of the Duponts, Rockefellers, Morgans, and their kind. My children need so many little things that my husband and I are anxious to get our share. My husband says that President Roosevelt got a mandate from the people at election to redistribute wealth. He says the common people have woken up, and are not going to be slaves any more to keep the Duponts and Rockefellers and Morgans in luxury. And he says, too, that the mass of the people are not going to be satisfied with any increases in wages or bonuses. They demand their share, and they are going to get it, or they will give the multimillionaires a bloody revolution. Our neighbor, who is a Republican, says that President Roosevelt was just "conning" the people with his radical promises in order to get elected. He says that all your family care about is money and their actions show it. He asked my husband what he thought about your son getting engaged to the Dupont girl right after election, and showing his contempt for the common people who voted for your husband. He, also, asked my husband what he thought of your son-in-law begging a job from Hearst. Both Dupont and Hearst did all they could to beat President Roosevelt at the election. My husband said that he had to admit that your son and son-in-law were two despicable and contemptible men, but that he was sure the President would not turn traitor to the people and let his name go down in history with that of Benedict Arnold. I think my husband is absolutely right. We have been in this country for four generations. We are entitled to our home, and money for our children just the same as the Rockefellers, Duponts and Morgans. Yes, and we are entitled to have just as much money as they have got. My husband says that anyone who trifles with the people at this time had better be careful. He says the old order of slavery has gone, and the people are going to work to pile up wealth for others. I am sure I don't know as much about it as he does. But I do hope you will ask our dear President to divide up the wealth as soon as possible.

Yours very truly
Mrs. M. B.

---

172. No other president ever had it so hard

Colorado Springs, Colo.
August 16—1937.

Mrs. Franklin D. Roosevelt,
White House,
Washington, D. C.
Dear Mrs. Roosevelt:—I am writting to you in regard to Our President. About that third term. It would mean chaos if he did not again be President.

It looks that for <u>us at the foot of the ladder</u> just another depression. This one so deep.—That our "Master" would have to come, and take us home. Do have President Roosevelt reconsider.

No other President ever had it so hard. There were others to go on But this time. —Who?—

The W.P.A. nurses across the street on S. Wahsatch Ave., come three times a week and bathe me. I am a cripple. So I am hoping that Franklyn D. Roosevelt will be our next President.

Sincerely
Mrs. F. B. S.

---

173. Our sons will never be sent to them foreign war mad countryes as long as President Roosevelt stays in office

Orangeburg S C
March 12 1936

Mrs Franklin D Roosevelt

Dear friend   I take this means of having a little talk with you a bout the situation of our country and its Progress   when President Roosevelt taken the office as President the People of this country was most of them on starvation with no work to do to Provide eny thing for them Selves and meny that was not yet on starvation was rite too it   of which class we was one   I am 66 years old a mother of 9 children and we are all getting work enough now to provide us a fair living and ever body down hear mostly is getting work and Business seems to be 100 percent better now than it was 3 years a go for which this country gives our President and his faithful work honor and the mothers of this state is doing ever thing tha can through our clubs and eny other way we can for his reelection we feel that he has Brought us out of a great depression and will continue to keep us going for Peace and Prosperity   we as mothers feel that our sons will never be sent to them foreign war mad countryes as long as President Roosevelt stays in office   it made our harts regoice when we read his Pledge he made to stay out of the entanglements of war with our countryes as far as he Posible could for we no that by gods help all Powr over our country lyes in his hands no matter what them felloes in Congress does so let us Pray for America to remain at Peace and for god to direct our President in the way for Peace and prosperity for our country   no mother wants to see her son sent to war . . . Pleas excuse this Plain little letter as I have only a scant education if you Pleas will ans I will appreciate your encoragement as I am almost a shut in as I haft to care for my invalid son the youngist of 9 which is 14 years old the 25th of April 1936 Crippled sence Birth

Yours Truly

Mrs. M. H.

Orangeburg SC

Happy days are here again . . .
1941: war and prosperity.

NOTES, SOURCES, AND INDEX

Notes

Preface

1. Fisk University, *Unwritten History of Slavery: Autobiographical Accounts of Negro Ex-Slaves*, eds. Ophelia Settle Egypt, J. Masuoka, and Charles S. Johnson (Nashville, 1945, unpublished typescript), pp. 45–46, as quoted in Lawrence W. Levine, *Black Culture and Black Consciousness: Afro-American Folk Thought from Slavery to Freedom* (New York: Oxford University Press, 1977), pp. 443–44.

Introduction

1. According to William R. Emerson of the Franklin D. Roosevelt Library, in an interview with the author, July 1975.

2. A complete list of such works would constitute a bibliography on the Depression and New Deal and cannot be attempted in a footnote here. A few of the most useful books of these types include Irving Bernstein, *Turbulent Years: A History of the American Worker, 1933–1941* (Boston: Houghton Mifflin, 1967); John Braeman, Robert H. Bremner, and David Brody, *The New Deal: The State and Local Level* (Columbus: Ohio State University Press, 1975); Robert Burke, *Olson's New Deal for California* (Berkeley and Los Angeles: University of California Press, 1953); Lester V. Chandler, *America's Greatest Depression, 1929–1941* (New York: Harper and Row, 1970); Bert Cochran, *Labor and Communism: The Conflict That Shaped American Unions* (Princeton: Princeton University Press, 1978); Paul K. Conkin, *Tomorrow a New World: The New Deal Community Program* (Ithaca: Cornell University Press, 1958); David Conrad, *The Forgotten Farmers: The Story of the Sharecroppers in the New Deal* (Urbana: University of Illinois Press, 1965); Len De Caux, *Labor Radical: From the Wobblies to the CIO, A Personal History* (Boston: Beacon, 1970); Melvyn Dubofsky and Warren Van Tine, *John L. Lewis: A Biography* (New York: Quadrangle, 1977); Sidney Fine, *Sit-Down: The General Motors Strike of 1936–37* (Ann Arbor: University of Michigan Press, 1969); Frank Freidel, *Franklin D. Roosevelt* (4 volumes to date; Boston: Little, Brown, 1952–73); Walter Galenson, *The CIO Challenge to the AFL* (Cambridge, Mass.: Harvard University Press, 1960); Otis Graham, *Encore for Reform: The Old Progressives and the New Deal* (New York: Oxford University Press, 1967); Donald H. Grubbs, *Cry from the Cotton: The Southern Tenant Farmers' Union and the New Deal* (Chapel Hill: University of North Carolina Press, 1971); Ellis W. Hawley, *The New Deal and the Problem of Monopoly, 1933–1939* (Princeton: Princeton University Press, 1965); Irving Howe and Lewis Coser, *The American Communist Party: A Critical History* (New York: Praeger, 1962); Bernard K. Johnpoll, *Pacifist's Progress: Norman Thomas and the Decline of American Socialism* (Chicago: Quadrangle, 1970); Richard S. Kirkendall, *Social Scientists and Farm Policies in the Age of Roosevelt* (Columbia: University of Missouri Press, 1966); R. Alan Lawson, *The Failure of Independent Liberalism, 1930–1941* (New York: G. P. Putnam's Sons, 1971); William E. Leuchtenburg, *Franklin D. Roosevelt and the New Deal* (New York: Harper & Row, 1963); George H. Mayer, *The Political Career of Floyd B. Olson* (Minneapolis: University of Minnesota Press, 1951); Donald R. McCoy, *Angry Voices: Left-of-*

Center Politics in the New Deal Era (Lawrence: University of Kansas Press, 1958); Raymond Moley, *After Seven Years: A Political Analysis of the New Deal* (1939; reprint ed., Lincoln: University of Nebraska Press, 1971); James T. Patterson, *Congressional Conservatism and the New Deal* (Lexington: University of Kentucky Press, 1967); Patterson, *The New Deal and the States: Federalism in Transition* (Princeton: Princeton University Press, 1969); Frances Perkins, *The Roosevelt I Knew* (New York: Viking, 1946); Van L. Perkins, *Crisis in Agriculture: The Agricultural Adjustment Administration and the New Deal, 1933* (Berkeley and Los Angeles: University of California Press, 1969); Arthur M. Schlesinger, Jr., *The Coming of the New Deal* (Boston: Houghton Mifflin, 1958); Schlesinger, *The Crisis of the Old Order* (Boston: Houghton Mifflin, 1957); Schlesinger, *The Politics of Upheaval* (Boston: Houghton Mifflin, 1960); Murray B. Seidler, *Norman Thomas: Respectable Rebel* (Syracuse: Syracuse University Press, 1961); David A. Shannon, *The Socialist Party of America: A History* (New York: Macmillan, 1955); Robert E. Sherwood, *Roosevelt and Hopkins: An Intimate History* (New York: Harper, 1948, 1950); Bernard Sternsher, ed., *Hitting Home: The Great Depression in Town and Country* (Chicago: Quadrangle, 1970); Sternsher, *Rexford G. Tugwell and the New Deal* (New Brunswick: Rutgers University Press, 1964); Rexford G. Tugwell, *The Brains Trust* (New York: Viking, 1968); Tugwell, *The Democratic Roosevelt* (Garden City: Doubleday, 1957); Tugwell, *In Search of Roosevelt* (Cambridge, Mass.: Harvard University Press, 1972); Tugwell, ed., *The Secret Diary of Harold Ickes*, 3 vols. (New York: Simon and Schuster, 1953–54); Howard Zinn, ed., *New Deal Thought* (Indianapolis: Bobbs-Merrill, 1966).

3. Schlesinger, *Crisis of the Old Order*, pp. 168, 252.

4. "The Depression Experience in Family Relations and Upbringing," unpublished MS., Berkeley, California, 1966, cited in Glen H. Elder, Jr., *Children of the Great Depression* (Chicago: University of Chicago Press, 1974), p. 74.

5. Cabell Phillips, *From the Crash to the Blitz, 1929–1939*, The New York Times Chronicle of American Life (New York: Macmillan, 1969), p. xii.

6. Fred Davis, *Passage through Crisis* (Indianapolis: Bobbs-Merrill, 1961); Elder, *Children of the Great Depression*, p. 4; Milton Meltzer, *Brother Can You Spare a Dime? The Great Depression, 1929–1933* (New York: Alfred Knopf, 1963), p. 3; Studs Terkel, *Hard Times: An Oral History of the Great Depression* (New York: Pantheon, 1970). Another slight drawback to Terkel's book as a means of access to the thoughts of "ordinary" Americans is the sprinkling of well-known, upper-class personalities throughout his pages. None of this alters the fact that Terkel's achievement is a magnificent one.

7. Alice Lynd and Staughton Lynd, *Rank and File: Personal Histories by Working-Class Organizers* (Boston: Beacon Press, 1973).

8. Gabriel Almond and Harold D. Lasswell, "Aggressive Behavior by Clients toward Public Relief Administrators: A Configurative Analysis," *American Political Science Review* 28 (August 1934): 643–55; Robert Cooley Angell, *The Family Encounters the Depression* (New York: Charles Scribner's Sons, 1936); E. Wight Bakke, *Citizens Without Work* (New Haven: Yale University Press, 1940); Bakke, *The Unemployed Worker* (New Haven: Yale University Press, 1940); Jessie A. Bloodworth and Elizabeth J. Greenwood, *The Personal Side* (1939; reprint ed., New York: Arno Press, 1971); Ruth Shonle Cavan and Katherine Howland Ranck, *The Family and the Depression: A Study of One Hundred Chicago Families* (Chicago: University of Chicago Press, 1938); Ewan Clague, Walter J. Couper, and E. Wight Bakke, *After the Shutdown: The Readjustment of Industrial Workers Displaced by Two Plant Shutdowns* (New Haven: Yale University Press, 1934); Benjamin F. Culver, "Transient Unemployed Men," *Sociology and Social Research* 17 (July–August 1933): 519–34; Solomon Diamond, "A Study of the Influence of Political Radicalism on Personality Development," *Archives of Psychology*, no. 203 (June 1936): 3–53; Philip Eisenberg and Paul F. Lazarsfeld, "The Psychological Effects of Unemployment," *Psychological Bulletin* 35 (June 1938): 358–90; Ernest R. Groves, "Adaptations of Family Life," *American Journal of Sociology* 40 (May 1935): 772–79; O. Milton Hall, "Attitudes and Unemployment: A Comparison of the Opinions and Attitudes of Employed and

Unemployed Men," *Archives of Psychology*, no. 165 (March 1934): 65; Alfred Winslow Jones, *Life, Liberty and Property* (Philadelphia: Lippincott, 1941); Mirra Komarovsky, *The Unemployed Man and His Family* (New York: Dryden, 1940); Arthur W. Kornhauser, "Attitudes of Economic Groups," *Public Opinion Quarterly* 2 (April 1938): 260–68; Harvey J. Locke, "Unemployed Men in Chicago Shelters," *Sociology and Social Research* 19 (May–June 1935): 420–28; Robert S. Lynd and Helen Merrell Lynd, *Middletown in Transition: A Study in Cultural Conflicts* (New York: Harcourt, Brace, 1937); Ruth McKenny, *Industrial Valley* (1939; reprint ed., New York: Greenwood, 1968); James M. Reinhardt and George R. Boardman, "Insecurity and Personality Disintegration," *Social Forces* 14 (December 1934): 240–49; Rosemary Reynolds, "They Have Neither Work Nor Money," *The Family* 12 (April 1931): 35–39; Sidney Roslow, "The Attitude of a Group of Relief Workers toward Work Relief," *Psychological Bulletin* 32 (October 1935): 576; Edward A. Rundquist and Raymond F. Sletto, *Personality in the Depression: A Study in the Management of Attitudes* (Minneapolis: University of Minnesota Press, 1936); Flora Slocum and Charlotte Ring, "Industry's Discarded Workers (A Study of 100 St. Louis Relief Families)," *Sociology and Social Research* 19 (July–August 1935): 520–26; Samuel A. Stouffer and Paul F. Lazarsfeld, *Research Memorandum on the Family and the Depression* (New York: The Social Science Research Council, 1937); Edwin H. Sutherland and Harvey J. Locke, *Twenty Thousand Homeless Men: A Study of Unemployed Men in Chicago Shelters* (Chicago: University of Chicago Press, 1936); Esther F. Swerdloff, "The Effect of the Depression on Family Life," *The Family* 13 (January 1933): 310–14; James Mikel Williams, *Human Aspects of Unemployment* (Chapel Hill: University of North Carolina Press, 1933); Howard B. Woolston, "Psychology of Unemployment," *Sociology and Social Research* 19 (March–April 1935): 335–40; Pauline V. Young, "The New Poor," *Sociology and Social Research* 17 (January–February 1933): 234–42.

9. Federal Writers' Project (U.S. Works Progress Administration), *These Are Our Lives*, ed. by W. T. Couch (Chapel Hill: University of North Carolina Press, 1939); Tom E. Terrill and Jerrold Hirsch, eds., *Such As Us: Southern Voices of the Thirties* (Chapel Hill: University of North Carolina Press, 1978); Ann Banks, ed., *First Person America* (New York: Alfred Knopf, 1980).

10. Richard Lowitt and Maurine Beasley, eds., *One Third of a Nation: Lorena Hickok Reports on the Great Depression* (Champaign: University of Illinois Press, 1981).

11. Leila A. Sussmann, *Dear FDR: A Study of Political Letter-Writing* (Totowa, N.J.: Bedminister Press, 1963), pp. 16, 65; unidentified clipping included with a letter, W. C. M., Berkeley, California, to Eleanor Roosevelt, 11 March 1935, Eleanor Roosevelt Papers, Box 2708, FDR Library; Mrs. F. G., Chicago, Ill., to ER, 8 April 1938, ER Papers, Box 2751; Mrs. P. D., Chicago, Ill., to ER, 16 May 1938, ER Papers, Box 2749.

12. Mrs. C. C., Petersborough, New Hampshire, to ER, 10 January 1934, M. C., Montgomery, Alabama, to ER, both in ER Papers, Box 2679.

13. Lorena Hickok to Harry Hopkins, Report from New Orleans, Louisiana, 8 April 1934, Lorena Hickok Papers, Box 11, FDR Library.

14. Leuchtenburg, *Roosevelt and the New Deal*, p. 331; Sussmann, *Dear FDR*, pp. 11, 60, 72, 87, 139–41. Sussmann has calculated that FDR's mail during the Depression represented 160 letters annually per 10,000 literate adults in the population. This compares with rates of 44 in Lincoln's years, 47 for Wilson during World War I, 4.7 for McKinley in 1900, and 11.8 for Hoover in precrash 1929. Louis McHenry Howe, "The President's Mail Bag," *American Magazine*, June 1934, pp. 22–23; Schlesinger, *Coming of the New Deal*, pp. 526, 571–72.

15. An analysis of the mail addressed to FDR and received in a one week period in March 1934 found 46 percent coming from laborers, 14 percent from clerical workers, and 15 percent from farmers. A combined total of only 20 percent originated with businessmen and professionals. FERA, "Analysis of General Run of All Mail Addressed to President Roosevelt, March 23–27, 1934," cited in Sussmann, *Dear FDR*, pp. 140–41.

16. United States Department of Commerce, Bureau of the Census, *Historical Statistics of*

the United States, Colonial Times to 1970 (Washington: Government Printing Office, 1975), Series D-86, vol. 1, p. 135. See also Paul Webbink, "Unemployment in the United States, 1930–1940," *Papers and Proceedings of the American Economic Association* 30 (February 1941): 250–51.

17. The estimate was made by Herman Kahn, former director of the Franklin D. Roosevelt Library. Sussmann, *Dear FDR*, pp. 87, 127n.

18. Sussmann, *Dear FDR*, pp. 73, 155, 180–81; Kenneth Burke, *The Philosophy of Literary Form: Studies in Symbolic Action* (2nd ed., Baton Rouge: Louisiana State University Press, 1967), 293–304.

19. Ira Smith, *Dear Mr. President* (New York: Julian Messner, 1949), 211–13; U.S. Congress, Senate. Special Committee to Investigate Lobbying Activities, *Hearings*, 74th Cong., 1st Sess., Part I, as cited in James F. Ragland, "Franklin D. Roosevelt and Public Opinion, 1933–1940" (Ph.D. dissertation, Stanford University, 1954), p. 86. Leila Sussmann concluded from her study of political letter writing that "the evidence available does not indicate that pressure groups are the stimulating agent behind most political mail." Sussmann, *Dear FDR*, 133.

20. E. P. Thompson, *The Making of the English Working Class* (New York: Vintage, 1963), 55; Robert S. Lynd and Helen Merrill Lynd, *Middletown: A Study in Contemporary American Culture* (New York: Harcourt, Brace and Co., 1929), p. 6.

21. Kornhauser, "Attitudes of Economic Groups," pp. 261–65.

22. Interview by Albert Levy, Texas WPA, with a fifty-five-year-old subforeman on a WPA paleontology project. WPA Division of Information Files, Box 482, National Archives.

23. Martha Gellhorn, report to Harry Hopkins on Rhode Island, December 1934, in Harry Hopkins Papers, Box 66, FDR Library.

24. Cavan and Ranck, *The Family and the Depression*, pp. 153, 159; Almond and Lasswell, "Aggressive Behavior by Clients," p. 655; Bernard Sternsher, "Victims of the Great Depression: Self-Blame/Non-Self-Blame, Radicalism, and the Pre-1929 Experiences," *Social Science History* 1 (Winter 1977): 149, 155.

25. Melvin J. Vincent, "Relief and Resultant Attitudes," *Sociology and Social Research*, 20 (September 1935): 27–33. The groups are presented here in a different and, it seems to this writer, more logical sequence than that given by Vincent. The subjects of Vincent's survey were mostly Californians. Hickok to Hopkins, 14 February and 2 September 1934, Hickok Papers, Box 11; Schlesinger, *Coming of New Deal*, p. 275.

26. Vincent, "Relief and Resultant Attitudes," pp. 27–33.

27. Eisenberg and Lazarsfeld, "Psychological Effects of Unemployment," p. 372; Cavan and Ranck, *The Family and the Depression*, p. 153; Sternsher, "Victims of the Great Depression," p. 154.

28. Lynd and Lynd, *Middletown in Transition*, p. 127.

29. Almond and Lasswell, "Aggressive Behavior by Clients," pp. 645–46; Sternsher, "Victims of the Great Depression," pp. 155–70.

30. Frances Fox Piven and Richard A. Cloward, *Regulating the Poor: The Functions of Public Welfare* (New York: Pantheon, 1971), pp. 61–62.

31. Cavan and Ranck, *The Family and the Depression*, p. 153; *Fortune* survey, July 1935, in *Public Opinion, 1935–1946*, ed. Hadley Cantril and Mildred Strunk (Princeton: Princeton University Press, 1951), p. 893.

32. Interview by Miss McEachern, Minnesota WPA, with "Paul D.," a fifty-one-year-old former streetcar conductor, and "Florence B.," a twenty-eight-year-old displaced by the automation of her job, which was packaging cookies and candies; interview by Frederic S. Schouman, Michigan WPA, with a fifty-eight-year-old former building contractor in Detroit; interview by Paul D. Shriver, Colorado WPA, with a forty-seven-year-old WPA white-collar worker in Denver; and other interviews in "Interviews of Project Workers in Twelve States" (February 1940), WPA Division of Information Files, Box 482.

33. Lynd and Lynd, *Middletown in Transition*, pp. 111–12; "Several of the men that need Help," Portland, Michigan, to FDR, 29 October 1935, FERA Central Files, Box 88, National Archives; "An S.E.R.A. Worker," Los Angeles, California, to FDR, 13 May 1935, FERA Central Files, Box 90. See also anonymous, Athens, Georgia, to FDR, 14 August 1935, FERA Central Files, Box 89.

34. Mrs. H., Cornellsville, Pennsylvania, to Col. Arthur Woods, 9 December 1930, PECE Central Files, Tray I-1, National Archives; "An Unemployed Home Owner," Cincinnati, Ohio, to "Department of Labor, President's Organization," 16 April 1932, POUR Central Files, Tray XVI-1, National Archives.

35. Sussmann, *Dear FDR*, pp. 95–97, 124–25; J. F. M., Sycamore, Kansas, to Senator Robert F. Wagner, 16 December 1933, Wagner Papers, Drawer Q-3, Georgetown University Library; anonymous, no address, to FDR, April 1935, FERA Central Files, Box 90, National Archives; anonymous, Massachusetts, to Hopkins, 7 January 1936, FERA Central Files, Box 88; anonymous, Maryville, Missouri, to Harry Hopkins, 15 February 1936, FERA Central Files, Box 87; anonymous, no address, to FDR, 7 March 1935, FERA Central Files, Box 91; anonymous, Kentucky, to FERA, June 1936, FERA Central Files, Box 96. On the gap between promises and results, see also memorandum from David M. Maynard to Harry Hopkins, 10 December 1934, Hopkins Papers, FDR Library, Box 60.

36. Anonymous, Chicago, Illinois, to FDR, 13 March 1935; FERA Central Files, Box 91; J. W. C., Loyalhanna, Pennsylvania, to Eleanor Roosevelt, 4 March 1935, Eleanor Roosevelt Papers, Box 2697, FDR Library.

37. W. L. D., Jacksonville, Florida, to A. R. Forbush, Chief, Correspondence Division, National Recovery Administration, 23 April 1934, copy in Wagner Papers, Drawer 1-A-3, Georgetown University Library; L. K. S., Cedarburg, Wisconsin, to Eleanor Roosevelt, 5 March 1934, Eleanor Roosevelt Papers, Box 2691; W. M., Kansas City, Missouri, to Eleanor Roosevelt, 14 October 1936, Eleanor Roosevelt Papers, Box 2723.

38. Mrs. G. W. B., Springfield, Missouri, to Eleanor Roosevelt, 13 July 1936, Eleanor Papers, Box 2716; H. H., Atlanta, Georgia, to W. M. Aicher, Emergency Relief Administration, 19 October 1934, copy in FERA Central Files, Box 5; "A Perplexed Friend and Wife," Arkansas, to Eleanor Roosevelt, FERA Central Files, Box 86.

39. A. G., Seattle, Washington, to FERA, 12 December 1934, FERA Central Files, Box 4; I. H., Lawndale, California, to FDR, 1 February 1934, CWA Administrative Correspondence, Box 54, National Archives; anonymous, Glendale, California, to FDR, 4 January 1936; FERA Central Files, Box 87; E. B. L., Tampa, Florida, to Eleanor Roosevelt, 19 May 1936, Eleanor Roosevelt Papers, Box 2723; G. S., Schenectady, New York, to Eleanor Roosevelt, May 1936, Eleanor Roosevelt Papers, Box 2727.

40. Sternsher, "Victims of the Great Depression," p. 150.

41. See David Montgomery, *Workers' Control in America: Studies in the History of Work, Technology, and Labor Struggles* (Cambridge and New York: Cambridge University Press, 1979); Montgomery, *Beyond Equality: Labor and the Radical Republicans, 1862–1872* (New York: Alfred Knopf, 1967); Herbert G. Gutman, *Work, Culture, and Society in Industrializing America* (New York: Alfred Knopf, 1967); Alan Dawley, *Class and Community: The Industrial Revolution in Lynn* (Cambridge, Mass.: Harvard University Press, 1976); Leon Fink, "Workingmen's Democracy: The Knights of Labor in Local Politics, 1886–1896" (Ph.D. dissertation, University of Rochester, 1977).

42. Evidence from many different sources and types points toward the emergence or reemergence in the 1930s among working-class Americans of the belief that morality ought to have a role in economic activities. The author is currently at work on an extensive study of working-class values and culture in the Great Depression. In that study this evidence will be explored in detail.

43. William B. Hesseltine, *The Rise and Fall of Third Parties: From Anti-Masonry to Wallace* (Washington: Public Affairs Press, 1948), p. 82.

44. *Historical Statistics of U.S. to 1970*, Series G-319-336, vol. 1, 300–302.

45. Ibid., Series D-804, E-188, E-194, E-195, D-725, vol. 1, pp. 169–70, 213, 164.

46. Bureau of Labor Statistics figures, as cited in Irving Bernstein, *The Lean Years: A History of the American Worker, 1920–1933* (Boston: Houghton Mifflin, 1960)), pp. 319–20; Schlesinger, *Crisis of the Old Order*, p. 249; Alan Johnstone, FERA field representative, to Harry Hopkins, 17 July 1933, Hopkins Papers, Box 53, FDR Library.

47. *Historical Statistics of U.S. to 1970*, Series G-347, vol. 1, 302.

48. Gladys L. Palmer and Katherine D. Wood, *Urban Workers on Relief* (Washington: Works Progress Administration, Division of Social Research, Research Monograph IV, 1936), part 1, p. 36.

49. Joseph L. Hefferman, "The Hungry City," *Atlantic Monthly* 149 (May 1932): 538–40; J. S. H., Latrobe, Pennsylvania, to Bruce McClure, Secretary, Civil Works Administration, CWA Administrative Correspondence, Box 54, National Archives; John Kenneth Galbraith, *The Great Crash: 1929* (Boston: Houghton Mifflin, 1954), p. 134; Bernstein, *Lean Years*, pp. 332, 422; Woolston, "Psychology of Unemployment," p. 336; *Historical Statistics of U.S. to 1970*, Series B-166, vol. 1, 58.

50. Schlesinger, *Crisis of the Old Order*, p. 242; Ragland, "Franklin D. Roosevelt and Public Opinion, 1933–1940," p. 211; Bernstein, *Lean Years*, pp. 330–31; David A. Shannon, ed., *The Great Depression* (Englewood Cliffs, N.J.: Prentice Hall, 1960), p. 29.

51. Bernstein, *Lean Years*, p. 331; *New York Times*, 4 February 1933; Palmer and Wood, *Urban Workers on Relief*, part 1, p. 44.

52. Caroline Bird, *The Invisible Scar* (New York: David McKay, 1966), p. 26; "Kentucky Miner" to Arthur Garfield Hays, *Nation* 134 (8 June 1932): 651; Leuchtenburg, *Roosevelt and the New Deal*, p. 3.

53. *Fortune* poll, January 1937, in Hadley Cantril and Mildred Strunk, eds., *Public Opinion, 1935–1946* (Princeton: Princeton University Press, 1951), p. 829. The same survey found a clear majority of the prosperous responding that such opportunity still did exist. *Business Week*, 7 October 1931, pp. 32–33; *New York Times*, 10 February 1933; Ragland, "Franklin D. Roosevelt and Public Opinion," p. 167.

54. Bernstein, *Lean Years*, pp. 294, 422–23; anonymous letter from Massachusetts to Harry Hopkins, FERA Central Files, Box 88, National Archives.

55. As quoted in Schlesinger, *Crisis of the Old Order*, pp. 242, 165.

56. POUR advertisements contained in a letter from H. L. C., Rome, Georgia, to Walter S. Gifford, POUR Director, 16 March 1932, POUR General Correspondence, Tray XVI-1, National Archives.

57. Joan Hoff Wilson, *Herbert Hoover: Forgotten Progressive* (Boston: Little, Brown, 1975), p. 6.

58. Ibid., p. 156.

59. Piven and Cloward, *Regulating the Poor*, pp. 46–48; Robert H. Bremner, *From the Depths: The Discovery of Poverty in the United States* (New York: New York University Press, 1956), pp. 16–17; Bird, *The Invisible Scar*, pp. 30–31.

60. Josephine Chapin Brown, *Public Relief, 1929–1939* (New York: Holt, 1940), p. 99; Harry L. Hopkins, *Spending to Save: The Complete Story of Relief* (New York: W. W. Norton, 1936), pp. 74–75; Piven and Cloward, *Regulating the Poor*, p. 53.

61. Piven and Cloward, *Regulating the Poor*, pp. 57–60, 45, 117.

62. Ibid., chapter 2; Schlesinger, *Coming of the New Deal*, pp. 263–96; Leuchtenburg, *Roosevelt and the New Deal*, pp. 120–25, 133–34; Sherwood, *Roosevelt and Hopkins*, pp. 38–77; Harold Ickes, *Back to Work* (New York: Macmillan, 1935); Searle F. Charles, *Minister of Relief: Harry Hopkins and the Depression* (Syracuse: Syracuse University Press, 1963).

63. Bird, *Invisible Scar*, pp. 198, 54; Piven and Cloward, *Regulating the Poor*, pp. 95–98;

Leuchtenburg, *Roosevelt and the New Deal*, p. 130.

64. Interview by R. D. Dutchcraft, Kentucky WPA, with a twenty-eight-year-old WPA employee; interview by Karl Minderman, Ohio WPA, with a twenty-nine-year-old Toledo project worker (a writer), B. Wissmann, both in WPA Division of Information Files, Box 482.

65. *Historical Statistics of the United States to 1970*, Series D-86, vol. 1, 135. The most complete, if somewhat overstated, argument that public welfare expenditures have been used as a means of regulating the poor, and that federal welfare spending responds to outbreaks of social discontent, is in Piven and Cloward, *Regulating the Poor*. See especially pp. xiii–xviii, 3–4, 45, 80, 109, 111, 117.

66. The most widely read and well-stated such argument is in Barton J. Bernstein, "The New Deal: The Conservative Achievements of Liberal Reform," in Barton J. Bernstein, ed., *Towards a New Past: Dissenting Essays in American History* (New York: Pantheon, 1968), pp. 263–88. Bernstein, who makes a number of important and valid points, seems a bit sad that Roosevelt did not allow more to starve, thus furthering the revolution. "In providing assistance to the needy and by rescuing them from starvation," Bernstein writes, "Roosevelt's humane efforts also protected the established system; he sapped organized radicalism of its waning strength and of its potential constituency among the unorganized and discontented" (p. 267). Piven and Cloward, in *Regulating the Poor*, express similar notions. Howard Zinn also makes the point (which, of course, is valid in itself) that modest reform defused discontent (*New Deal Thought*, p. xxv).

67. Theodore Saloutos and John Hicks, *Agricultural Discontent in the Middle West, 1900–1939* (Norman: University of Oklahoma Press, 1951); Don S. Kirshner, *City and County: Rural Responses to Urbanization in the 1920's* (Westport, Conn.: Greenwood, 1970); William E. Leuchtenburg, *The Perils of Prosperity, 1914–1932* (Chicago: University of Chicago Press, 1958), 100–103; David M. Chalmers, *Hooded Americanism* (Garden City, N.Y.: Doubleday, 1965); Schlesinger, *Crisis of the Old Order*, pp. 105–10.

68. *Historical Statistics of the United States to 1970*, Series K-259, vol. 1, 483.

69. Schlesinger, *Coming of the New Deal*, pp. 34–84, 201–2, 373–79; Leuchtenburg, *Roosevelt and the New Deal*, pp. 48–52, 137–39; Perkins, *Crisis in Agriculture*.

70. John Hope Franklin, *From Slavery to Freedom: A History of Negro Americans*, 4th ed. (New York: Knopf, 1947, 1974), pp. 396–413; Ralph J. Bunche, *The Political Status of the Negro in the Age of FDR*, ed. by Dewey W. Grantham (Chicago: University of Chicago Press, 1973), p. xxii and *passim*.; Raymond Wolters, *Negroes and the Great Depression: The Problem of Economic Recovery* (Westport, Conn.: Greenwood, 1970).

71. Bernstein, *Turbulent Years*; Fine, *Sit-Down*; Galenson, *CIO Challenge*; De Caux, *Labor Radical*; Dubofsky and Van Tine, *John L. Lewis*; Art Preis, *Labor's Giant Step: Twenty Years of the CIO* (New York: Pathfinder Press, 1972).

Chapter 2

1. William E. Leuchtenburg, *Franklin D. Roosevelt and the New Deal* (New York: Harper & Row, 1963), p. 165.

Chapter 3

1. Donald H. Grubbs, *Cry from the Cotton: The Southern Tenant Farmers' Union and the New Deal* (Chapel Hill: University of North Carolina Press, 1971).

2. See File 150.1, Eleanor Roosevelt Papers, FDR Library.

Chapter 5

1. Mrs. B. H., Connorsville, Indiana, to FDR, n.d. (1934), CWA Administrative Correspondence, Box 54, National Archives.

Chapter 6

1. Matthew 21.16.

2. Glen H. Elder, Jr., *Children of the Great Depression* (Chicago: University of Chicago Press, 1974), p. 64.

3. United States Department of Commerce, Bureau of the Census, *Historical Statistics of the United States, Colonial Times to 1970* (Washington: Government Printing Office, 1975), Series A-119-134, B-1-10, vol. 1, 15, 49.

Chapter 9

1. Caroline Bird, *The Invisible Scar* (New York: David McKay, 1966), pp. 27–39; Mirra Komarovsky, *The Unemployed Man and His Family* (1940; reprint ed., New York: Octagon Books, 1971), pp. 130–33.

2. Robert S. Lynd and Helen Merrell Lynd, *Middletown in Transition: A Study in Cultural Conflicts* (New York: Harcourt Brace, 1937), pp. 256, 475–76, 482–86; *Fortune* poll, January 1937, in Hadley Cantril and Mildred Strunk, eds., *Public Opinion, 1935–1946* (Princeton: Princeton University Press, 1951), p. 829.

Chapter 11

1. For a fuller exploration of the nature of Coughlin's support, see Robert S. McElvaine, "Thunder without Lightning: Working-Class Discontent in the United States, 1929–1937" (Ph.D. dissertation, State University of New York at Binghamton, 1974), pp. 219–31.

Sources of Letters

Chapter 1

1. President's Emergency Committee on Employment Central Files (PECE), 003, Tray I-1, National Archives, Washington, D.C.
2. President's Organization for Unemployment Relief General Correspondence (POUR), 002, Tray XVI-1, National Archives.
3. Ibid.
4. PECE, 003, Tray I-1.
5. Ibid.
6. Ibid.
7. POUR, 002, Tray XVI-1.
8. PECE, 003, Tray XIII-15.
9. POUR, 002, Tray XVI-1.
10. Ibid.
11. PECE, 003, Tray I-1.

Chapter 2

12. Eleanor Roosevelt (ER) Papers, Box 600, Franklin D. Roosevelt Library, Hyde Park, N.Y.
13. Civil Works Administration Administrative Correspondence (CWA), Box 55, National Archives.
14. ER Papers, Box 2197.
15. CWA, Box 54.
16. ER Papers, Box 612.
17. Federal Emergency Relief Administration (FERA) Central Files, Box 4, National Archives.
18. Ibid., Box 5.
19. POUR, 003, Tray XVI-1.
20. ER Papers, Box 2220.
21. Ibid., Box 645.
22. Ibid., Box 2220.
23. FERA Central Files, Box 5.

Chapter 3

24. ER Papers, Box 645.
25. Ibid.
26. FERA Central Files, Box 4.
27. Ibid., Box 5.
28. Ibid., Box 88.
29. ER Papers, Box 600.
30. Norman Thomas Papers, Box 10, New York Public Library.
31. Ibid.
32. ER Papers, Box 2197.
33. Ibid., Box 2220.
34. FERA Central Files, Box 4.
35. ER Papers, Box 2220.
36. Ibid.

Chapter 4

37. FERA Central Files, Box 91.
38. Ibid., Box 88.
39. Ibid., Box 86.
40. Ibid., Box 88.
41. Ibid., Box 4.
42. CWA, Box 55.
43. FERA Central Files, Box 90.
44. ER Papers, Box 2220.
45. FERA New Subject File, 002.
46. Ibid.
47. Ibid.
48. Ibid.
49. Ibid.
50. Ibid.
51. Ibid.
52. Ibid.
53. ER Papers, Box 2721.
54. FERA New Subject File, 002.
55. Ibid.

Chapter 5

56. ER Papers, Box 600.
57. Ibid., Box 631.
58. Ibid.
59. FERA Central Files, Box 4.
60. ER Papers, Box 612.
61. FERA Central Files, Box 5.
62. ER Papers, Box 612.
63. Ibid., Box 612.
64. Ibid., Box 600.
65. Ibid.
66. FERA Central Files, Box 5.
67. Ibid.
68. CWA, Box 54.
69. ER Papers, Box 2220.
70. FERA Central Files, Box 5.
71. ER Papers, Box 2197.
72. FERA New Subject File, 002.

Chapter 6

73. FERA Central Files, Box 88.
74. ER Papers, Box 2197.
75. FERA Central Files, Box 87.
76. ER Papers, Box 631.
77. FERA Central Files, Box 87.
78. ER Papers, Box 2220.
79. FERA Central Files, Box 5.

Chapter 7

80. FERA New Subject File, 002.
81. Ibid.
82. Ibid.
83. FERA Central Files, Box 86.
84. FERA New Subject File, 002.
85. FERA Central Files, Box 88.
86. Ibid., Box 5.
87. FERA New Subject File, 002.
88. FERA Central Files, Box 5.
89. FERA New Subject File, 002.
90. FERA Central Files, Box 88.
91. FERA New Subject File, 002.
92. FERA Central Files, Box 87.
93. Ibid., Box 88.
94. FERA New Subject File, 002.
95. Ibid.
96. Ibid.
97. FERA Central Files, Box 86.

98. FERA New Subject File, 002.
99. FERA Central Files, Box 90.
100. Ibid.
101. Ibid., Box 89.
102. FERA New Subject File, 002.
103. Ibid.

Chapter 8

104. ER Papers, Box 2735.
105. Ibid., Box 2727.
106. Ibid., Box 2730.
107. FERA Central Files, Box 4.
108. Robert F. Wagner Papers, Drawer 1-A-3, Georgetown University Library, Washington, D.C.
109. FERA New Subject File, 002.
110. Ibid.

Chapter 9

111. FERA Central Files, Box 4.
112. FERA New Subject File, 002.
113. CWA, Box 54.
114. FERA New Subject File, 002.
115. Ibid.
116. Ibid.
117. Ibid.
118. Ibid.
119. FERA Central Files, Box 88.
120. Ibid., Box 91.
121. FERA New Subject File, 002.
122. FERA Central Files, Box 4.
123. FERA Central Files, Box 88.
124. Ibid.
125. Ibid., Box 4.
126. Ibid., Box 88.
127. Ibid., Box 4.
128. Ibid., Box 88.

Chapter 10

129. FERA New Subject File, 002.
130. Ibid.
131. ER Papers, Box 2721.
132. Ibid., Box 2697.
133. Ibid., Box 2714.
134. FERA New Subject File, 002.
135. Ibid.

Chapter 11

136. ER Papers, Box 2697.
137. FERA Central Files, Box 88.
138. FERA New Subject File, 002.
139. FERA Central Files, Box 88.
140. ER Papers, Box 2691.
141. Ibid., Box 2725.
142. FERA Central Files, Box 89.
143. FERA New Subject File, 002.
144. ER Papers, Box 2708.
145. FERA New Subject File, 002.
146. ER Papers, Box 2712.

Chapter 12

147. FERA Central Files, Box 87.
148. Ibid.
149. FERA New Subject File, 002.
150. ER Papers, 2735.
151. Ibid., Box 2708.
152. FERA New Subject File, 002.
153. ER Papers, Box 2751.

154. FERA Central Files, Box 91.
155. Ibid., Box 86.
156. FERA New Subject File, 002.
157. Ibid.

Chapter 13

158. Wagner Papers, Drawer Q-2.
159. ER Papers, Box 2691.
160. Ibid., Box 2197.
161. Ibid., Box 2719.
162. Ibid., Box 600.
163. FERA New Subject File, 002.
164. FERA Central Files, Box 4.
165. FERA New Subject File, 002.
166. FERA Central Files, Box 4.
167. Ibid., Box 86.
168. Ibid.
169. FERA New Subject File, 002.
170. Ibid.
171. ER Papers, Box 2716.
172. Ibid., Box 2741.
173. Ibid., Box 2721.

Index

DATE DUE

APR 2 6 2010			